Confessions and Memoirs
of an Airline Pilot

Captain Enrique "Blyhe" Horta

authorHOUSE®

AuthorHouse™
1663 Liberty Drive, Suite 200
Bloomington, IN 47403
www.authorhouse.com
Phone: 1-800-839-8640

First published by AuthorHouse 5/19/2009

ISBN: 978-1-4389-2815-9 (sc)
ISBN: 978-1-4389-2814-2 (hc)

Printed in the United States of America
Bloomington, Indiana

This book is printed on acid-free paper.

Myself doing an exterior preflight on my bird.

FOREWORD

THIS IS A BOOK ABOUT LIFE, ADVENTURE, PASSION AND LOVE.

IT IS ALSO AN ACCOUNT OF MY EXPERIENCES AS AN AIRLINE PILOT, SURFER, ADVENTURER, OFF-SHORE SAILOR, TRAVELLER, DREAMER AND LOVER.

IT EXPRESSES MY VIEWS ABOUT SEVERAL AREAS FROM AIRLINE SAFETY, AVIATION INDUSTRY DECADENCE, AIRPORT SECURITY, AIRLINE CREW RISKS DUE TO ACCUMULATED FATIGUE AND POSSIBLE RISK SCENARIOS.

I ALSO WOULD LIKE TO APOLOGIZE BEFOREHAND IF I HAPPEN TO REVEAL THINGS I SHOULD NOT REGARDING WOMEN IN MY LIFE, AND THANK THEM FOR THE LOVE THEY SHARED WITH ME. ALTHOUGH FOR THE PROTECTION OF REPUTATIONS I WILL SLIGHTLY ALTER THE LADIES' NAMES.

EVERYTHING I WRITE HERE HAS REALLY HAPPENED TO ME AND NOTHING IS CREATED OUT OF THE IMAGINATION.

MY STRONG OPINIONS AND OPEN MINDED VIEWS REGARDING AIRLINE SAFETY AND FLIGHT RISKS ARE MY PERSONAL VIEWS ONLY, SO PLEASE USE CAUTION WHEN READING THIS SECTION BEFORE A FLIGHT.

I HOPE YOU AS READERS WILL ENJOY AND UNDERSTAND MY LIFE. I ALSO HOPE MY WRITINGS CAN SERVE AS AN INSPIRATION TO OTHER DREAMERS AND LOVERS OF PASSION , LIFE AND ADVENTURE.

ENJOY IT WITH AN OPEN AND HUMOROUS MIND AND PLEASE DON'T TAKE ANYTHING PERSONAL.

CONFESSIONS AND MEMOIRS
OF AN AIRLINE PILOT

So here I was, at 39,000 feet with my bottom (derriere) looking down towards Planet Earth, stuck in a 800,000 pound time metal capsule speeding below the tropopause at 1,100 kilometers an hour (650 miles an hour). Getting younger by the day, you see, in a Boeing 747 when you're going across the International Dateline 180 Degrees East, flying from Japan to Honolulu you really do gain one day or go back in time one day. That is where East meets West at the 180 degree East line of Longitude. Sort of like a time warp, when you get to the end of the time count a new count begins with a difference of 24 hours.

The degree and time count starts from the Prime Meridian in Greenwich England, moves Eastbound 180 degrees until it meets up with the West 180 degrees, then continues until it completes a full counter clockwise direction in one day (24 hours). The Earth rotates in a counter clockwise direction at a speed of 15 degrees per hour so multiplying 15 times 24 you get the full 360 degrees in 24 hours. Where it meets up for the International Date Line change is where both 180 degrees East and West meet up, which is right down the middle of the great Pacific Ocean, just like an orange cut in half, with a few slight direction changes. Crossing this 180 degree line is where time skips to the next day if going Westbound or rewinds one day if traveling Eastbound.

Up here in thin air there isn't much to do except make position reports every hour or so and check that you are indeed going in the correct direction, and that you make sure that you keep the airplane upside up at all times. We do a few more things such as checking the fuel status, the estimated time to the next waypoint and the proper heading during every waypoint or crossing of Latitudes or Longitudes.

Since the Aircraft is on Autopilot from the Departure phase to the Approach phase, hand flying is left only for the Takeoff and Landing. Landings can be made completely on Autopilot with the Auto-land system, however, it is rare when we let the Autopilot land because it's probably the only fun thing to do during the whole flight.

All Boeing aircraft are built with alternate redundant systems so if you loose for example one Auto-Pilot, you still have two more, and most of the other systems are also backed up by three alternate systems. Well, besides staying in an alert mode at all times, you must always know where you are and which way you'll turn the Aircraft in the event of a sudden emergency, such as a Decompression (loss of air cabin pressure), Engine failure, sudden severe turbulence, medical emergency, fire, etc.

And no, the Aircraft will not fall out of the sky if we hit sudden light to moderate turbulence, for those of you that are terrified of it. It's only uncomfortable as it is when you hit a pothole on the road when going fast. You just should have your seat belt fastened as you would when driving.

Your mind should always be ready to react with a decision and a plan of action. Flying across the Pacific Ocean doesn't leave you much choices as to where to divert the aircraft to. Except, Midway Island, Wake Island further West-South-west and that's pretty much it between Honolulu and Japan. You do however have four engines on a Boeing 747, so chances of loosing all of them are almost nil. Although it has happened due to volcanic ash over Indonesia and Mt. St. Helens some years ago, it is rare. (The crew did manage to start two or three engines and were able to make a safe emergency landing).

A west bound flight in the winter time, flying into strong headwinds, can take up to ten hours from Honolulu to some cities in Japan. But flying back to Honolulu can take as little as five and a half hours with the help of 200 knot tailwinds in the jet stream (jet stream winds are high altitude winds that reach 200 knots or more during the winter, they flow normally in an Easterly direction and they are snake shaped in northern latitudes mostly like a river current). Fortunately, these jet streams can be used to our advantage by our Flight Planning Department when going downstream. In other words, picture a free ride with

3

winds on our tail pushing us at around 200 knots an hour faster when our flight path has been intentionally filed precisely inside of the jet stream. It saves fuel and flight time, therefore also saving the environment at the same time (Add the 200 knots of tailwind to our normal speed of 500 knots an hour and you get 700 knots ground speed).

When flying Westbound in the winter time, then we are encountered by strong head winds from the west on our nose and all we can do is have our flight path arranged so that it avoids the strongest part or the jet stream itself. This way it meets the minimum resistance of the strong jet streams that would slow down our progress, increase our fuel burn and greatly increase our flight time. (In this case subtract 100 knots of the slowest head wind component away from the core of the jet stream, from our normal 500 knot speed and we end up with a true ground speed of 400 knots and hour) So the normal 3,400 Nautical mile flight from Honolulu to Japan in the winter time would take us almost nine hours. Coming back from Japan to Honolulu at 700 N. miles an hour would only take us five hours, what a difference isn't it.

Managing the flight is what the Captain of the Aircraft does mostly, besides the flying that we share with the First Officer or Co Pilot (same person). The Flight Engineer, on Aircraft that still have them, does the fuel management and aircraft systems monitoring, and the First Officer when not flying, assists the Captain. (Flight Engineers have been for the most part retired from modern two man cockpits except on older Aircraft that still use them to monitor and operate aircraft systems). We use a multinational group of professional Flight Engineers, from countries from Europe, Canada, Australia, Persia and the US. Most of them are super great guys and it really has been an enjoyable experience working with them.

It's a joint operation, a well organized team effort beginning from the cleaning up of the aircraft, the catering, the boarding of passengers and the cabin preparation by the Cabin crew.

The Flight Planning has been done hours in advance by this Department, using the latest weather information and meteorology conditions to flight plan the aircraft at the most convenient altitude and route of flight.

They also take into consideration the weather along the route, if possible avoiding turbulence and weather systems and therefore choosing the best route that allows a Minimum Time Track or MTT. The Flight Crew then shows up at dispatch one hour and thirty minutes before the estimated time of departure and reviews the Flight plan, fuel to be carried and mechanical condition of the Aircraft. The Captain makes the final decision on what altitude to accept, fuel and Aircraft acceptance, we then sign the Dispatch release, Flight plan and fuel forms.

When arriving at the Aircraft, the Captain also does an exterior inspection of the Aircraft, reviews the logbook and prepares the Cockpit with the assistance of the First Officer or in some cases the Flight Engineer.

That's where our workload is the highest, those first two hours or so from show up until 30 minutes after take off. Before passenger boarding takes place, we meet with the Flight Attendants for a short briefing regarding the flight. There are around eighteen F. Attendants and they're all petite and generally cute, some above average and others below. We have a saying that if they're good looking we rate them as Tennis players, if they're average then they're Soccer players, and if below average we rate them as Hockey players. We then (The Flight Crew) stand in front of them at the very nose section of the Aircraft Cabin to introduce ourselves, and when it's their turn to introduce themselves they raise their right hand and pronounce their short nick names along with their Emergency Door Duty, e.g. "Wong Sir, L3 duty", they have funny names such as; Wee, Ping, Pong, Ying, Yang, Aw, Aom, Sing, Song, Poon, Tang, Pee, Apple, Pie, Oh, Eh, Porn. I came close to rolling in laughter the first time I stood in front of them for the briefing. I'm pretty serious, these nick names usually mean something pretty in Thai, and you should hear their real complete names, they are much longer and sound pretty interesting. I remember one cool older Captain who leaned over towards my ear during the briefing and said to me, "This is were you make your selection for the night", I had to bite my lower lip to avoid laughing out loud.

Once passengers start boarding we get locked up in our little time capsule right above the nose of the aircraft, for security reasons. Then someone hangs a sign at the Cockpit door that says, "Do not feed the Animals". Just kidding, but it feels that way sometimes. (We have a camera screen inside our cockpit so we can make sure no one is close to the door before we open it.)

By regulations, we can only exit the cockpit to use the bathroom, gone are the days when we could stroll down the cabin checking out and inviting the cute chicks to visit the Cockpit. (Have you ever wondered why it's called a Cock Pit?) Well, at certain Airlines they call it the Box Office.

After all passengers are boarded, luggage is secured in the cargo area, and we receive our additional required paperwork such as the Weight and balance Manifest, we're ready to push back and roll. Since we can't just put the Aircraft in reverse to push back out of the gate, we have huge Tow Vehicles that push back the Boeing 747.

Then we start all four engines on the taxiway, get our taxi clearance and taxi to our assigned runway. This is where it could get tricky at some complicated airports. We have to listen carefully for our taxi instructions and write them down so we don't get on the wrong taxiway or worse, cross an active runway. Runway incursion happens often at some airports around the world and is usually caused by a language barrier problem from Foreign Crews with limited "Engrish Knowredge and Undelstanding".

Finally, once we have completed our final cockpit checks and pre-take off Checklists we let the Tower know we're ready for Take Off. And we begin our Take Off roll, the Pilot Flying that leg does the Take off and Landing, not necessarily the Captain but it's the Captain's decision based on the weather conditions, Co Pilot experience and other factors mostly related to Flight Regulations.

The Take-Off Roll on a heavy jet (sometimes close to 820,000 lbs) is the most critical part of the entire flight for most aircraft. The high speeds needed to achieve lift at these weights can reach up to 220 miles per hour, and it has been calculated to have the Aircraft lift off the runway with at least two thousand feet remaining runway at the other end. Actually, there are three important speeds we use for every takeoff, and they vary with weight, atmospheric conditions and field elevation. These speeds are based on the Accelerate Go or Stop distance calculations allowed by the actual Runway Length and conditions. There are three more speeds called Vmcg, Vmca, and Vmca2 and they relate to a Minimum Control speed on the ground and in the air after one or two engines fail.

The three more important speeds are V1, which is Take Off Decision speed, Vr, which is Rotation speed, and V2, the Safety climb speed.

By the time we reach Decision speed, we should have decided whether we Reject or Continue the Takeoff in case of a serious mechanical failure, (Take off should be continued unless the Aircraft is unable to fly) in most cases, it is far safer to continue the Take off with the remaining engines. Every second counts in this split second decision and this could mean the difference between a successful Lift Off even with only three engines or an uncontrolled over run and crash off the runway with disastrous results.

A heavy Aircraft loaded with jet fuel (up to 380,000 pounds) is the most dangerous position to be in when trying to abort the Take-Off at very high speeds close to the Decision speed. Generally it has been calculated that the Aircraft can be stopped within what remains of the two and a half mile long Runway, if the Captain follows the Reject procedure properly and timely prior to that Decision speed. Many accidents have happened this way, the Flight crew trying to reject and stay on the runway when they should have continued with the Take-Off to a safe altitude and returned for a controlled landing even with minus one engine. All aircraft are flight tested and certified to lift off and land with one engine failed. Once in the air, a minimum Vmca, (a minimum of 160 knots for two engines failed) Minimum Control Speed in the Air must be maintained at all times.

This is why they pay us the big bucks, (hah, not enough for the responsibilities we have) to be the heroes and save the day of hundreds of passengers.

Anyway, after we're beyond that V1 speed, Rotation speed comes next and that's when we start rotating the Aircraft's nose gradually to around 15 degrees pitch up (14 to 18 degrees depending on weight and other factors) on the Artificial Horizon or Attitude Director Indicator. The Aircraft should start lifting off and reaching the next speed of V2+10 knots until establishing a positive climb that should guarantee clearance of all obstacles in the Climb out phase and path. There are precise numbers for every take off and they always vary depending on all the conditions mentioned before.

Then we start cleaning up the aircraft, raising the Landing gear, retracting flaps, etc. The climb to our initial cruise altitude could take up to twenty five minutes and burn up to 20,000 pounds of fuel. The initial climb up to 10,000 feet is the most demanding since we have to continuously monitor our flight path, outside watch for other traffic, weather radar for possible cloud build ups and listen carefully to Air Traffic Control instructions, all this without making unnecessary conversation due to the Sterile Cockpit Rules. (No talking below 10,000 feet)

Once the Aircraft is leveled off at it's initial cruising altitude with the Autopilot and the Auto throttles engaged, then we can start to relax. From there on we check the status of the fuel, route, time and position reports every hour or so. It's all recorded on the Flight plan to keep track of the progress of the flight. We also plan and calculate our Equal Distant Points (ETPs) in case an Emergency Diversion is necessary. We always have a Contingency plan for any unseen or unplanned scenario. The fuel is constantly monitored at every waypoint to ensure there isn't a fuel leak. There are times when the headwinds can be stronger than predicted or when we're not able to get a higher altitude due to other traffic at our desired altitude. In cases like this then we must monitor the fuel remaining more carefully at every waypoint and not allow it to drop below acceptable levels.

We always carry contingency fuel, (which is around 5% of our burn off fuel to our destination, it's calculated for unforeseen contingencies such as unexpected weather, stronger headwinds, undesired flight levels, etc.) extra, emergency, alternate airport and holding fuel on every flight so it's very difficult to run out of fuel. As the Aircraft gets lighter due to fuel burn, we are able to climb higher and closer to an optimum altitude that gives us the most economic fuel burn conditions, comfortable ride and on time arrival if possible. We always have enough fuel to cover for an unforeseen problem, such as engine failure Enroute or Depressurization of the Aircraft which would call for the need to descend to very low altitudes such as 13,000 feet above sea level. At these lower altitudes the Aircraft burns much more fuel per hour so it is already calculated and included in our total fuel.

Jet airplanes are only fuel efficient at very high altitudes. On a Boeing 747, fuel burn off for all four engines at it's best optimum altitude (at a lighter weight of 600,000 pounds for instance at 37,000 feet) will be approximately 22,000 pounds per hour for all four engines, but at takeoff at sea level at a heavy take off weight, it can burn up to 14,000 pounds or more for each engine.

Our Flight Levels or altitudes assigned to us by ATC in our Flight plan ensures we don't encounter other Aircraft at our same level. For example, going West towards Japan we get even Flight levels, (32,000, 34,000, 36,000, 38,000 feet, etc.) While going East we get odd levels (31,000, 33,000, 35,000, or up to close to the maximum ceiling of the aircraft if it's very light, which could be up to 45,000 feet, limited by the pressurization limits of the cabin fuselage). We're also separated from other Aircraft by 50 miles laterally and ten minutes or more ahead or behind us. Vertically, we usually have one thousand feet of separation from Aircraft meeting us in the opposite direction if we are on RVSM rules, Reduced Vertical Separation Minima. That should be plenty enough since we also have TCAS, Traffic Collision Avoidance System. As long as we don't turn it off and don't misunderstand our altitude clearances, we consider these distances safe from a possible head on collision. (over the Amazon region, two years ago two aircraft met almost head on and one actually lost part of it's wing when the winglet of the other jet sliced thru it like a knife thru a cake. It lost control and plunged to earth, disintegrating in flight and killing all 140 plus passengers. Air Traffic Control and Pilot error where to blame in this accident.)

It doesn't get busy again until about 45 minutes prior to our arrival at our destination. It normally takes around 25 to 35 minutes from the start of our descent to the point of landing. 15 to 30 minutes prior to our descent, we start planning our approach and landing, reviewing the latest weather conditions at our landing airport and just in case our alternate airport too.

We review our charts, our expected Arrival Procedures and Approach procedures charts, also our Airport layout. Sometimes taxiing the Aircraft at a Complex Airport such as Tokyo Narita International Airport can be more demanding than the whole flight if you haven't been there before. Driving the Aircraft on the ground is a lot of fun and is done with a small tiller that's on both sides of both pilot's side panels. It helps turn the nose wheel around sort of like a tricycle. But because the airplane is so large we must be very accurate to stay on the centerline of the Taxiways. During a turn we must overshoot the desired turning line until it's abeam of our seating position to ensure the wheels under the wings don't run over taxiway lights and therefore avoid mowing the lawn with them.

Everything in Japan is made complicated so you do want to review everything well in advance.

The taxiways are the most complicated because of a few land properties that were not sold to the Airport Authority and therefore the taxiways had to be designed around these properties or ancient sacred burial sites. There are quite a few S turns because of this on the taxiways in between the Terminals and the runways in Narita.

Normally, the flying legs we do are shared between the Captain and the First Officer. The Captain decides which legs he assigns depending on the current weather conditions. This way the First Officer eventually gets the experience necessary to qualify for Captain Upgrade training in a few years. This could take a couple of years if the F. Officer has been a Captain on an Airliner before, if not it would take more years to accomplish.

Whoever is doing the Landing briefs the rest of the crew on the approach and landing procedures, approach speeds, etc. Since we're all supposed to follow the same Company Operating Procedures there's no need to explain exactly how we plan to execute the approach and landing. A similar briefing is also done prior to Taking off. So it's all about timing, time management, and completing every task in an orderly and safe order.

Time can really drag on sometimes unless you occupy it with reading or studying to prepare for the next Simulator checks that we are subjected to (in the Torture Chamber) every three to four months.

Also, we converse, eat, drink coffee or take turns power-napping ten to twenty minutes during night flights sometimes. Really, it's actually recommended by NASA who made extensive studies with Military test Pilots. Power-napping is the safest way to go. It makes time easier and makes a flight safer to manage. Although, the trick is to keep one pilot awake while the other power naps. Any Pilot that denies that they sleep in the Cockpit is a liar, (of course there may be some exceptions, but it's not safe to force yourself to stay awake all night because then your mental awareness would be decreased during the approach and landing), I've seen those that condone it just fall sleep for a few minutes without even knowing it. That's when it can be risky if both pilots at the same time fall sleep. This is why I think it's safer to manage controlled power naps where only one at a time does it, while the others make sure they stay awake.

It's a great feeling after we complete the final parking Checklist. It gives us a feeling of satisfaction unlike any other job I can think of. Well, that is if the flight was a good flight, with a nice landing and a harmonious atmosphere. Otherwise it might not be so satisfying.

Most of the time it will be a good feeling with a Happy Ending, well not the kind you're thinking of. Specially when the Flight attendants comment on the nice landing. Hmm, maybe this would be the time to make your choice for the night?

Once we get off the airplane, which is after every one of the nearly 500 passengers and eighteen Flight Attendants have gotten off, wheelchairs and all. We have a bus or shuttle to transport us to our Hotel which is normally a 4 to 5 star Hotel in a nice part of town hopefully. Sometimes we have a "table for one" experience for dinner but most of the time we can hang out together and have food or drinks at a Restaurant or bar in our area. Sometimes the girls (Flight Attendants) join us or we join them, other times they stick to themselves and we to ourselves, it depends.

In the old and early days of aviation, Pilots didn't have reliable Auto Pilots. Those pioneer Aviators where true adventurers and masters of their skill. The death rate of those aviators was very high during the early 1900's. It's no wonder that there were very few people that wanted to get into aviation in those days. Only the brave and truly adventurous would qualify for a Pilot job back then.

Times have changed, thanks to many of these individuals and technology, Aviators like myself and many others have come to enjoy and pursue an Airline career without risking our lives as much as they did. Although there is some risk to it, the risk is very low compared to other jobs such as, elephant trainer, crocodile hunter, lion tamer, bull riding, formula one driver, porn star, (well there is risk there too) etc.

It is interesting to note that every aspect of the flight and the aircraft itself has been carefully designed to cover all areas of safety, comfort and reliability. However, the most important piece of this puzzle is sometimes neglected or abused, that is us, the Pilots. Due to flying long hours into the night, different time zones and very little rest at times, we are exposed to physiological and adverse reactions caused by lack of sleep and jet lag. The FAA (Federal Aviation Administration) and the NTSB (National Transportation Safety Board) are always trying to look for the causes of aircraft accidents and eventually when it becomes a Pilot Induced Accident, they close the case as solved but the problem persists and continues to exist worldwide.

Airline Management and Crew Scheduling Departments are unaware or don't care about the side effects and exposure we are subjected to from flying too often into different time zones, from being up all night flying or from getting minimum required rest periods.

For example, a late evening arrival into Manila at around 10 pm, would have us at our Hotel room by 12 midnight. Then our wake up call would be at 6 am the following morning. Do the math, there are only six hours in between and I assure nobody can sleep right away, it takes a couple of hours to wind down, get settled into the room before we're able to relax and actually rest, so with only four hours of sleep if lucky, we start the next day for another flight, feeling tired and groggy. Our rest period would get further reduced if we have a departure delay out of our originating Airport, which happens often. According to Regulations, this is considered legal, but has anyone asked us if it's safe?

Not to mention the ultra violet radiation that we are receiving from the sun at high altitudes and from the Cathode Ray tubes in glass cockpits. This continues to be a problem and I will discuss it more in detail later on in this book. It's no wonder International Airline Pilots only reach an average life span of 66 and a half years according to statistics.

The biggest challenge in a modern Airline Flight crew position is how to occupy our time during a long Trans-Pacific nine hour flight.

Time seems to come to a standstill and sometimes you can even hear every sound the Aircraft makes in rhythm with your heart beat, it's almost like you become one and the same.

You must be wondering what Pilots do in the cockpit when we're not busy. We converse a lot amongst ourselves but sometime we avoid talking politics and religion (the two institutions that have been responsible for most world problems). The typical conversations are about women, airplanes or boats. Sometimes we fly with more evolved worldly crew members so we talk about other interesting open minded subjects. We also tell a lot of jokes to soften the atmosphere. Since we are a multi national crowd it happens often that we fly with other pilots from different cultures, ideas, religions and backgrounds. So sometimes our conversations get pretty interesting, some even play chess in the cockpit.

Other ways of occupying our time in flight besides studying the Aircraft manuals, reading the newspaper or a book are, just thinking of the things that you have to do once you get back on the ground. Or how about letting your mind race back to the past, into it's memory bank, sending intermitent flashbacks and fragments of your life, contemplating and rejoicing on good old times you've had.

Myself in my cowboy boots in Moorpark California,
late 1960s.

THE GOOD OLD SIXTIES.

Good old times, yeah, that's my favorite way to describe it. Life hasn't been bad really, I must say I consider myself privileged to have lived an exciting and plentiful life, so far. Love Memoirs pass thru my mind, traveling experiences and life adventures.

I was born in Port Hueneme California on July 19th 1960 something, that is Ventura County for those of you who have never heard of it. My earliest and happiest childhood days take me back to Moorpark California, where we lived near a chicken farm where my Father worked. Our house had a large yard and garden and we had many cute little animals and grew many things like corn, watermelons, and other edible plants (Noooo, not marihuana). I used to love going for walks in the late afternoon with my Family, to the fields and the water channels surrounded by huge walnut trees, the aroma of those trees are still fresh in my mind.

My first solo traveling experience was actually when I ran away from home, or tried to. I was three and a half years old and I was pissed off at my Mom for having slapped my butt for something I did, or didn't do. So I decided I was leaving. I slipped out the back door while my Mom did the laundry and started walking along the side of the road sniffling along. I must have continued on that country road for a couple of blocks before my Mom found out and went after me, I think she was laughing because she didn't believe I meant it when I said I was running away. After that first time, I made it a habit to threaten to run away if she would spank my butt again. And twice I did, but this time I was around thirteen and seventeen (to be told later).

I almost didn't live to tell my story because I almost got run over by a train when I was little. I remember all the details in full color and it happened when I was barely four. My Mother was driving our old tanker of a Caddy (without a license or much driving experience) around Moorpark while my Dad was working. She was so petite she looked like a little girl driving, anyway, I was in the backseat with my brother and my sister was in the front seat. My Mom thought she could make the railroad crossing (back in the days when crossing at your own risk was allowed) before the train but because she gassed the pedal nervously she choked the engine right as we were almost over the rails. The engine died, then I heard the loud horn of the train, it was impressive because I could see it from my left side of the window as it approached us in full view from a curve. My mother was trying desperately to start the engine while she gassed the pedal even more, choking it more. In the meantime the train kept getting closer and louder and then I said to my Mom calmly, "Mom, the train is coming", without realizing that we were about to die. Luckily two men rushed from their cars behind us and pushed us out of the way. Phew, that was pretty damn close and it used up one of my nine lives. I thought it was a cool experience because I was impressed by the size and the sound of trains.

We lived in various places in California, Cucamonga, Orange County, Watsonville and Moorpark.

I remember my first day in school in Moorpark California very clearly, I cried all day until my Teacher got fed up with me and ended up taking me home (later on when I was sixteen I thought about using that trick and wished my 'hot' high school teacher would have taken me to her home for the night) at lunch time after I threatened to walk by myself. Of course the second day I had to go back but this time I didn't cry because my Mother promised to flatten my rear end if I did. My brother Joe and Lulu were both at the same school and often we would hang out together. My brother Joe was sort of my body guard since he was one year older and more aggressive. Too aggressive and it got him in a lot of trouble and fights. I was the quiet and shy one but I occasionally had a fight or two in my grammar school days. Usually over some girl that made another boy jealous or something like that. My sister Lulu the Snitch was the brains in her class and she often volunteered to tutor kids in my math class.

One day as she sat next to me, I pulled out the chair from under her to try to be funny but as she fell, she rolled on her back, whined like a piggy in pain and complained to the Teacher about me. Of course I was detained and got in trouble with the General at home, (my Mother). Another time, I don't know why I pushed a go kart that a kid was pulling with a bucket of water during cleaning chores at the Cafeteria, and it all sloshed and spilled all over the floor. I tried to hide and so I ran back to my classroom and hid in a closet. I could hear a posse looking for me all over the school. Nobody saw me clearly so they couldn't identify me as the culprit and I lived another day.

Everyone thought I was the good little boy and I appeared to be because I was shy and quiet. My brother was the aggressive and restless one so the teachers sometimes would hint that he should be like me. What they didn't know was that I could do evil things too, but in a quiet sort of way. One day we went grocery shopping and my parents told my brother and I to stay in the car while they shopped. We were somewhere near Anaheim California at a Safeway store (which wasn't really that safe with me around) and my Dad had parked our mid 60s tanker Cadillac sort of on a downhill slope but without the hand brake set. I inmediately jumped to the front seat and told my brother I was going to drive, so I started pretending I was driving. I pushed the gear handle out of the Park position from the steering wheel pedestal and the car suddenly started moving very slowly at first. My brother screamed at me to stop it but it kept going without hitting anything because the parking lot was almost empty. We were headed towards the end of the lot which was at high ground with the rest of the streets around it and at the end of the parking lot there was a Gas Station right in front of it. I knew I had to stop the beast so I stepped on both petals and obviously hit the correct one, which brought it to a stop at the same time it hit a wooden log at the skirt of the lot. Phew, that was close because it could have gone over the log, down the slope and into the gas station. (imagine the mess after the explosion, at least I would have escaped a good beating from the General)

I made my brother promise he wouldn't say anything and we ran in to tell our parents that the car had mysteriously moved by itself four car lengths. Of course as soon as my Mother asked who had jumped in the driver seat my brother the traitor pointed his finger at me. I was so terrified from the experience that my parents didn't whip me for doing that, they just didn't let me play outside or watch TV the rest of my life, no, just that week. As a result my Father had to hear the wrath of my Mother's mouth the whole day for not setting the hand brake on the car. Normally we both would have been smacked, me for being the mischievous one, and my brother for not telling on me right away, or vice versa, which was usually the case. For example, if he got in trouble at school such as for picking a fight, he would get smacked and then I would also get smacked. "But I didn't do anything," I would say, to which she would reply, "exactly, you should have told me right away". It was like standing in between two shotguns because if I squealed on him, he would beat me up, and if I didn't, she would smack me. It wasn't easy being me, sometimes I wished I could grow all of a sudden so I could defend myself. So I chose to take his side if he took mine, besides, sometimes I was more scared of him than of my Mom. He was like a double edged sword, he protected me at school but he also would throw stomach punches at me sometimes.

We traveled a few times between Mexico and California by train. Boy, that was an adventure. We sometimes lived in Mexico for a few years at a time. When we returned to California after a few years it was sometimes a culture shock. Things were so different in California from Mexico and we loved coming back. In the early 70s when jogging started being popular only few people jogged on the street. I remember the first time I saw a man jogging, I thought he was being chased, then I saw a woman running in hot pants and I thought she was being chased by her husband who caught her in bed with another man.

Growing up in both places allowed me to experience the best and worse of both worlds but it also awakened my curiosity for the unknown and for faraway places. Traveling by train for three days at a time was like a true adventure in those days. The deserts, mountains and dozens of tunnels we crossed along the way were like watching a 3D movie from the windows of the train.

I loved the rolling and shaking of the train and it's musical sounds coming from the tracks. The railroad track sounds would make my mind race ahead of me while I dreamt of faraway places. I dreamt of driving a big bus, then a big train. That lasted until I saw my first jet plane, then I knew that's what I wanted to drive. It wasn't long before I wanted to be an Astronaut. What else after that, a startreck explorer after watching Star treck. At the time I thought that Pilots were like angels that had to fly to get to the jet planes high above, I thought they were supernatural beings with amazing powers and I wanted to be like them.

On our way to Mexico, our first stop was at my Aunt's ranch style home in Ciudad Granja, at the outskirts of Guadalajara City. I had five male cousins there, Javier, Eugenio, Bernardo, Daniel and Alejandro and they were all older than me and my two siblings. I remember the excitement of seeing farm animals in the back of the house. I loved that place and I kept going back every few years until they sold the place. They taught us to ride goats, donkeys, sheep and finally horses once we mastered all the others. One of my earliest scares in life happened here. There was my Aunt's maid who used to enjoy scaring me to death. One day I was alone with her and she said that if I didn't finish my breakfast I was going to get kidnapped by an evil man and sold to the circus. She even gave me details of what the evil man looked like and at what time he would show up. At first I didn't believe her but almost as she predicted it, a man dressed in white overalls and fitting the description she gave me, showed up to the gate. (It happened to be the Electrician who she knew was coming to read the meter). Now I was terrified because I believed her, he was here to take me away and I was going to hide no matter what. I ran into one of the many rooms and hid under the bed for a long time. I kept hearing her call me and I thought she was going to sell me to the Evil man so I didn't make a sound.

I was crying and praying they wouldn't find me and I must have been under that bed for probably over two hours. Finally I heard my Mom and Aunt arrive and I ran out of the room with the accusation on the maid. My Aunt might have fired that maid because I never saw her again.

I've always had a lot of imagination. But the real kind of imagination, not the wild unachievable type. For example I wished to be an Astronaut (actually, I preferred the Pilot life because it seemed more fun after all and besides, there aren't that many babes up in space except for the occasional love crazy nut they put in that space shuttle sometimes), or an International Airline Pilot that would travel to places like Paris, Rome or other exciting cities. I would imagine myself as an adventurer, sailing across an ocean or just traveling around the world. I would see myself speaking other languages, having many beautiful girlfriends and having beautiful children. Somehow dreams and wishes can come true because I have made everything I dreamt as a child come true (except for becoming Raquel Welch's lover during her movie 'One million years BC', and going to the moon, well I've been there in a different sense). I think it was my desire and passion to know, to visit, to explore other worlds and to fly big jet planes.

I think it was my adventurous imagination that made me visualize everything, therefore setting the arena in my subconscious mind to organize and prepare my future life as I imagined it to be. That, is basically called Visualizing, the power of the mind has no limits when it comes to programming your subconscious mind with positive information. It also has the reverse negative effect for people who constantly think negatively.

I have proven one thing, everything you wish for is possible if you really want it with a passion, if you visualize it and wish it to come true.

I have surpassed obstacles, difficulties, financial, cultural and emotional blockades to reach my goals. How I did it sometimes I wonder, it seems like I also must have had a good guardian Angel. One thing is for sure, never do anything dishonest to achieve what you want because in the end it will bounce back in your face. Everything comes around and the laws of Karma are very real. When you do good to others, good will come to you. And the opposite is true too.

I don't know for sure if I should consider myself to be gifted or damned in respect to love, love of women, sometimes confused as lust passion or just animal sexual desire. I don't think I was unusually handsome, maybe a mixture somewhere in between the looks of El Zorro (the newer Zorro) and the Hunchback of Notre dame. I considered myself unattractive and skinny as a kid, but I guess I wasn't that unattractive when I grew up because I had a pretty good reaction from pretty girls. Ever since I was a little kid I've been attracted to the female kind, specially their breasts. I do have a good excuse for being weak to women's breasts, ah yes those beautiful mounds of joy and nutritious liquid that I never received as a baby, my Mom said she didn't have any for me (maybe she just didn't trust me because of my big curious eyes fixated on what I thought I was just about to receive). So instead I got the imitation, the bottle, I was disappointed and now I was destined to search for the eternal breast to satisfy my curiosity and desire.

Sometimes at the park or market place, watching young mothers breastfeed their babies in public made me feel envious of those babies, I couldn't help staring until my Mother would suddenly smack me in the back of the head. I wished sometimes I could have been friends with the babies and have been invited for breakfast. I remember one day in grammar school, fifth grade I think it was, I got caught looking down the blouse of a little girl I was playing with, she called me a pig and walked away.

Another time I wanted to see my cousin naked while she was taking a shower so I purposely kicked a ball into the shower and pretended to accidentally push the door open. She screamed and then I screamed in shock for what I saw wasn't what I wanted to see, she was so hairy I thought she needed a banana to disguise herself as a hairy ape.

THE GREAT SEVENTIES

Well, let's just say I started being interested in the female kind since I was little kid. When I was 9 or 10 we had some girl friends who were my Dad's friends' daughters. We were neighbors so we played often together. Barbara and Lorena were their names. They were both cute girls and they liked us. One day they decided I had to decide who I liked best so that they shouldn't have to fight over me, (I wish I had that problem now) . So I decided on Lorena because she wasn't as pushy like her older sister and she was cuter or so I thought. Barbie said she would pick my older brother after promising she wouldn't be angry if Lorena picked me, but she didn't keep her word when I picked her little sister and she still got mad at me. One night we were all playing in the garage and their little brother suggested we kiss his sisters because he wanted to see what it was like. My brother wasn't' so interested so Barbie had to convince him by offering to give him one Hot wheel little car in exchange for 7 kisses. He obliged but he closed his eyes and demanded his Hot wheel as soon as it was over (after wiping his lips clean with his shirt sleeve). Lorena and I had our first warm kiss in the lips and we almost got caught by her Dad looking thru the window.

It seemed so natural to me so we kissed later again in the dark and those innocent first kisses remained in my memory for many days. However, I remained only in a short lived bliss because a couple of weeks later we got bored and broke up peacefully. Ironically, Lorena was my first girlfriend and I would continue to encounter that name thru out my life.

Then in 5th grade at Central School in Santa Ana, I had a little friend called Joy, I think we liked each other but were too shy to show it. We were just little friends but when I left town we stayed in touch. We used to write each other pretty often and we kept in contact for a few years. Then when I moved to San Diego in 1979 I called her. We agreed to meet and she said she would drive to my house so we could meet again after so many years. I was pretty excited and I'm sure she was too. Then finally she showed up with a cute friend of hers who also lived in San Diego. She was still cute, petite with the same cute little face. We couldn't believe it. After so many years of staying in touch and now here we were. But I didn't feel anything and instead I actually got interested in her cute friend who also happened to go to my School.

After they spent a couple of hours at my house they were getting ready to go, and then I blew it. I really didn't think of it at the moment but I spontaneously asked her friend for her phone number, I really feel bad about it now. I mean, we didn't have a commitment with Joyce or anything but I do realize it now, I shouldn't have done that. It was very bad timing and it was probably a disappointment for Joy that after so many years of looking forward to seeing me again I would end up hitting on her cute blonde friend. Well, I didn't exactly hit on her, I was just thinking we could be friends too. She did give me her phone number and I thought she was even flirting with me. But later when I called her she sounded not interested because she said Joy didn't like that. I guess she was protecting her friendship with her friend which is perfectly understandable. Joy, wherever you are, I apologize for disappointing you.

Another time as I was working as a teenager at a bookstore with a cute girl called Coco, her and I were alone in the back room storing books and we started liking (not licking) each other. She was standing on a ladder storing some books on a high shelf and she kept asking me to pass her some more books. I couldn't help it looking up and seeing her panties and she didn't seem to mind so I clearly assumed she was teasing or seducing me. Well she was, so I kept passing her books in exchange for kisses and a few flashes of her legs and panties. Ah, what a beautiful new discovery, girls. Now life was much more fun and exciting.

GIRLS, SENNORITAS.

So know I was a teenager and had my first touch and taste of the beautiful longed for breasts. It was a girl that my friends and I knew, she was as easy as pie, friendly with the opposite sex, very cute and willing to experiment. Perfect specimen, so one day she asked me to walk her home at night, I suspected she was on to something but I wasn't quite prepared for her demands. We arrived to her dark street and there she led me into a dark corner by a post. We started to kiss and before I knew it I was like a baby looking for that nurturing breast, so she let me touch them and kiss them.

Oh, it was the nicest feeling, I though they smelled like roses and tasted like honey, actually at first I thought they felt like licking an inflated balloon. Then she said to me, " I want you to give me something" . Hmm, I wondered if she wanted my bicycle or perhaps my roller skates, I was so naive I didn't get it and it wasn't until later that I realized that she wanted the whole chorizo (bratwurst, sausage, burrito) treatment.

Eventually she gave up when I didn't get her drift, she said she had to go and was gone. The next day I told my friends and they laughed at me. In a couple of days one of the guys called Luis in my group of friends ended giving her the full treatment, so he became our hero after that.

I had my share of close encounters while living in this small city in Mexico. Including close encounters with the rotten corrupt antagonistic police. One day a friend of mine and I went hiking to the nearby hills when we were around 15 years old when suddenly we were surrounded by the Federal police in plain clothes. They had shotguns pointed at our faces and had planned a posse to go hunt down two innocent teenagers on the false assumption of a nosy neighbor of the nearby rich neighborhood. One cop in particular I did recognize, he was a bloody midget with a huge gun and enormous sunglasses that made him look like an extraterrestrial from a lost planet. He was a real bossy prick and he pointed his gun at me and said, "Don't run punk or I'll shoot you down", while he held my friend with his other arm around his neck. I froze in panic because I really believed he would have done it. (I heard he'd been killed in a shoot out some time later). Remember what I said about Karma?

Apparently there had been a few house break-ins during that week and the rich and spoiled people of that area called the police on us on the false assumption we might be part of that gang of midnight robbers.

They carried us on a private police car and locked us up for half of the day, interrogating us and trying to convince us to put the blame on each other while threatening to hang us by the thumbs if we didn't talk. It wasn't until I demanded a phone call while letting them know that my Dad was related to the Mayor of the nearby city, which happened to be true. I called my parents and my Dad came by right away, the police apologized over and over again and I walked out of there terrified and furious. My friend wasn't as lucky but he did get picked out of there by his uncle a short while later.

Another incident with the police was when some local gang picked a fight with me over some girl and as we were roller skating they surrounded me. I didn't chicken out. I took off my roller skates and we started fighting, I had no experience in fighting except for the private karate lessons I had had by my buddy Bruce Lee, from movies. I guess my karate chop hand and arm position got my opponent nervous and he didn't dare to attack, but his buddies tripped me over with their bicycles and then he jumped on me and tried to bang my head against the concrete.

That's when I realized people could be very mean and bloodthirsty, my innocence was shattered all of a sudden when I felt the first blow on the concrete with my head. I managed to grab Julio the coward's hand interlocked and as he sat on my chest I raised my long legs and banged him on his head with my feet while occasionally his little satanic brother and friend would kick me in the head as I tried to fight Julio the creep of me. I'll never forget the stench from his pants as he sat on my chest trying to bang my head on the concrete, it was disgusting and he smelled like a pig.

Eventually someone yelled that the cops were coming. We happened to be right in front of the City Hall building which was also the Police Station. All the creeps ran off and I stayed, thinking that I was innocent. A few people had gathered around us and when the cops grabbed me by the arm a few ladies stepped in to defend me, telling the cops that the other guys had picked a fight with me. The pig cop that had me by the arm said he didn't care and proceeded to drag me across the park towards the police station, while grinning, the son of a ....

I was terrified and kept fighting him off but he was stronger than me, then once there I demanded to see the Chief of Police which happened to be a relative of my Father. He knew my Father and said to the cops that we were good people, he also warned me to avoid those troubled teens sons of a rich man called Viscaino, he said they were rich and rotten cowards. So I walked out of there sniffling and swearing I'd claim revenge someday against that stupid cop. So that was my experience as an outlaw.

As a result of standing up to Julio the coward's gang they all started to respect me and knowledge me, I didn't want to be their friend but I was no longer their enemy and most of Julio's friends became sort of friendly towards me. I had another short encounter with Julio shortly thereafter when he was surrounded by his gang, but this time he didn't dare to fight me because his gang just stood by and didn't help him like they did the first time.

RUNNING AWAY.

I had a fun and partly innocent teenage life during those years in Mexico but my mind and imagination longed for more. I was one of the fastest roller skaters (roller skates with steel wheels with bearings) in town and could ride my chopper bike on it's rear wheel for up to three blocks at a time, while eating an ice cream and holding on to one handle bar only. I had also sort of befriended and earned the respect of the toughest kids in town and at least they weren't trying to slam my head into the concrete anymore. But it was time to go and life had more to offer me, besides, I had already imagined myself traveling thru Europe and courting cute French mademoiselles.

By now, we could outrun my parents if they wanted to whip us for something and nothing they said would stop us. Like my Mom's typical threat, "if you run away from me, the earth is gonna swallow you alive", I actually believed that shit at first and would stop on my tracks terrified, giving her the chance to grab me and smack me, until I saw my brother one day who kept running and nothing happened to him. My Dad rarely hit us except when Mom ordered him to, or if we touched his precious Lulu who was sacred to him. One day I accidentally ran into her chest area when she tried to stop me from entering the house to hide from my Dad, I knocked her down and she screamed in pain. Now my Dad was really going to kill me, so I slid under the bed and he couldn't pull me out because I kept kicking away like mad, I stayed under until he went to sleep.

My brother and I tried to run away again to escape my Mothers Regime at home, we were 13 or so and had a plan. The plan was to walk out of Sunday church while my parents where there, walk back to the house and grab our little prepared packs from under the bed, grab some money from (the General) my Mom's hidden stash and take a bus to the train station, once there we would board the freight trains going North to the good old California.

But our plan was ruined by our sister who had spied on us and knew about the whole thing, she then told my parents and they pretended not to know anything. However, they followed us home and caught us getting ready to split. They didn't beat us up this time, but it did teach my Mom a lesson that we did not want to be there any longer because of her abuse and lack of respect. She cried and promised she'd cut us some slack and I think it did work out better for us after that (at least she cut down on the beatings, but not on the face slaps). But we still longed to return to California. I must thank Joy for her letters from California which kept my dream alive of returning there.

I had been observing and asking my Dad for driving lessons since I was 15. So whenever I was alone I would practice in my Mom's VW 1972 Bug while it was in the garage. Soon after I was practicing on a friend's old beat up Bug until I crashed it. There were three of us in the car when this happened, my cousin Alex, my friend Sergio (Sergio was my best friend and I was sad to know that years later he was murdered in a crime related incident) and myself. As we were driving down a dead end street and I was preparing to make a tight 180 degree turn I felt that the brakes weren't stopping the car so I told Sergio that it didn't want to brake. It wasn't until much later that I found out he forgot to tell me that sometimes they didn't work that well.

We were going too fast to make a 180 degree turn and gearing down only slowed it down a bit, so I drove straight into a cement post knocking it over. We bounced off with our heads into the windshield and the car was pretty damaged from the front. Oops, now the owner of the car who was Luis the stud wasn't very happy and he tried for some time to get me to pay for the damage. I didn't have a penny to my name and used the "it wasn't my fault the brakes didn't work" excuse.

My second crash happened with my Mom's car. I knew where the second set of keys were hidden and I developed a trick on how to open the garage gate while it was locked. I would push the metal sock (where the center of the gate engaged) deep down inside until the gate cleared and just opened freely. Then I would drive away and pick up my friends and go cruising. My Mom never found out because I timed it right when I knew she would be in church for a long time.

One afternoon as I was practicing driving down a wide busy street with my brother in law Carlos. I tried to race a coming truck by passing a parked pickup truck but there wasn't much space for both of us. The incoming truck was bigger, faster and I didn't brake on time so I crashed into the parked vehicle and totally crunched the right fender. It was totally my fault and Carlos disappeared right away after we dropped off the car.

I was terrified and thought my Mom would kill me. I hoped that night that she would walk right into the house without checking the car, but somehow she sensed something and went back outside to check on the car. I heard her scream and cuss at me, " Oh sheeet, my car, hijo de…sonafa…" and knew I was in deep shit. So I locked myself in my room for safety and peace of mind until the next morning when she left for church again.

That's when I made my escape. I grabbed some money from the kitchen stash, my backpack and told my sister Lulu the snitch where I was going because I knew she would eventually tell Mom and I didn't want her to worry too much about me. I rode the bus to my cousins beautiful ranch style home in the outskirts of Guadalajara City. They were the ones that had cows and horses and were surrounded by land and orchards. I loved it there, most of my best childhood memories originated there. I helped my cousins Alex and Daniel pretty much with everything a farmhand does. Feed the animals, wash them, ride the horses, water the trees and even make goat milk by hand.

The nights were quiet and the stars were bright almost every night and I loved the smell of cows and horses. I was locally racing a fast horse for my cousin Daniel, bareback but strapped with a leather belt to the horse. I was really good at riding Indian style and even my cousin Daniel couldn't catch up with me when he would try to whip me with the horse whip for riding without wearing a cowboy hat.

I spent around three months there until things were calm at home and I returned with promises from my Dad that we would all return to California soon.

My Dad was by the most part pretty cool. However, he was The General's hit man and if she would order him to whip us for something she thought we did, then he would do it if he thought we deserved it. If he thought we didn't deserve it, he pretended to hit us and hit the wall instead while signaling us to scream. He just didn't want to hear the wrath of her mouth running all night for disobeying her orders. I think we saw him more as a big brother than a Dad and we could talk to him about things we couldn't talk to our Mom about. My Mom was good in heart but she didn't know how to show love. She had a lot of compassion for animals, the poor, beggars, and was often helping with charity. She just didn't have a lot of patience for kids and we knew that if we pushed her limits we might end up as decorations on the Christmas tree. She wasn't like that before during our first years in Moorpark, I remember she had more patience and did more stuff with us.

During those years we had a Maltese white shaggy dog called Daisy. I know, we gave him a girl dog's name even thou he was a boy dog. My Mom taught him to sit, salute and walk on his hind legs and he became like part of the family. Daisy was a dog but he thought he was a cat, he would chase rats and kill them, walk on the tiles of the roof chasing cats to play with them and get so excited whenever we tried to catch a mouse. He also had nine lives because after getting run over twice, poisoned, electric shocked, shot at, falling of the second story of the house, and abused by our experiments he lived up to 15 years.

My brother Joe and I were sort of like the Wright brothers, well, not quite but we tried to invent stuff. From huge kites to gliders and parachutes. So naturally we needed a test pilot and Daisy would sort of volunteer, well not exactly volunteer but he didn't say NO. So we would make him wear goggles, head gear and tie him up to the parachute made out from bed sheets. Then we would climb with him to the roof and drop him into a trampoline down below, or one of us would be ready to catch him in case the parachute didn't open. Of course it didn't open and Daisy would bounce of the trampoline and end up all wrapped up on rope and sheets.

We also tried the scuba gear invention but Daisy hated water and tried to bite us if we tried to submerge him. I know, it all sounds cruel but we didn't think so at the time.

Daisy left his mark on my face when he accidentally bit me right above my upper lip (I know you're thinking I deserved it well). I still have two fang marks barely visible. It was accidental because as I was trying to lift him up over the fence, I must have crunched his nuts accidentally and as he cried in pain his fangs dug into my face. He started

29

apologizing and whimpering and I knew he didn't mean it. Another time he did mean it when he bit me in the hand for trying to smack him because he peed on the couch. I had to go to the clinic and get the necessary shots. He was so almost human, those big dark eyes, his expressions of laughter, anger and fear.

He was also sort of the meteorologist of the house because every time there was a storm system approaching he would start shaking by the door, terrified and begging to be let in the house. So we knew it would be raining soon. I think Daisy remained a virgin all his life even after he tried with the chickens, the goat, the rabbits and even the cats. We tried to help him mate with a neighbor's dog a couple of times but he was too stupid, maybe he was gay I don't know. The funniest thing was to watch how he would try to mount the goat that was taller then him. The goat who was my pet that I milked every morning (I was allergic to cow milk so I drank fresh goat milk instead), would be hopping away with Daisy on his hind legs attached to the goats butt with his fore paws and bouncing behind it while trying to get lucky, his ears bouncing up and down and his tongue hanging sideways. Of course he also tried to hump my little cousins but we smacked him for that. We didn't smack him hard, just sort of with a wrapped up light newspaper. Eventually he died a slow and painful death. Up to this day we think he was poisoned by the evil neighbor who had it in for him for quite a while for braking his tiles off his roof.

BACK TO GOOD OLD CALIFORNIA.

Shortly thereafter we returned to California. Initially we lived in Watsonville, near Santa Cruz and there I worked at the Happy Burro Market, got my driver's license and started driving myself to night high school. My Mom wasn't very cooperative with my plans and tried to hinder me from going to night school because of her fear of me driving late at night on those narrow country roads. Also because I'd already crashed her car and my Dad's friends car on one of those curvy country roads (my Dad and I lucked out on this one when I skidded off a curve and we S turned into someone's fence coming to a stop within one foot of a gas tank, then the owner of the house pulled me out by the shirt neck like a rabbit by it's ears and demanded to have his fence fixed, which I did the very next day), and the fact that I liked speedy driving.

I was always sort of a thrill seeker since I was a little kid. As kids, I used to challenge my older brother to do things that I could do and that I knew he couldn't due to his fear of heights or speed. That was my way of showing him how tough I was compared to him being aggressive and a tough fighter. One day I was swinging from a monkey bar over concrete and letting myself fall backwards while sitting on the bar and then swinging while holding on tight with my knees. My brother wanted to show me that he could do that too even thou he was afraid of heights. When he let go he forgot to tighten his knees and he fell straight on his head. I was so scared because when his head hit the partly hollow cement it bounced like a ball and it resonated into a deep echo. He was delirious and in a lot of pain.

My parents where outside at the moment so I thought I'd make something else up to cover for his accident. What was helping me was that he'd lost his memory and didn't know what happened or where he was. So while I was running thru my head a lied up scenario of the accident, the walls and the floor started shaking. We started getting hit

31

by a strong earthquake and just then the idea clicked. My brother kept asking were we where and what had happened while he complained about his head. I told him to follow me and led him by the hand as we ran outside while we were being bounced left and right into the walls from the continuing earthquake.

My parents where outside on the street with other neighbors screaming at us to come out to the street. When we finally made it out and my Mother inquired what had happened to my brother, I told her that as we ran out, we fell off the stairs and Joe hit his head on the bottom of the stairs. Up to this day she thinks that's what really happened. Joe had a slight concussion and his memory came back a couple of days later but I think he's slightly brain damaged now, no, just kidding Joe.

Another time in Watsonville I was showing off to him that I could ride half way down a steep hill on my skateboard. He then challenged me to do it but from the top of the hill which I couldn't chicken out from. I said of course I could and went along to the top of the hill. I started rolling down hill really fast and about half way down I hit a little pellet or rock which destabilized my skateboard. It started wobbling right and left to the point of oscillating violently. I knew I had to jump off before it ejected me head first so just like in the movies I tried to land on my feet and curl into a little ball. As soon as I touched the concrete with my feet and tried to run, I flew into a ball and must have rolled about five times like one too. Fortunately, I covered my head with my hands over it and just let myself roll. I couldn't believe I didn't break anything in my body but every corner on me such as my knees, elbows, shoulders, hips etc. had blood and skin torn away and I was in pain. Just at that moment I saw my brother running down the hill screaming after me, he really thought I was badly hurt. I just sat and crouched on the sidewalk as a cop passed by.

I started laughing from the whole thing in a nervous way and my brother thought that I was crying. Later on he made fun of me and said that I was crying like this,,, iiiiiiiiiii,,,iiiiiiiiii.

On another occasion I was playing Evil Knievel on my bicycle trying to jump up and down car ramps from the sidewalk, it had just rained and it was of course slippery. I was really trying to impress the little girl neighbors next door and just when I thought that I made a really cool jump I landed with my front tire on a slippery patch and my bicycle disappeared from under me. I flew over the handlebars with my hands still on them. Ouch, that really hurt because I landed on my chin and then my front tooth chipped and got loose. I had little pellets inside my chin skin for a few days. My Mom refused to take me to the dentist and I kept my broken tooth like that until I went to the dentist to fix my first cavities when I was 28 years old.

It was a very beautiful area on the outskirts of Watsonville where we lived, my Parents, my Brother and I, next to a golf course below a big mountain. My sister had remained in Mexico married to Carlos who deserted me after the VW crash. We used to gather lost golf balls in the bush by the golf course, wash them and sell them for a profit. At night we had wild deer jump into our backyard to graze on our grass sometimes. It was beautiful for the moment but we didn't get along very well. My brother was "awol" from the Navy so he was sort of in hiding and he was often pretty aggressive towards all of us. To make matters worse I didn't like to be controlled any more by my Mother so we fought a lot. I felt my independence coming since I'd just turned 18 so her threats didn't scare me anymore.

I had dreams to become an Air force Pilot and maybe an Astronaut and I was willing to pursue them but my Mother seemed to get in the way. Eventually my Parents understood that they could not change or force us into their simple ways.

We argued a lot and again I tried to leave home, until they realized we couldn't live together anymore so they decided to retire back to Mexico. I stayed on my own after I turned 18 and that's when my real life adventure really began.

INDEPENDENCE, SWEET EIGHTEEN.

After my Parents left I moved to San Diego. (Actually, I stayed at my grandparents for about nine months until I got established with a job and enrolled again in school). I hung out pretty much with neighbors at the nice neighborhood where my grandparents lived, there were many girls in the next door family and the ones across the street. Enrique next door had six sisters and Omar across the street had five. It was fun because we would all pile up into my beat up Plymouth station wagon and cruise to the beach or out on the town, I did that occasionally with my cute cousins too, I had about five of them and they all ranged in ages from teenagers to a bit older than me.

Being eighteen was a great time but it was also a little scary, I was enjoying my new found liberty, girls and independence. I realize now how scary it must have been because I was pretty much on my own and except for my job at Safeway, I didn't have much security, moral or financial support.

By the way, the only job I've been fired from was at Safeway. I was working as a courtesy clerk, pushing shopping karts, bagging groceries, etc. The manager was a fat ugly guy called Marky and he was always hitting on the young cashiers. He was a hard ass and always tried to treat other employees like slaves. One hot summer day, I was gathering the shopping karts outside in the parking area with this stupid little sissy black ribbon tie we had to wear, and so I took it off so I could breathe easier in the heat.

Well, he saw me and threatened to fire me if I did it three times, so on the second time he saw me he had a very negative and demoralizing talk with me, telling me I would be fired because I didn't follow rules, he also said I would amount to nothing and that people like me didn't have futures. The asshole really laid it on me just for that. I really was furious when I drove home and it really upset me to the point of being demoralized about work. So the next day I took off the bloody sissy

34

tie and hoped to get fired, and I did. I walked out of there feeling so free and peaceful and drove home feeling good about myself because I stood up to this jerk. The idiot Manager got fired shortly thereafter because he was caught having an affair with some other manager's wife. Hah, isn't it funny how things turn out, I wish he could see me now.

Now I had to worry about getting another job quick. In the meantime my room mate Bud suggested selling our plasma for $50.00 Dollars at the nearby clinic. It paid for groceries for a week but it was uncomfortable having to lay on a bed for two hours while they pumped the plasma out of my blood. I never did it again because fortunately I got a job right away at a Pharmacy.

I was a shy kid but somehow often attracted cute girls towards me, the outgoing type. Like the cutie big green eyed teenager who used to shop with her Mom at the Safeway Store, she used to talk to me a lot while her Mom did the shopping. She was a very pretty girl, I didn't realize she liked me until one day that she walked outside with me to gather shopping carts. She said she wanted to give me something and told me to close my eyes. I did, and she gave me a warm kiss on my lips, then she said she liked my eyes and enjoyed my company. So I got her phone number and told her I'd call her that week to go to the movies. I was so stupid because I didn't call her because of the chick I was currently having sex with. So the week thereafter when she came back to the store she didn't want to talk to me anymore. I should have called her, I know.

I had always liked classic Mustangs and Camaros since I was a little kid so I started looking around for a cheap one. One day while looking at the paper I saw an add that advertised a 1969 convertible Mustang for $660 Dollars. I had saved close to that amount so I drove inmediately to look at it. It needed some work but it ran. I inmediately made a $600 dollar offer and drove away with my dream car. It had been in an accident and the doors were different colors but it ran great. I loved the smell of old leather and the sound of the 289 eight cylinder engine. I was so stoked that I failed to notice the hood latch, it didn't latch properly and as I was on the freeway I-5 South going at about 65 mph, it suddenly opened up with a loud slam as it banged into the windshield blocking my view and cracking the windshield.

I managed to slow down and exit the freeway with my head sticking out the side window. The hood was pretty crunched up and my windshield was still in place with a huge crack down the middle. I was still stoked to have my dream car which I eventually restored to a cherry condition.

Shortly thereafter I crashed it with my Grandmother inside of it. She wasn't hurt but she had a slight stroke some time after. I didn't think it was my fault because I managed to avoid hitting the pickup truck that suddenly crossed in front of me, partly, I did hit it's bumper and again it ruined my new hood. I felt really bad for my Grandma because she was a little bit scared.

I think that car was jinxed because it eventually got stolen later on but I'll tell you the story later.

BECOMING A MAN.

My first experience was with a young mother in her teens who needed a man to satisfy her needs, I happened to be introduced to her by my cousin Adam and before we knew it, my old Mustang was warming up it's shocks. Of course it was a little chaotic the first time, in the backseat of my 69 Mustang parked at the Humphrey's Memorial Wing Park on Beyer street.

Now, she'd been around the block and had dated a guy in his late 20s that obviously taught her some dirty tricks, I assumed that because she asked me as we were ripping our clothes off if I would have back door sex with her. I was still innocent and a virgin so I declined her offer, sorry but I wasn't that easy and experienced for my first time anyway.

Everything was going fine until it was time to aim the cannon into it's target, somehow the cannon blew it's cannonballs before entering the target and oh boy what a mess, it took a short while to recharge and try again and then it was quite a success. Of course until we were caught stark naked by I think the police or some guys with a flashlight, they flashed their flashlight right into us and we just froze like iguanas in panic, naked iguanas that is. They must've had pity on us so they just left in a hurry, laughing of course. So now I thought I was the man, I was showing off with my close friends and brother and didn't wash my hands so they could enjoy the smell of womanhood.

Well, it didn't take long after that to find the second volunteer. Her name started with a C, she was experienced and had been married for three years. She was 21and I was18 or so. She was my private teacher, I learned all about sexual pleasures from her. But we were only secret lovers, sort of, so I was able to date other girls in the meantime. She actually suggested to have a threesome, mélange a troi, with her big breasted girlfriend, but I didn't like her friend very much so I declined. (What an idiot.)

My third victim or should I say voluntary specimen, was my Judo partner in College, her name was Katy. She was tall and blonde, nice figure, sporty, pretty and outgoing, my favorite kind. She was pretty feminine and sexy but had a thick voice for her looks, (of course she was a woman).

Anyway, one day while wrestling on the dojo matt during judo class she ended up on top of me and then me on top of her, we got each other in a lock with our legs around each other and arms around our heads, so close for a kiss, our pelvises rubbed and other items in the area as well. I noticed her blush with excitement and sensed she wanted what I wanted. So after class as she taking off on her moped, I caught up with her on my Mustang and signaled her to stop. We talked for a few minutes and then we made a date for that night.

I picked her up at around 5 pm and we went to a movie or dinner I don't' remember, what I do remember is that on the way to her house that night I told her of a nice park in the Bonita area and she agreed to go since it was still early. Well, let's just say that she was a very keen volunteer, we were in the middle of things, actually I was now playing the role of a gynecologist when two other cars full of high school kids showed up and spoiled our party, so I suggested we go to my house and practice the Judo locks in private. She smiled and then agreed, so we went there and finished our business.

She had long hair down to her lower back and a beautiful body, we made love until the middle of the night and then she had to go at around 5 am. I still remember details of that night, her naked reflection against the light of the full moon and her beautiful long blonde hair over me as she smiled with beautiful music of sounds of pleasure emanating thru her pretty lips. We went out a couple of other times until I guess we got bored or something happened, I really don't remember anymore.

There was also my distant relative, I'd rather not mention her name, she was hottttttt. Long black hair with a petit little exotic figure with full lips and a radiant smile and personality. She was also very curious about the opposite sex, we were roomating for a few months with her and her brother.

Then one evening after jogging we got to the apartment and we both ran to get to the shower first. We ended up wrestling on the bed,

I felt her heartbeat like a rabbit's heartbeat and saw that desire in her eyes, her skin was so hot and she just kept rubbing herself on my body like a cat in heat, her legs were now pretty much around me and our breathing was getting louder and deeper. I was kissing all over her legs when I had the terrifying thought of her brother walking in on us and just then I heard a slight noise. I rolled off the bed and she dashed right into the bathroom, just as her brother swung the door to the bedroom open. He must have suspected something because he gave me a message, saying that if he ever caught me messing with his sister he'd use me as his punching bag.

So I decided to keep my distance from her, it helped that I moved out shortly thereafter with College friends due to misunderstandings with them. She was a little hot tamale waiting to get someone in trouble (and she did because she ended up pregnant by her new boyfriend shortly thereafter) and besides she wasn't always paying her share of expenses.

I was soon after occupied with my cute neighbor across the parking lot. Perla, we didn't get that far beyond second base because every time we wanted to be alone, her weird neighbor Ronald who was in love with her would knock on her door. So one evening I had to climb to her apartment via the trash bin on to her balcony and then crawl on my knees across the window of her weird neighbor to avoid being seen by him. We did smooch all evening but we decided not to go further because she had a distant Christian boyfriend and I didn't want to go to hell for messing with her. We remained good friends for a while after that. Her and her sister lived in La Jolla where I visited them there a couple of times whenever I went surfing to Wind and Sea.

Then there was my new roommate's friend from College, she had pretty oversized boobs and a pretty smile. She was usually nice to me when she visited us but I didn't think much of it cause I knew she had a boyfriend, he seemed like a redneck and looked like a football player built like a tank. Then one day she walked into my room and sat on my bed. She was wearing a sort of sporty tights, she laid down with her legs hanging down which showed very clearly the formation of her love nest underneath her tights. She looked at me and waited for me to make a move. I knew I was playing with fire so I walked out and said I was busy, whew, that was close because her boyfriend came to visit often and one day we almost got into a fight because of his jealousy of me. He probably thought I had shagged his girl. He threatened to slug me and towered over me as I sat on the couch but I was ready to kick him in the balls as I dared him to slug me. My bluff worked because he backed off. We actually all became good friends after that.

Then there was my roommate Bud who was more like a little brother to me. We got along great and often had fights like brothers. We got into the habit of playing jokes on each other and sometimes it got out of hand. One day Theresa who went to my College left me a note on my car's windshield, the note said it was a girl who was my admirer and her phone number was there for me to call.

So when I got home I called the number all excited and it turned out it was the phone number to the State Garbage Collection Agency. They were all listening outside my door when they heard me calling to ask this girl out and they rolled in laughter when I walked out of my room. Another time, Bud put some overly ripe banana's under my sheets so when I got home late at night I just got under the sheets without checking. When I felt the soft banana's in a row looking and feeling like a snake I jumped off my bed screaming that there was a snake in my bed. Bud had a good laugh with this one but I was now determined to get him back.

One evening as he was stoned watching a horror movie, I tied a fishing string to the end of his pillow, placed his pillow at the edge of his bed and left his sliding door to his room open. The couch where he sat was only a few feet from his room so when I started pulling on the line he could see from the corner of his eyes that his pillow seemed to move on it's own. At first he ignored it the first time but the second time I made the pillow jump to the floor and that's when he jumped off the couch and was ready to run out the door very scared. I couldn't help it laughing so he eventually realized it was me behind this prank.

Another time as he was about to sit on a rocking chair with some snacks in his hands I pulled the rocking chair from behind him and he ended up doing a barrel roll on the carpet with the snacks all over him. This time he did get really pissed off and started to chase me around the house.

Bud was a pretty cool guy but he was very superstitious. One Halloween I dared him to go with me to the Graveyard near our house in National City at midnight. To show him that there were no ghosts coming out of their graves as he claimed. It took a couple of six packs of beer to get his courage up and accept my challenge. When we got to the Cemetery, we sat in a little isle in the center of a small lake in the middle of the burying grounds. Just at around midnight he jumped up and I saw his eyes bulge out as he pointed at something on the next hill. He said he saw a ghost and was so terrified he wanted to jump in the lake to swim away as fast as he could. I grabbed him by the shirt and said I would prove to him it wasn't a ghost.

Then I saw it too, there were two white spots floating around the trees. They did look like ghosts but I felt there had to be an explanation to that so I grabbed our empty beer bottles and started throwing them towards the assumed ghosts, while yelling to them, "are you human or ghosts". They started scattering and hiding behind the trees and then we heard voices. It turned out to be a young couple who were wearing a white pants and a white shirt so that's all that we could see with the reflection of the moon. They thought we were ghosts throwing things at them so they were pretty terrified too. We all had a few laughs afterwards and Bud later thanked me for not letting him jump into the cold lake.

I really enjoyed living with my roommates, Bud, Theresa and Jim who eventually became almost like family because their Mom Leona always made me feel like part of the family. I lived with them for two years until I decided to go backpacking to Europe.

Kicking back on my bike while watching the sunset at Imperial beach.

THE EXCITING EIGHTIES.

Life was good, I was going to South Western College, I was taking my aviation related classes, meteorology and navigation, etc. I had a fun job at a pharmacy in Chula Vista and part of my job was, at the end of the day I would deliver prescription drugs to the elderly at other retirement homes in Pacific Beach and La Jolla. The Pharmacist, Steve Fazziolla was a pretty cool guy and usually called me Monsieur Henri.

I was still trying to find my bearings as a teenager with lots of freedom and no discipline. Sometimes I missed having a family but knew I was better off this way since I didn't have to constantly argue with some family member.

One of my first discovered passions after girls was surfing. The moment I saw surfers flying up and down waves I was hooked and determined to learn to surf.

So naturally I would carry my garage sale special $15.00 surfboard with me and stay the rest of the evening at the beach. I was still trying to learn to surf so I was obviously pissing off the experienced surfers at the PB Pier, getting in the way or cutting them off, I didn't know the proper surfing etiquette at the time. I had a used beat up hollow epoxy board called a WAVE, it was a small single fin five foot ten or something, too small to learn and plus, it was leaking water in. I must have looked ridiculous lifting it out of the water every so often to let the water out. I also had an old beat up upper divers' wetsuit which was all I could afford at the time. Eventually I learned because I had the passion for surfing and was determined to learn no matter what.

Thanks to surfing constantly I got a good physical build, I also let my hair grow and soon had long dark curly hair to my shoulders. Now I was more marketable to the chicks. I eventually became a decent surfer and surfed all the known spots from; Blacks, Wind and Sea, Bird rock, Tourmaline park, PB pier, OB pier, Sunset cliffs and Imperial Beach, including some of the great breaks down south into Baja.

Then came number four or five, I was dressing up after surfing at Imperial Beach when I noticed a cute girl coming up the beach, I had noticed her and she had smiled at me as I was on my way to the water. Now she was walking towards me with some beach bum hanging by her side, I knew she was trying to get rid of him so I thought I'd help her out. She said Hi as she walked by and then I asked if she needed a ride, she said yes but the guy sticking to her like chewing gum also said he needed a ride too. So I thought I could just dump him overboard at the next light, (just kidding) . Well he did get off eventually, said he was heartbroken or something and took off. I gave cute Pocahontas a ride to her home, she was sort of a volunteer for a certain World Aid organization. She was a pretty Indian girl from Arizona of Navajo descent with full lips, a cute smile and a nice little body to go with that. Hmm, I liked that.

So I asked her out for that night and picked her up to go to the Drive- in theater, 'drive in' (drive in and out) what an appropriate name for those theaters, you get it? Well, inside the theater we started kissing almost before the movie began. My driver's seat in my Mustang was broken at the hinges and holding it up straight was a large brick I would just remove and Voila', a reclining seat. She started taking off her jeans without me asking her to, then her panties and before I knew it she was riding me like a wild Indian pony.

Those were the safe days so condoms were pretty much unheard of. It was great, we didn't wait for the movie to end before we drove to my home that I shared with my college friends and continued our pony riding lessons there. Man, I loved drive-ins.

There was also a cute beach beauty from Imperial Beach, she worked as a nurse helper at the retirement home, had a nice set of big breasts and a very pretty face with long hair. We went out a couple of times and again ended up at the "drive-in" for a movie we never saw.

Then there was Tita my cute neighbor, her Mom looked mean and overly protective so I had second thoughts about the whole thing. Also, my roommate Bud was in love with her since childhood and once as we were making out in my room, we could have continued to third base but my roommate kept knocking on my door asking what we were do-ing in there, I really considered hanging him at that very moment. So I made a missed approach on that one. But then came Li, she was barely (I think) eighteen and was my roommate's friend's friend. I didn't think much of her at first, she was cute but childish and kept flirting and slid-ing in my way. So we sort of started dating, she was still a virgin and had obviously picked me to be 'the chosen one'.

I really wanted to avoid sex with her because her Dad happened to be my Martial Arts instructor at my school and I didn't want to piss him off. One day during practice he gave me the message, he pinned me down while twisting my arm behind my back and said with a smirk on his face, "This is what I would do if someone hurts my little girl." I got the message, but she insisted I spend the night at her place one weekend when she was alone and I could not resist what was develop-ing, I actually had feelings for her by now but the thought of her Dad walking in on us was scary because I thought he would have killed me. So I took the chance anyway and we spent a weekend night together at her house. I couldn't sleep at all, worrying her Dad would show up any moment. Oh man, that was exciting, the adrenalin rush of near death.

Well, needless to say she fell in Love with me and didn't want to let go, it was too much for me and I wanted out. Fortunately, I was going to Europe that summer anyway so I split and said "I'll see you soon after the summer". Actually, we had a sour end now that I remember. It was her Prom night and I was supposed to be her date. So I rented the tux and drove her and her best friend and boyfriend to the Prom. First of all, I hated the hair- do style she got, it was like the Piza tower on her head, it didn't look good, in fact it looked terrible and I couldn't hide my disappointment. Even her friend's boyfriend was making fun of it, well we both were. We weren't on good terms the whole night at the Prom and when we headed for the beach at Coronado to a Bon fire, we all got drunk on Tequila. Then she started accusing me of ruining her night and started crying and having a fit, so I let her cool off and fell sleep on the sand. When I woke up in the morning with the sun on my face I was alone, they had left in the middle of the night. I was so hung over that I felt like jumping in the ocean, but I was so thirsty so I decided to look for drinking water first. I noticed that sitting next to me there were two little kids with sodas in an ice chest so I asked them if they could spare one and they gave me a Coke, that tasted like the best Coke I'd had in years. I didn't call her anymore I think. Well, I didn't come back from Europe until a year later so that took care of that.

During this time I had been attending College, I had also taken a few airplane flights on a Cessna 172 with my College Instructor Mr. Brannon but unfortunately I didn't have much money to start or continue so I had to stop. I thought I had decided to join the Air Force, they had a ROTC program (reserve officer training) for students with two years of college were they would have continued to pay my college tuition fees. But in the end I changed my mind when the recruiter said they couldn't guarantee me a flying slot.

My hunger for traveling took over and I packed my backpack, gathered my one thousand dollars from my savings and bought a cheap ticket to Frankfurt Germany on Capitol Airways (my first time ever on a jet airplane and it almost ran off the end of the runway, it actually rejected the takeoff due to an engine problem prior to lift off). Now I was finally on my way after packing all my belongings into my Mustang and storing it at the Sav-On open storage place. Little did I know that was the last time I'd see my loyal Mustang with the good shocks and all my belongings.

Me in Bruxelles, mid 1980s Summer.

TRAVELLING THRU EUROPE IN THE EIGHTIES. FROM HELSINKI WITH LOVE.

I never really met anyone that interesting until I went to Europe, I was young, pretty tanned and still had long curly black hair past my shoulders. That was the eighties man. Germany was having a late prolonged hippie age (they called them freaks) and long hair was in. I couldn't help noticing I got a lot of looks from the Frauleins, specially the Scandinavians chicks. It was great backpacking thru Europe. I hooked up with Krista, a gorgeous Finnish hottie on the Ferry from Stockholm Sweden to Helsinki in Finland. Our eyes and smiles had crossed as we walked around the ship earlier but I saw her with some dude and thought they were together. Later in the night as I was trying to break away from my berth neighbor, I ran into her again at the Disco. They played a Rolling Stones song called 'wild horses' while we danced tight close to each other, within minutes we were French kissing or should I say Finnish kissing.

Then she said she wanted to get some air so we went on deck and were just in the middle of passionate kissing with her shirt open and her lovely breasts staring at me, (European girls didn't wear bra's) so we looked around for an empty place. We rocked that boat all night in the men's room because that was the only place on the boat where we could be alone. We locked ourselves in a bathroom stall where she took off her jeans and panties and very swiftly took a seat over me. Whenever someone walked in we just made sure to pick up her little feet, held our breaths and didn't make a sound until it was empty again. Yes, that was my quickest pickup time, (and she wasn't even drunk) 15 minutes (except she picked me up). So from French-Finnish kissing with Krista we Finished, made it to the Finnish Line, get it?

We spent the rest of that night on that ferry with her sitting on my lap enjoying my caresses and kisses seated on a comfortable love-seat at a lounge, then that geek guy from Boston that I had originally seen her with showed up and started bitching that I had taken her from him, so she told him that she didn't want to be with him and didn't want his company. It wasn't until I told him to take a hint and hike that he left us while bitching about "free spirited" people like me. (that was after he asked me where I was from and I told him California).

That weekend I spent at her parents house while they were gone, she made me pizza and talked a lot, we also had a lot of wonderful sex with all her dolls around her bed while listening to Rock music. I was shocked when she told me she was still sweet sixteen but then added not to worry because the legal age in Finland was 15 at the time. Then on Sunday morning while we were on her bed playing nurse and doctor the phone rang, she looked worried when she hung up the phone and her look told me my dream was just about to end.

She said I had to go because her boyfriend was on his way to her house, she was only a teenager and already so free and wild. It had been a great experience but I was bummed out that my Penthouse story came to a sudden end. Man, she was so gorgeous and I didn't want to shower that afternoon so I could smell her aroma all over me, my hands, my breath, my face and all over my body. I was exhilarated by that experience but I also felt like the loneliest man on earth the rest of that day.

That afternoon as I was waiting for my train I was laying on the grass at a park and fell sleep. I woke up feeling my arm around my backpack move. I jumped up instinctively when I noticed four bums, winos trying to steal the contents of my backpack. I managed to punch one out and push another one down, the remaining two didn't dare to step in, I guess they had never seen a pissed off Latino before.

Helsinki was a very pretty city in the summer time, girls were eager to meet strangers and would often walk up to me and ask where I was from. Sometimes they would touch my dark long curly hair and ask if it was real. Other times I would get an invitation to meet them at some club or café' later that night. Getting sex was so easy and these girls were real blonde pretty girls, not silicone inflated fake blondes like the ones you generally encounter in Los Angeles or Las Vegas.

Now I was on my own again and eventually made my way the long way around, around North Finland, crossed Sweden then on to Narvik Norway, here I met Karl Hiller who at first I thought looked like Mick Jagger with curly hair or a rabbit with two big front teeth, he would later become my best friend and brother in Germany. Then I continued further down thru Northern Germany and then Amsterdam Holland. I stayed at the Adam and Eve Youth Hostel and what a perfect name they picked for it. One morning as I was taking a shower, in walks a naked female, she said "Hi" and proceeded to take her shower, at first I thought I was in the women's showers and then I had to make an effort to command my soldier not to get up and salute.

There I hooked up with a cute girl named Anna and her friend from Sweden, also a cool and funny Israeli guy was with us, we hung out for a few days and then I moved on. I took the ferry to England, hitchhiked across to the west side and took the other ferry to Ireland. What a great fun place with friendly people everywhere and easy to make friends. I had met Ayla, a German girl on the ferry and over a few beers we struck a friendship so she invited me to join her and visit her friends in Don Leary, suburb of Dublin. I did join her and her friends who were all Teachers, we had a great time, drinking lots of Guinness and hanging out at the beach, making music and other fun stuff.

She was a lot of fun to be around and I later visited her in Berlin, but I 'll tell you about it later. Ireland was a great place, specially at the small suburbs like Don Leary. Every evening we met at the local pub and had a few pints of Guinness beer. They were the friendliest people I'd encountered in Europe. The funniest part was hitchhiking from the Port town towards Dublin. The Lorie (truck) drivers were always eager to take us along and have a few laughs and chat with us. The roads were so bumpy but it didn't deter them from speeding up and the more they could make us jump and bump our heads on the ceiling of the truck cabin the more they rolled in laughter. I loved the Irish people.

SOUTHERN EUROPE. RUNNING WITH THE BULLS. ANTTIBES FREE LOVE.

Next I was on the ferry to Calais France and further south to meet Karl, the friend I had met in Norway. We were supposed to meet in San Sebastian for the Pamplonada or the running of the bulls. Karl had been a police man in Mainz Germany but his career didn't last long when he got reported by a wealthy man in a new Mercedes. He was accused of only ticketing new fancy cars parked illegally while the beat up ones he ignored, he was like my long lost Bro.

We actually coincidently met before we got to San Sebastian, at the train station of the nearby town. We arrived on time for the Pamplonada and hooked up with other people there, mostly Germans, also three cute American girls from New York, Beth was one of them and we liked-lusted each other for a few days and nights. That night I hadn't eaten much but drank cheap wine and beer and obviously smoked something that I thought was tobacco rolled in a big cigarette paper, it tasted a little sweet and I liked the taste. Obviously my head and body didn't like it and I got sick, I couldn't walk back to the camping grounds and the Germans had to carry me while I screamed like a madman, thinking in my hallucinations that they were going to kill me. I tried to run away but I would drop like a rag doll to the floor, they just laughed and carried me some more.

Thanks to the Germans I was okay the next morning, I had become popular with the camping neighbors and they just looked at me and laughed. I remembered most of it the next day and was embarrassed about it. I swore never to drink or smoke weird tobacco again and I celebrated to it the next day again.

The next day we ran with the big horny bulls (big horns) without anyone getting trampled or gored. Well to be honest I didn't run that much and the bulls did all the running. Once I was inside the fenced up street I tried to get out after having second thoughts and the cops guarding the fence wouldn't let me out anymore, so I sort of tried to make myself invisible and spread myself like butter on the walls when the bulls went by, then I sort of ran behind them. It's actually a pretty hairy experience but if it's something you want to do to prove something to yourself then that's it. You just have to be smart and not be the last one on the pile when all the drunk and hung over people running in front of you, trip over each other. This is when the first bull gets it's laughs because when it sees this pile of people trying to get out of it's way, it kind of helps them by adding a new asshole to the last asshole on the pile, ouch that's got to hurt.

There have been some deaths in the past but every year someone gets gored and survives. I was smart enough to avoid those people piles and stood sideways to let the bulls run by. That's not always the smart thing to do because some bulls have gored people standing on the sides of the walls too. Nevertheless, it was a blast and a great experience and I walked away without any additional holes on my body.

From there, Karl and I hooked up with two eighteen year old German Frauleins, Melanie and Ute, they were traveling for the first time on their own and were hesitant to try hitchhiking so we volunteered to pair up with them and hitchhike in pairs, Karl liked the dark haired one and I was left with the blonde bitchy one, she was cute but Oh what an attitude. We didn't hit it, she somehow was unfriendly and didn't show any interest in jumping into my sleeping bag, Karl on the other hand was all lovey-dovey with his girl Melanie and didn't want to part. After a week, I met two cute Swedish girls alone and naked in their own private beach cove near (that's probably where my original ancestors originated from my Father's side of the family) a small town called Hortas de Tabul in the south of Portugal and I told Karl I was going to join them, Karl was sad to leave his new love but he joined me.

A few days later, we rode the train to the Mediterranean Coast of France, Anttibes, we rode the night train for free, laying on the luggage racks above peoples' heads to avoid the ticket officer. When the ticket guy was walking down below us asking people for tickets I was awake laying on my sleeping bag above his head on the luggage rack while

---

Karl was sound sleep with his hand dangling down. I was holding my breath because I thought that anytime the guy would see his hand and then kick us out both in the middle of the night. But luck was on our side and he didn't see us, the passengers around us who were all travelers like us just laughed and cheered at us after the guy left. At Anttibes we met a lot of people, specially cute student girls from all over the North.

There was the British cutie with the big floating devices, Jette from Denmark, Hanna from Sweden, Brita from Stuttgart and a few others. I switched girls almost everyday like switching swimming shorts. I was about to leave Anttibes one day after a week of hanging out there, mainly because of the troubles I got into with Hanna's boyfriend, (he showed up later and noticed we had something going) Swedes are pretty open minded and after she admitted she'd had sex with me, he didn't want her talking to me anymore. Hanna and I shared her tent and sleeping bags for a couple of nights to sort of keep the French-Moroccan hippies off her, she was hot. She was always topless at the beach (like every other girl) with a beautiful set of breasts. We were inseparable by day and night and made love by the light of the full moon, then swam and slept on the beach by day, that is until her boyfriend showed up. We almost got into a fight when he saw us hugging and kissing good bye one night, I was going to kick his ass but she stepped in and saved my ass probably, he was over 6 foot plus and built like a wrestler.

Above, Me looking up, Vipsy and Anna with friend from Youth Hostel. Below, hanging and camping at the beach cove of Anttibes, the love beach.

Anyway, I was bummed out and just when I was packing to leave when Brita arrives to the beach where we camped. Beautiful face with long blonde hair, wide hips and a radiant smile, we connected right away. After we talked for a few minutes and when I told her I was leaving to go South she looked disappointed. I didn't want to leave but I did. Later at the train station in Nice, I was waiting for my train to Italy and started conversation with a group of Norwegians, two girls and a guy. Two sisters, Marit and her older sister, Marit was so cute, petite, brunette and had a high pitch baby voice (which later used to nerve me). They had just come back from Greece. We exchanged addresses with Marit and she invited me to visit her in Norway if I stayed longer in Europe.

I was so preoccupied with Marit and enchanted with her that I forgot all about my train to Italy and missed it. It must have been destiny. So guess what, I trailed back to the beach in Anttibes and there was Brita with her tent all set up. She smiled when she saw me and I was happy again to be in her surroundings, my friend from Germany, Volker, friend of Karl from Mainz was also still there.

We all hung out together, there were about six or seven of us, two Swedish 17 year old girls, Brita and her girlfriend Theresa, a Britt called Joe Cool and another Britt called Duncan I think. At night the local gipsy gang would come and join us sometimes. There was one called Freddie who was stoned out of his head for good and was always trying to impose on the girls. One night he started trying to fondle one of the Swedish young girls even after she told him to go away. He just laid there on her sleeping bag and kept trying to fondle her, so I being the protector there told him to get up and leave, he wouldn't move so I grabbed his feet and dragged him off on the sand. All of a sudden he jumped up and I saw his hand go to his waist to his dagger, it happened so fast and I managed to punch him in the forehead and nock him down while his dagger rolled on the sand. I thought, Oh shit, now his friends are all going to jump me. But to my surprise, they told him to get up and leave, I couldn't believe it but they understood it was his fault. Everything returned to normal and we resumed our usual activity of drinking French wine by the fire at the beach surrounded by good company, cute girls and the stars.

That night Brita and I decided to test her tent and we got engaged in some hot passionate love making. It was embarrassing because she was a little loud and everyone was cheering us the next day when we came out of our love quarters. I had some very happy days hanging out with her and her friend so I suggested for them to join me to Greece, they said they were supposed to meet friends in Avignon and that there was a big festival carnival going on. They invited me to join them but I said I would try to make it to Greece first. So while we waited at the Nice train station for our trains while playing guitar, I missed my train for the second time so I decided to accept her invitation to join her and her friend to Avignon. (I sort of regretted that outcome because I never got around to going to Greece).

That night on the train there, some French geek followed us to our cabin and tried to fondle her friend Theresa while we all tried to sleep. At first I pretended to be sleep but was watching the creep from the corner of my eye. First he tried on one of the other two German girls who were in the cabin with us but she kept pushing his hands off. At first I almost wanted to laugh at the show he was making but when he then turned his sight to the right towards Theresa and started trying to slip his hand towards her legs, I intercepted it by putting my foot on the seat. That didn't stop him because he slipped his hand under my foot and kept trying to grab her legs. She started pushing him away and that's when I decided the show was over. I stood up and said to him in French, "Enough, Stop, Arrete", I pushed him out of the cabin and threw his jacket at his face, he just said, "Je suis desolee', bon voyage" (I'm sorry, have a good trip) and left us alone.

SUMMER CARNIVAL IN AVIGNON.

We arrived in Avignon early the next morning, tired and hungry. Everyone was camping all over the place by the River but we chose to camp out in the Cathedral's gardens at night, we had to jump the fence without being seen and had the garden of Eden all to ourselves, we made love next to her sleepy friend Theresa by the moonlight in the church garden, romantic and religious huh. The next early morning the priest saw us sleeping there in our sleeping bags and politely told us to leave, it was a good thing we were dressed and in our own sleeping bags by then. (See Mom, I did go to church).

By day we would hang out in the Main Plaza where everything was happening, music, shows, circus acts, it was a great atmosphere and I had my guitar always with me so we always joined somebody else with more musical instruments. Brita and I really enjoyed each others company, that is until her ex-boyfriend came to town.

Her ex-boyfriend from Peru, who played in a local band showed up. He still loved her and wanted back with her, she was confused and I felt like I was in the way so I elected to leave, I thought it was for the best.

She was wearing my long white shirt (that used to belong to my friend Karl) over only her bikini bottom, with her long blonde hair over my shirt, she looked like an angel, a sad angel. I was very sad too. I clearly remember when she pulled my shirt off over her head, revealing her bare breasts, handed me my shirt and put on a tee-shirt. She looked at me intensely with her deep blue eyes and said "you said you would stay with me here" I answered back "yes, but that was before your ex-boyfriend showed up, do you want me to stay"? She didn't answer anything and I knew she was confused and didn't know what to do. She was very silent thereafter and we kissed and hugged for a long while until the train to Germany showed up. She just stood there as the train started to move, I hung out over the window and stared at her, waved and said good bye for the last time, it was just like a sad goodbye in a love movie.

I wanted to jump out of the train and stay in Avignon but I knew it was best to leave. That night in the train, when I went to the bathroom I kicked the walls a couple of times and released my disappointment and frustrations. It sucked to be alone again after meeting someone you thought you were in love with. We did talk on the phone a few weeks later and we made plans to meet again in her hometown of Stuttgart, but somehow I didn't get around to it because I had other girls to visit in Scandinavia.

When I returned to Germany a few months later I called her home and her Mom told me she had moved to Paris with her boyfriend and that she was having a baby. Gulp, I wondered if it was mine, I still wonder that today. Someday I'll try to find out for sure.

I continued my journey to the town of Mainz where Karl had invited me to visit. I knew my time in Europe was about to run out in a week so I decided to spend the last of those days with my friends Karl, Volker and his friends. It wasn't the Germany I had imagined, it was crawling with activities, musical concerts, pubs, chicks and really cool young people reliving a late hippie age. I stayed with Karl and his girlfriend Kristina in a little studio at first, until she had enough and told Karl to either move me out or it was over. So Volker rescued me and invited me to his parents house. They were so nice and hospitable and his Mom was always trying to practice English with me. His Dad was a Police man and was also very nice.

Volker was one of the nicest people I've ever met, he was so unselfish and easy going, didn't talk much but listened very carefully. We're still friends up to this day. Anyway, Karl suggested I work at his parents grape fields with him and his other friends in a town nearby, also making the wine, and that caught my attention. I knew I had to decide to either stay and let my plane ticket expire, or leave and regret it for not staying.

I was also supposed to join the Air Force on my return but by now that I had discovered my wings of freedom I wasn't too sure anymore if Military life would be for me. Besides, the chances of getting a flight slot were very slim.

So I made a decision to stay and I didn't regret it. We picked the grapes with all of Karl's friends, had lots of good food that his Mom cooked for all of us and had all the wine we wanted. (his Mom was such a nice lady and his step Dad was nice too but very quiet). We all crashed exhausted in the barn after crushing the grapes with our feet and then pushing them into the huge barrels down below in the cellar of the barn. That's how they make wine the traditional way In Germany. Eventually I made some more money playing music in the streets with other musicians. The best idea was that of Ingo a friend of Karl's, he said I could probably get a job at the Military Army casernes near Mainz. So I went and applied as a civilian US and got a job as a Gymnasium attendant right away. I guess the nice girl in her mid twenties at the Personnel office took a liking towards me and moved me up on the job waiting list because otherwise as a civilian US I would have been below the German Nationals looking for jobs too.

It was great because I had already run out of money by then.

It was the beginning of a new life for me, I felt more at home in Germany than I did in California and the people at first appeared unfriendly but they were easier to make real true friendships, which compared to California it's the opposite, you meet many people that are only superficially friendly but it's hard to make true friendships.

NUDITY THE GERMAN WAY. ME NUDE, NEVER.

That October after I worked with Karl's family making wine, Karl and I took off for Munich for the famous October Fest. It was definitely a big Feast we couldn't miss. We hitchhiked there and were invited to crash at a lady's house who picked us up on the highway. Every late afternoon we would party till late, sleep until noon and then head for the English gardens to relax by the park and watch the naked girls play around the park.

Not kidding, everyone was naked at the park, it was still summer weather and the German's were very open minded with nudity. I was still trying to get used to it and wasn't planning to undress to my birthday suit but Karl suggested we both do that because we were the only idiots in shorts in that section of the park. He went first and then he insisted I do it too otherwise I might look out of place. Okay, so I took my shorts off and just laid on my towel without moving for fear of being seen naked. Ha, little did I know that I was gonna roast in the sun and I needed to crawl to the edge of the stream to cool off.

I started crawling on my butt slowly until I reached the edge of the water. When I got to the stream and sort of floated in it, I thought it wasn't so bad because nobody could really see me from the waist down. Then I let myself float with the strong current thinking I would be able to swim or walk back. When I was ready to return to my towel and tried swimming or walking against the current I realized I couldn't do it. Now I was in a naked predicament, I couldn't return to my towel via the stream so I had to walk stark naked back to my towel amongst all the other naked people playing in the park. I was so terrified to be seen so I just pretended to be invisible and walked as quietly as possible to make sure nothing jumped around too much. I probably stuck out like a sore thumb because I was very tanned and had a mop of black long curls on my head so I must have looked like a mop upside down. I was so embarrassed when I returned to my towel and Karl just had a few laughs on my behalf.

BACK TO THE FUTURE.

Oh, back to the future, time for another position report, let's see, where are we now, at the 180 degree Longitude, the International Date Line. I'm about to go back one day in time, I am now one day younger. The perfect moment, I do feel younger you know, so to celebrate I will request a fresh brewed black coffee from the upper deck Flight Attendant.

After verifying that the position report has been sent, we'll also check fuel status, altitude and heading, etc. Fortunately we now use CPDLC, (Controller Pilot Data Link Communication) to automatically relay position reports thru ADS to the appropriate Oceanic Control Area.

Let's see, where is our closest emergency airport just in case, still Midway airport, in the middle of nowhere. But it's the only emergency airport just past the International Dateline, it's less than 9,000 feet long, it feels kind of short for a Jumbo 747-300 but long enough in case of a real emergency. Midway Island is run by the US government and is the only Emergency Airport we use on Japan to Honolulu flights.

Two engine aircraft such as Boeing 767 or 777 follow different over water rules that are called ETOPS, meaning, Engines Turning or Pilots Swimming, no just kidding, it actually means Extended (or Emergency) Two Engine (Over Water) Operations. They are required to remain within two or three flight hours of an Emergency Airport that they are able to reach on one engine only, in case they loose one engine. On the Jumbo we have four engines so we don't follow that procedure. All Heavy two engine jet planes are able to, and certified to maintain flight on one engine and continue flying to their closest airport as long as there is sufficient fuel on board.

The Boeing 767 and most other Boeing aircraft are actually certified to maintain fire suppression for up to three hours and 15 minutes in the cargo area, scary huh. It makes me wonder how they came up with that certification and if it actually has been tested at high altitudes, loaded with fuel and passengers and in the middle of the Indian Ocean while three hours away from Mauritius, Cocos Island or Diego Garcia Island. I used to fly that route some years ago and it was the longest and loneliest ocean crossing I can think of.

You know what they say about the safety of having two engines, the remaining engine takes you to the scene of the accident, also kidding there. (That applies mostly to twin prop aircraft).

Normally on long ETOPS flights of nine hours or more we used to have a supplemental crew member pilot on board, so that we all take turns sleeping or resting. We even used to get a first class seat or bunk to use at our leisure. That way on an eleven hour flight say, Mauritius to Manchester, we could each get up to three and a half hours of rest or sleep. That is crucial on night flights.

Unfortunately there are different regulations from country to country and differences between Pilot Unions. With an Asian Airline, we Foreign crews (Gaigin Pilots) are allowed to fly without a supplementary Pilot for up to eleven hours. Although on the Classic Jumbo, with a Flight Engineer it still is a very tiring flight so it is necessary to take the occasional Power Nap. On two man cockpits it's more critical to keep one guy awake at all times. As I mentioned before, it makes us and the flight safer.

POSSIBLE FLIGHT RISK SCENARIOS.

Now, here is the interesting thing, here we have a plane load full of passengers, 200, 300 or maybe 500 (including crew, I once had 501 on the Jumbo). All boarding with their loved ones, children, wives, girlfriends, lovers, parents, inflatable dolls, etc.

They are all trusting their lives on two or three single individuals, who they know nothing about. They see us walk up to the airplane and figure these are extraordinary people who are taking their lives into their hands to transport them safely from point A to point B.

Ironically, most people feel safer if they see that the Pilots look aged, bald, white hair, etc.

It's a false impression of safety probably given by the older day movies of Pilots being portrayed like that. That is not the case anymore because now we have a new generation of younger better prepared (and better looking) Pilots. What I mean by better prepared is that thanks to Simulator and Aircraft advanced technology, Pilots are easier to train in all kinds of Emergencies by simulating exact scenarios of what can go wrong in flight. (What I mean by better looking is that we are better looking, lol).

Therefore, sitting in a cockpit for many years and moving from Mechanic to Flight Engineer, then Co Pilot and finally Captain after twenty years or more, isn't necessary anymore like in the old days.

The passengers see that the aircraft looks good, safe, clean, humongous and impressive. The Flight Attendants look attractive and always remain cool and friendly (not always, have you ever seen a 200+ pound sixty something year old and with the attitude of a wrestler on a Major US Carrier? For safety reasons huh, right).

Well my brave flying friends, in the perfect world it would all go fine and dandy, oky dokey and no problemo mon. But according to Murphy's Law, anything that can go wrong will go wrong, We must remember and never forget that nothing is perfect in this world and that to err is human.

Let's look at all the scenarios that could mess up your hairdo, ruin your manicure or just send you to meet your creator.

Terrorist attack? Very low chances of it happening again in my opinion. Unless we allow it to happen, again. Beefing up Airport security even more and subjecting passengers to more abuse and nonsense won't make it any safer. I know they keep saying on the news that they will be training TSA agents even more to prepare them for more possible terrorist detection. It's not going to work if they keep using the same stupid techniques and all they are doing is harassing the flying public even more.

For example, they are still making us Flight crew members go thru their metal detector secondary inspection with their magic wands, grabbing our nuts and ass like they're enjoying it and then releasing us to fly a huge bomb-like airplane with wings, loaded with explosive fuel and hundreds of passengers. Even our own personal stuff e.g. a nail clipper or mini screw driver set won't be allowed thru, as if they didn't know that we carry a huge sharp axe in the cockpit (It is carried on every aircraft as an emergency item). Does that make any sense? Oh, and guess who is paying for all of this increased security, you are my dear flying fans.

Aircraft catching fire on Takeoff? Maybe an engine but not the aircraft itself, unless the aircraft rejects the takeoff run late and ends up rolling off the end of the runway, breaking up in pieces and burning up because of the large amount of jet fuel it carries. Yeah, those chances could happen more often than others.

Aircraft not touching down properly and bouncing or floating down the runway therefore cart wheeling and breaking up, which would probably lead to a fire. Yes, that's also on the top of the accident list.

Actually, many accidents like this have happened due to poor weather, poor Pilot technique or just plain GET-HOME-ITIS by the

Flight Crew. (which could be possible due to accumulated Pilot fatigue).

Pilots falling sleep and overshooting their destination until they run out of fuel? Maybe, but I don't know of any cases yet. It almost happened to me many years ago. There have also been two cases over the Hawaiian Islands by the new Airline that opened up just before Aloha Airlines went out of business. Apparently the two pilots fell sleep and were incommunicado for 30 minutes or so. Fortunately they did not run out of fuel before and where able to return and land, otherwise it could have had fatal results.

Now, commuter airlines such as the one I just described follow different FAA rules when it comes to Pilot rest periods. Commuter Pilots don't get enough sleep sometimes on a four or five day pattern and have many late arrivals followed by early departures for a few days in a row, that is exactly why the accident rates are higher amongst Commuter Airlines. Add to that, that most Commuter Pilots are much less experienced since they are just starting their professional careers and they are more apt of making mistakes or not recognizing a possible mistake due to accumulated fatigue. Also the age factor, most commuter Pilots are young in their twenties and early thirties, therefore, they are more susceptible to partying, drinking or late night girl chasing. Add to that, a young male ego when they're given the position of Captains and voila', a bitter cocktail.

ACUMULATED FATIGUE, in my opinion is the main source of pilot induced accidents. Sometimes we are scheduled to operate flights that are eight or nine hours duration each way with a 12 to 24 hour layover, then one or two more flights day after day in the same direction, duration and time zone crossing. All that is very strenuous on our bodies due to the time zone difference and confusion of our biological clocks. Also, going there by day and back by night three times in a week would seriously affect our performance and alertness level. Imagine being up all night three times in a week while shooting thru the same time zone difference back and forth three times. It makes you feel like you've aged all of a sudden and it takes up to three full days just to recover and feel normal again.

Our own companies corner us into doing flights like this sometimes because they say that it's legal, although not safe. Normally the FAA doesn't allow crews to fly the next day after an International arrival, but with foreign Airlines it's a different story because they have and make their own rules that are not always subject to US FAA Regulations.

With our alertness level reduced, jetlagged, sleepy and in the event of an abnormal condition or a heavy work load approach due to bad weather, it could create the arena for a pilot induced accident or violation. Crossing time zones more than once in a few days is very hard on our bodies and even thou it is legal according to Company and Foreign FAA rules, it is NOT SAFE. So when a Pilot screws up and falls sleep like in the Hawaiian incident, he just gets fired and the company continues to operate with very minimum rest periods for Flight crews. It's up to the flying public to lobby with their lawmakers to sanction aviation Management that allow Airlines to operate with tired crew. Unfortunately, many Airlines operate this way.

Aircraft perhaps blowing up in flight without any notice or reason? Maybe, it has happened with TWA, still a mystery today. It is very possible it was an accidental missile target and was kicked under the rug. It is very rare for an airplane to just blow up in midair except when a bomb gets detonated from the inside, Lockerbie Scotland for example.

Mid air crashes? Yeah, that could happen more often if it weren't for TCAS (Traffic Collision Avoidance System). There was a Saudi Jumbo and a Russian Airliner over New Delhi over a decade ago that had a mid air collision. The Russian Crew misunderstood the altitude clearance they were given and stayed at the same altitude as the other Aircraft. With the TCAS system we can actually see the approaching traffic on a screen, their direction of flight and their vertical flight path. RA's, Resolution Advisories also tell us which way to climb or descend in order to avoid them. That only works if the Pilot flying follows the directions given even if the Air Traffic Controller gives different instructions. There was a midair collision over Switzerland a few years ago were the controller didn't see the incoming traffic and gave instructions to the pilots to fly into the other aircraft. However, the final outcome could have been avoided if the Pilot would have followed the TCAS commands properly and disobeyed the controllers directions. In this case it wouldn't be considered a violation since it is a first priority to obey the TCAS commands first.

Language barriers causing accidents? Yes, the example above was one of them. Although English remains the official language in Aviation and all Flight Crews are required to speak it, many far Eastern Airline Crews have a very marginal grasp of it. Chinese and Russian being at the top of the list. Altitude clearance misunderstandings, wrong headings and Take off clearances have been misunderstood very often. The strong accents by the AT Controllers of some countries are so difficult to understand sometimes that it is necessary to verify what was said twice.

Death by Air Traffic Controller? It's happened and is bound to happen again as long as humans are manning the Air Traffic Control Areas and Aircraft. I have been given heading instructions on a few occasions that would have taken me into a mountain, another aircraft or the wrong direction. I questioned the controller in time and an accident was averted.

That works only if the Pilot always know where he is, where he is going and which direction he expects to be going next. Situational awareness is the key.

AT Controllers are also affected by stress and fatigue, they work long hours and get a little sleep sometimes due to insufficient Controllers and increasing Air Traffic. So they are prone to making mistakes when accumulated fatigue sets in, they are only human and to err is human, remember?

I've been told in the past by people unrelated to flying that they are more impressed by what AT Controllers do. They think that they directly control every airplane in the sky and that's why it sounds impressive to them.

It cracks me up to hear that because what those people don't realize is the following. The AT Controller sits safely in his office surrounded by screens and electronic radar equipment.

He can fly an airplane into a mountain or into another airplane only if the Captain in control allows him. He is only giving instructions to separate aircraft from others within the safe and legal parameters, directing them or vectoring them to line up so the aircraft can intercept the extended centerline of the runway and land safely. Kind of like a cow herder, directing cows and bulls safely from behind the fence, where the real difficult job is of the bull rider (in this case the Pilots), trying to stay on the bull without getting thrown off and gored. That would be the analogy between controllers and pilots.

Not only that, it takes just a few months to train an AT Controller. Pilot training requires up to four years or more of initial training which covers up to eight ratings. That only allows a new Commercial pilot for hire to fly a small propeller aircraft initially, or make flight hours from Flight Instructing other new pilots. He then must fly for various years as Copilot for different aircraft while increasing in aircraft size as his experience increases. He may become a Captain of a smaller aircraft and then start as Copilot again with a different Airline or a different type of jet aircraft.

Every time we change to another jet aircraft, we have to do new training to obtain a type rating for that specific aircraft and that normally takes three to four months. With some Asian Airlines, that takes up to a year. In addition to accumulating five to ten years of flight training and flight experience, a Professional Pilot wishing to reach the Major Airlines must also posses a four year or more University Degree. Preferably in a major related to Aeronautics.

Yes, all that costs money and the total bill could reach up to $100,000. The cost in time between graduation day and being a Captain on a Commercial Jet Airliner could take from ten to fifteen years. Of course there are unethical and dishonest pilots that have lied about their total flight time and have managed to slip thru the system and hired to fly something that's very automated such as an Airbus, where their poor pilot skills may go unnoticed, that is until they commit a serious offense or accident due to their insufficient experience.

Another scenario; Death by Flight (fright) Attendant? Possible from a love gone sour, passionate crime or simply poisoned in flight. I don't think it has happened to my knowledge but I did almost loose my precious goods once (family jewels). A pissed of Fright Attendant who was upset about not being the one and only love of my life, so she thought, (I never gave her that idea), she brought my coffee that another F. Attendant was preparing for me and tried to drop it on my lap while I was tending to my flight. Fortunately I recognized her perfume and turned my head in time while grabbing the coffee free falling towards my precious goods, it only burnt my fingers a little bit but the contents stayed inside the cup while the little Witch ran out in a hurry.

Now here's another Fright Attendant scenario. Picture you're on the Takeoff roll on a Major US Carrier where they allow overweight very mature granny Flight Attendants to work on airplanes. (Because of Union protection they cannot be replaced and can fly until well past 60, whatever happened to hiring young, fit and beautiful proper Flight Attendants like in the old days when they were selected for safety, pleasure to the eyes and excellent service.)

The aircraft rejects the Take Off due to an engine failure and the aircraft ends up on the grass (hopefully not over a cliff or rocky terrain) and catches on fire. Everybody starts screaming and running like headless chickens and the evacuation procedures begin. I don't see how a 200+ pound sixty something year old person in poor health is going to help passengers out of a burning airplane after an aborted take off. On the contrary, they might hinder the evacuation or even block the emergency door. That is if they don't get a heart attack first. I know it sounds exaggerated but if it hasn't happened yet, it's bound to happen sooner or later. I apologize if it offends some that fit the above description, but if it is for the safety of humans on airplanes I don't think it's safe to allow such Flight operations.

Last scenario, Death by Turbulence. Well, that's always possible if an airplane accidentally flies into a major Cumulonimbus cloud that generates excessive vertical winds as the Aircraft passes thru it at 600 miles per hour. It could destroy it and send it flying in all directions specially if it was a lighter displacement composite built airplane. A Boeing 747 is so strong I don't think it would be that easy to destroy it in midair. There where a couple of cases were in two different scenarios in the past, two Boeing airplanes were knocked out of the sky, plunged a few thousand feet and were able to recover almost intact except for the landing gear being ripped and pushed backwards due to the excessive gravitational forces exerted on them. In both cases, they were able to land safely.

Turbulence at cruising altitudes generated by atmospheric instability, temperature changes, pressure changes and high speed jet streams are usually the cause of in flight turbulence.

Also flying in the proximity of weather systems, large clouds and stormy weather. Flying thru light or moderate turbulence is not necessarily dangerous or unsafe, it's just like driving across a dented road with potholes in it, we just try to avoid the potholes and the ones we go over are not large enough to make us loose control of the aircraft. So don't worry about turbulence, it's not going to kill you, just make sure you're buckled up so you don't bounce of the ceiling, yes, that could hurt you bad or at least mess up your hairdo. Also, watch were your hot coffee might end up.

The other bad scenario could be caused by Passenger Rage. Strangely, there are more of those cases than you would think. Passengers that have some adverse reaction to alcohol in flight, maybe due to taking prescription drugs or other illegal drugs too. They could go crazy in flight and try to enter the Cockpit, that's happened a few times before our Cockpit doors were beefed up.

Alcohol plays a major part in most of these cases. You have to remember that at altitude, the amount of oxygen is much thinner. An airplane cabin is pressurized to remain at around 7,000 feet while it flies at altitudes of around 37,000 feet or more above sea level. Picture yourself downing a few heavy drinks at a mountain top of 8,000 feet and your body will feel drunk just with two drinks instead of 8 drinks when at sea level. Oxygen depletion mixed with alcohol don't get along very well and some people react aggressively when exposed to this situation. So my advise would be to limit alcohol consumption when flying. It still surprises me that most airlines still give uncontrolled quantities of alcohol to passengers in flight.

There was a case once on a previous Airline I worked for with a Deadheading Flight attendant. (Dead Head means a traveling Crew member for Duty the next day, we often Deadhead to another Airport to start our flight from there, Captain's travel in First class and get paid for this travel, not bad for drinking champagne, eating First class excellent meals and watching movies)

This Flight attendant had been taking some medication and didn't know she shouldn't mix it with wine at high altitude. She was getting drunk and obnoxious before anyone noticed her flirting with a man traveling with his wife. She ended up with the man in the bathroom sitting on him stark naked, apparently found by the man's wife after her husband was missing for quite a while.

She didn't get fired because she claimed she wasn't aware of the side effects the pills and wine at altitude had on her. I believe she even got a promotion eventually. (High altitude personal service girl?).

On one of my recent flights to Japan, the Chief Flight Attendant came to the cockpit to report a drunk and obnoxious male passenger. I instructed her to stop serving him alcohol and to issue him a warning letter if he continued being offensive and unruly. He continued demanding for alcohol and when he wasn't getting anymore he got more offensive and aggressive. So I signed the next and last warning letter and he was told this time that Airport Security personnel would be waiting for him if he didn't remain quiet and peaceful. Well, he wasn't stupid so he acted calm for the remaining of the flight, however, as soon as we landed he went to the KI ground staff and reported the Flight attendants for not serving him alcohol. Incredibly the Ground KI staff asked him to point out the Flight Attendants and then he called them over. Now the passenger got aggressive again and intimidated the girls accusing them of passenger abuse. He was trying to contact his lawyer so he could sue them and he wouldn't let them walk away.

I was unaware of this because by now we thought all the crew had made it to the waiting shuttle bus. 45 minutes went by and when the girls didn't show up, myself and my First Officer went looking for them. Then we saw them at the arrival gate, cornered by this drunk Ahole, raising his hand at them and intimidating them while he called his so called Lawyer. Only in Japan can someone get away with this abuse of women.

The girls were terrified and they didn't dare to move until they saw me. I told the girls to get their luggage and follow me just as the drunk idiot tried to give me his bullshit, but I stopped him with the palm of my hand in front of his ugly face and told him, " You misbehaved and have intimidated my Crew, go away or I'll call Security," I don't know if he understood but when I gently took the arm of the Chief F. Attendant to lead her out to the exit he leaped forward as if to stop her, I stood in front of him and suddenly lifted both my hands' palms facing him and said in a loud and authoritarian voice which scared him dead on his tracks, " Stay away now, go away". He was like a bullying dog that barked too much until someone stood up to him and knocked him off his pedestal. Then he kept saying he was calling his lawyer to accuse us all of wanting to attack him. The girls were pretty shook up and I really had to retain myself from letting the situation getting out of hand. Nothing came of this or at least we didn't hear anything else from the Company. It goes to show my point of why alcohol should be limited on long flights.

Now with the fuel prices sky rocketing, airlines are sometimes forced to make some cuts. In my opinion they should start with CEOs and top management. (Some CEOs in the US are known to make 400 times more than the average worker even if they suck at their job). Instead, they start with the employees, maybe a cut or two in maintenance here and there, maybe carry a little less fuel to destination? Or how about reducing the Flight crew's rest and putting them in cheaper noisier hotels while we make them fly longer hours with less pay. And all this is happening while Airport Security costs keep increasing, except that the flying passenger pays this bill.

To make the situation worse, some Aviation Brokers are taking advantage of the Pilot supply exceeding demand so they offer less pay, more flight hours per month and lousier conditions at Hotels in addition to lower per-diems. It's like being prostituted to the uglier clients for less cash, basically our Profession has been pimped by Bean Counters and greedy Executives.

The way I see it, if your time is not up, it's not up. We all have purposes and reasons to be here so why worry and cry before we get spanked, right? Pilots know the responsibility we have when given the keys to a heavy jet aircraft full of passengers. (Figure of speech, we really don't have a starting key to the aircraft). It's not going to be a ride in the park but the operation of the Aircraft can be both fun and safe.

Most of the time, we have near perfect flights in perfect weather and in a perfectly safe Aircraft.

While other times we might have poor weather at our destination, typhoons near by, low ceilings due to fog, thunderstorms, snow storms or wind shear and microburst conditions.

This is why the best way to describe our job is: LONG MOMENTS OF BOREDOME, PUNCTUATED BY SHEER MOMENTS OF TERROR.

It's all in a days work to deal with whatever problem we are facing. Whether it's caused by mechanical malfunctions, weather related or Air Traffic Control delays. I personally sort of enjoy the challenge of landing in adverse conditions, with strong 30 knot crosswinds or landing on snow or rainy conditions. It's definitely an adrenalin rush and you can feel your heartbeat accelerate after a landing in such conditions. Sometimes we let the Auto Land system do the landing when the weather visibility goes below certain legal minimums, e.g. less than 500 meter RVR (Runway Visual Range or 1,500 feet forward visibility) or below 150 feet cloud ceiling.

Remember that video of the Lufthansa Airbus trying to land in Hamburg Germany recently?. The cross winds where so strong that the Flight crew almost bought the farm. In my opinion, the Crew should not have tried to land in those conditions in the first place. They got very lucky when they recovered and executed the missed approach.

If we feel that safety is compromised by landing in adverse conditions, then we can execute a Missed Approach and divert the flight to our Alternate Airport which we carry enough fuel to get there plus 30 minutes of Extra Holding time. Every flight scenario is planned for, so it's very difficult for an Aircraft to run out of fuel just like that. Of course it's happened due to faulty fuel measuring systems, a fuel leak or basic human arrogance.

Nobody is perfect and I admit that, including myself, so I'm not denying any mistakes I've made in the past. Obviously none life threatening or I wouldn't be writing this book. Most of the small mistakes, misunderstandings or misjudging of my part were mostly due to FATIGUE. Being up all night on a long flight or having a series of night flights close together. Rushing to get out of there or landing also has led to some mistakes that have made me learn to not let me rush myself ever again. Rushing is a very sure way of forgetting things, doing procedures the wrong way or missing important checklist items. Like almost forgetting to put the landing gear down for example. The last two car accidents I've had on the road were also due to accumulated fatigue while driving home after many night flights.

So next time you're about to get on a jet plane be assured that you're chances of being wiped off the face of the earth are statistically six times lower than: Riding a taxi, driving yourself, or taking the train or bus. (Or crossing the street in Honolulu)

Ironically, most human deaths are caused by disease, accidental poisoning, crime, Doctor mistakes (100,000 deaths a year from malpractice or simple negligence), side effects from prescription drugs or suicide and, oh yeah, did I mention unnecessary wars?

Yeah, it sucks being up all night but my Airline career has mostly satisfied me. I always dreamt of being an International Pilot since I was a little kid, or an Astronaut. I somehow imagined what my life was going to be like or what I wished it would be like. Interestingly enough, it all pretty much has come true. Except for the Astronaut part and that Raquel Welch wasn't interested in me, (well, we were actually madly in love, me in her, and her in some other dude). The power of thought is amazing, all you have to do is wish for something, put a date on it, visualize it and make it come true. We all have the incredible ability to make thoughts become matter.

The long and slow road to an Airline Flying job isn't for everyone, nor for the weak or faint of heart. The only thing that can keep you going is passion and the love for airplanes (no, not the love for chasing beaver or big amounts of cash). Otherwise most people that give up are the ones that weren't meant to be Pilots. They just thought they wanted to be Pilots because of the traveling, money or Flight attendant chasing. In my opinion those are not good enough reasons to get into Aviation. Or their Daddies or Mommies put them there, it's not easy to refuse a nice easy life when it's served on a silver platter. However, it's more satisfying and gratifying to get there under your own impulse based on your dreams and passions.

Sure, nowadays fully automated airplanes such as Airbuses can make any mediocre pilot look good, but make a good pilot feel mediocre. You have to have good flying skills and fly the airplane with style and feeling. If you love what you do, and you do it with finesse and passion, then you will become good at what you do.

The slow and bumpy road to the Captain seat of a Boeing 747 or such is but for very few lucky and good aviators in the old fashioned sense. It all takes dedication, responsibility and guts, not forgetting the passion and love for whatever airplane you're flying. That long bumpy but exciting road has taken me around 19 years of Professional flying. (not counting flight training or flight instructing.)

I have completed my Circumnavigation around the world in about twelve years of International flying. Eventually I connected the dots and marked with a marker on my world map of my flights around the world. Except for one point, Los Angeles to Hawaii was missing, but I completed It in a different way, not as Pilot operating in an airplane but as the Skipper on my sailboat, that counts doesn't it? Approximately 2,400 Nautical Miles in 18 days. (I'll write about the details of that voyage later on in the book.)

I have Flown to most continents and major cities and lived in interesting places, e.g. Mauritius, New Zealand, Germany, Dominican Republic, Mexico, Japan, Hawaii and all over California.

The cities I flew to were usually major cities in different countries. In Europe e.g. London, Frankfurt, Paris, Geneva, Zurich, Manchester, Rome, Madrid, Vienna, Munich.

In the East: Bombay, Delhi, Indonesia, Bali, Jakarta, Singapore, Hong Kong, Bangkok, Saudi Arabia.

Africa: Mauritius, Reunion Island, Madagascar, Cape Town, Johannesburg, Durban, Zimbabwe, Mozambique, Kenya, Seychelles, etc.

The other side of the world, the great Pacific and Oceania: Hawaii, Fiji, Japan, Guam, Manila, Brisbane, Sydney and Perth.

And of course most major cities in the US and some in Canada, Mexico, South America and the Caribbean. I have also recently completed over 12,800 total flight hours of which around 4,300 hours have been as Captain in Command.

Most of those International flights were long distance flights so we usually had layovers from 24 hours up to seven days. The best were in Australia and Europe, but I also enjoyed and loved Africa and India very much. Something about the magic and charm of those places filled with misery, disease and poverty. People seemed to be more human, more conscious and alive. I always remember the children there with their wide smiles with shiny white teeth. The other party fun places were in Latin America and the Caribbean, abundant in exotic women, great music and excellent rum.

Europe was always nice to overnight because we usually had three to four day layovers. Rome was one of my favorite ones because I usually took a train to Firenze, Florence which was only 90 minutes away by train. I loved the language, the people and the cuisine there and my friends Alessandro and his girlfriend always showed me around the city. They used to live around two blocks from the Plaza de Michael Angelo in a cozy ancient apartment. We drove all around the city sites in their motorinas (fast mopeds) with me in the back seat of Rafaela's or Alex's bike. It was pretty scary at times because they would drive in any direction of any road, even on one way roads going the opposite way. I remember clenching my seat with my butt for fear of being thrown out on sharp turns. All this driving took place while they would turn their heads to talk to me so that even made it scarier. Alessandro had been a Flight Student of mine in 1989 and we had remained in touch ever since. He had told me he'd contact me whenever he would make it to a Commercial Airline, and he did. I was in Mauritius when I got his call. Then they visited me to Mauritius for a week and after that they always invited me to stay with them on my layovers in Rome. That's how I started to learn Italian, well and also with my sexy half Italian girl friend in Mauritius.

Whenever I had other long layovers of five days or more I would take a flight or train to stay with my little son Enriko in Wiesbaden. That was the best part of my International Flying, that I could see my son often and spend time with him. We established such a nice relationship that when he turned 16 he elected to move with me to San Diego, with his Mother's approval of course.

I've flown for six Airlines and one Corporate jet charter in my career and have had much fun at everyone of them, I remember all the great people I worked with, while the assholes I've forgotten about.

That's what most jobs are all about, not only Airline Flying jobs, it's all about your comrades, workmates, crewmembers, ground personnel, etc.

It also has helped me learn other languages, German (which I learned thru my ex wife while living in Germany almost three years, and by attending the Folkshochschule Mainz for two years until receiving my Certificate in German), French, which I learned mostly from my other sexy Mauritian girlfriend (also a little from College but I didn't really learn until traveling thru Morocco and living in Mauritius), some Italian (from sexy Kexy) in addition to English and Spanish, Portuguese is similar to Spanish so I can understand it and somewhat converse in it too (I traveled to Brazil a couple of times and self taught myself with Cds and a private pretty Brazilian tutor).

Japanese is my next challenge and even thou I've been exposed to it and continue to spend much time in Japan, I still only know the bare basics of survival, (e.g. what a pretty woman you are, would you like a massage?, another big beer please, I'm sorry, excuse me, how do you say 'shave' in Japanese?, which way to the closest bar, etc).

I always say that the best way to really learn a language is to either live in the country or to have a good pocket dictionary with sexy legs in a miniskirt. The latter one being my favorite one.

Many people in America that have had years in college of a foreign language claim to be fluent in it, however, fluent has a different meaning elsewhere. The word Fluent in America is grossly overused and normally is at a level of barely book language to a minimum in other countries.

You can't ever be fluent unless you've lived in the country or are living with people that only speak that language, where you would be always exposed to it and forced to speak it. Fortunately, I lived in those countries for a couple of years and had a good pocket dictionary with sexy legs. I was also brought up bilingual in my childhood and that made it easier to associate other Latin or Germanic languages with English or Spanish.

A Flying career can really be satisfying if you're the traveling, unstable and adventurous type.

Sometimes you're gone on long layovers with the same crew of Pilots and Flight Attendants and you end up sticking together everyday, having coffee, dinner, going out, sharing beds with a cute FA, etc. Sometimes it becomes more discrete and personal with a particular (FA) flight attendant and you end up dating her even to the point of being serious, that happens more often when the Crew are younger and single.

There are also many case of divorces due to Pilots having affairs with flight Attendants or other employees within the industry, being gone for too many days or simply loosing touch with their wives doesn't help. Flying for an Asian Airline has it's temptations too, because the majority of the flight Attendants are young, attractive and from various distinct countries such as Thailand, China, Japan, Taiwan or the Philippines. At my present Company, we've had over a dozen divorces due to the "yellow fever", meaning another Aviation Induced Divorce Syndrome (AIDS) case caused by an Asian love affair. These girls truly know how to treat a man and anyone who is already having a weak marriage is prone to falling for one of these girls.

There have been a few guys who've dumped their wives along with most of their wealth and started a new life with a new hot looking younger chick. I'd like to think that most of those guys end up having happy lives with them.

But you have to be very careful not to fall for the gold diggers, or the ones that are looking for "the eternal meal ticket". They'll do anything possible to get the guy to fall head over heels for them, and I mean anything, specially sexually. At first all you hear is, " I love you long time, you're my best lover, you're so handsome," then it starts changing to, "you don't respect me or take me seriously, you just want sex with me and nothing else, you're wife and kids are more important than me", etc. Then after they marry them and get them their green cards they start changing or showing their true colors. I've seen a few of those cases too.

In my opinion, the trick is not to take them too seriously and to let them know of it. That way, if they still want to play and not demand or expect anything, then in the end nobody gets hurt. Unless a guy honestly just want to marry one of them, they do make great wives I've heard.

This reminds me of the typical phrase you hear from different women of different cultures right after having sex, here it goes: (I heard it on a radio show, okay, some I made up).

The French girl, " Izz dat all yu can doooo".

The German girl, " Dass varr sehr gut JA, but you lacked Precision".

The Russian girl, " You possessed my body, but not my mind".

The British girl, " That was lovely, but you came too late".

The Japanese girl, "Thank you fol waiting".

The Thai girl, " Thank you for comiiiing".

The Latina girl, " You were my first man, what are you ganna tink of me now?".

The American girl, "What did you say your name was?".

The Aussie girl, " Good lay mate".

The Kiwi girl, " Maaa-aaaaybe we can do it agaaaain".

The Canadian girl, " Good lay, eh".

The Mauritian girl, "Cette' Mari-bo'n Ca".

I've had my share of these love adventures before I settled down, and at least once I seriously considered bringing a girl from an exotic country like Mauritius back to the United States. She was a very pretty young French Mauritian who seemed to be in love with me, she was a great cook, great in bed and had a good upbringing. But there was something psycho about her and I confirmed it when I met her Mom, she had that quality from her Mom and it was scary. I knew I had to try to break it up but I couldn't at first. Her tears and sweet lovemaking were really working on me initially. Then after the third try we broke up peacefully and remained good friends.

I came to my senses eventually and decided it wasn't a wise idea after seeing so many cases of sour endings with these girls. The girls some guys brought in were from different parts of the world, Russia, Philippines, Thailand, etc.

I know of a few cases were a few years after they brought them in and married them, they ended up dumping them for a younger guy, keeping their house and money and ruining their lives. Why did you think they call them housekeepers? Yes, because they keep the house and everything else. This could apply to girls of all nationalities.

Sure, every one will argue that it's natural for most women to be gatherers because it is in their nature. Only sometimes they take it to the limits and start gathering your house, your bank accounts, your boat, cars, etc.

It's just as bad as guys trying to lay most women that crosses their (our) path based on the theory that we were genetically designed to impregnate many women and populate the world, that my friends, doesn't apply anymore in our times. It seems like that impulse still remains ingrained in our deep subconscious minds thou.

AIR STORIES.

There are also personality conflicts or cultural differences amongst crewmembers or even ground personnel sometimes. I can give a few examples of my own experiences:

CAPTAIN ARROGANT.

While I was flying out of Las Vegas I was living in San Diego, so I had to jump seat to work in my Pilot uniform. Jump seating agreements amongst Pilots have been a privilege for years but now it tends to create some animosity from other groups. Why can we fly anywhere for free and they can not? This seems to bother some Ground or other aviation personnel that don't have our travel benefits So when it comes for us to ask for a boarding pass at their check-in counters, they see it in their power to sometimes make it difficult for us. Almost always they will be nice after we ask politely to board the airplane but sometimes that isn't the case.

Such was the case one morning in San Diego as I was trying to board an airplane to go to work. I approached the female Ticket agent, dressed in full uniform, and politely asked for a jump seat form in order to board so I could get to Las Vegas. The unpleasant agent looked at me with a very unhappy look and proceeded to tell me that they didn't take Flight Attendants as Jump Seaters.

Now, any one who has flown or seen Airplane movies, can tell the difference between a uniform of a Flight Attendant and a Pilot or Captain right? This woman was obviously trying to give me a hard time, although it was not in her power to deny me the jump seat because the power lies directly in the Captain of the flight. When she said that, I was caught off guard and I thought maybe I had forgotten to put the epaulets or four Captain bars on my shirt, so I put my hand on my shoulder to make sure they were there, while at the same time I said I was Cockpit Crew and not a Flight Attendant.

She took this as an excuse to describe me to the Captain and Flight Attendants as "Captain Arrogant wants to board" when she took my documents for the Captain of the flight to verify. So when I entered the cockpit to introduce myself, the Captain who was a very nice guy said to me, "Oh, so you're Captain Arrogant" sort of laughing. Then he said I should ride in the cockpit with them because the chicks in the back didn't want me there, all because of that ticket agent who spread the venom to get even at me for something she made up. I tried to explain what had happened but he said not to worry because he knew how they were sometimes. Unfortunately they expect us to kiss ass for a free ride sometimes.

Once I asked a Flight Attendant for a Takeoff drink as we usually were used to. She answered with a bad attitude that the drinks were in the rear galley and that I could help myself. So I asked her politely if she could fly the airplane while I went to the back to get our drinks, she said she couldn't fly, so I told her, "I guess that leaves you to get the drinks, doesn't it?" She did get us a box of OJ and glasses without poison this time.

The case of the missing passenger; After the passenger count prior to take off, the chief Cabin attendant who was German, notified me that the passenger count didn't match. He did it all over again and still there was one passenger missing even after they checked the lavatories. I tried to be funny and asked him if he checked all the ovens but he didn't think it was very funny. No sense of humor.

On another occasion I was the Captain on a Boeing 757 out of Las Vegas. We had quite a few young, inexperienced but attractive Flight Attendants who had been promoted very quickly to Senior Attendants in charge of the Cabin. On one particular flight to Miami, one of these cute anorexic blondes suddenly burst into the Cockpit with orders, (so she thought) "I need you to contact Med Link because I have a sick patient" (which is a phone patch with a Med Facility where a Doctor speaks on the Radio with the Flight crew regarding the patient's condition, or if necessary the Doctor on board the airplane speaks to the Doctor on the ground, it was allowed in the safer days of aviation before the 9/11 events).

Normally the procedure is for them to notify the Captain inmediately when a passenger gets sick, then on the Passenger Address system they should call for a Doctor or Nurse aboard, let them check the patient and then get the patient's details on a form, such as age, condition, appearance, allergies, etc. This information form gets passed to the Captain so that in the event the Doctor on board is unable to help, then we can contact the Med Link services for a Doctor on the Radio.

This Flight Attendant hadn't followed all the above procedures and here she was, acting in a bossy way telling me to contact the Med Link. She needed to be reminded, that it is the Captain who is in charge and makes the final decision if necessary to call the Med Link facility.

As diplomatically as I possibly could I told her to hold her horses, I then asked her if she had already asked for a Doctor amongst the passengers, a nurse or even a vet. How about the patient information form that she was supposed to fill out for me. I also asked her when the patient started getting ill and what the symptoms were.

She hadn't done any of the above and here she was giving orders. So finally I told her to follow the proper procedures and then if needed I would decide if a call to the Med Link was necessary or as a last resort, a diversion to an emergency airport along the way. In the end, it wasn't necessary because there was a Doctor on board and he handled the situation well. Once we landed, and on the way to the Hotel I overheard her talking to the other flight Attendants, telling them the proper procedures to use, as if it had been their mistake. When I was alone with her and in order not to embarrass her, I reminded her of the importance of communicating with the Captain inmediately during abnormal situations, as well as the levels of responsibility and Authority in an aircraft. She acknowledged humbly and went on her way with a bit of an attitude. Needles to say, a date for that night was out of the question. Maybe a massage? une petite pip peu-etre?

On another flight, the chief F. Attendant informed me that the ground agents had boarded a very drunk young woman but that she was behaving well and went to sleep in her seat right away. I asked him

81

if he wanted her removed, I would have her removed and he replied it wasn't necessary because she seemed to be okay. Well, right after take off, she puked her guts out and had an ugly smelly mess in her area. Of course the other F. Attendants were upset because I didn't remove her off the flight. (It is normally the ground agents job to load or remove passengers but if the Captain thinks it's safer to remove a certain passenger we can have them removed). In this case the Chief F. Attendant agreed to leave her there so it was now his responsibility to clean after her mess and look after her. She was behaving and appeared okay so it wasn't necessary to return to unload her. However, when I called one of the F. Attendants two hours later to ask what was on the menu, she answered, "a plate full of vomit". Witch, only in the US would they get away with such behavior.

On a different flight, from Miami to Las Vegas, I was at the Hotel entrance near the airport shuttle van ready to head for the airport, but there was a missing flight Attendant. The missing flight Attendant turned out to be a young male gay who was kissing his boyfriend good-bye, right in front of the Hotel and in front of me and the rest of the crew. I thought that was disrespectful and unprofessional since he was in company uniform.

I decided to handle it as diplomatically as possible, so once in flight I asked him to come to the cockpit to try to give him an idea of what was expected of us when in uniform. Once he entered the cockpit I reminded him of our Operation Manual's rules regarding one's proper behavior and professional attitude at all times. Inmediately he defended himself saying that "he was just like everybody else and that he was just showing affection", while wagging his hands all over the place. So I added that he should keep his affections to a more private level while in uniform, like to the confinement of his room. Well, he didn't take that very well and he stood up and headed for the door very upset.

That wasn't the end of it, the Lead Flight attendant came in later and said he was very upset and that he was going to report me for picking on him because of his sexual preference. Sure enough, as soon as we landed he took off to his direct supervisor who was also one of his kind and reported me.

Now I had to go thru the trouble of filling out my own report backed up by the First Officer's. My Chief Pilot said not to worry about it, but once I got interviewed by a lady from Human Resources it was very obvious they were backing up the pillow biter. They tried to make it look like something was wrong with me for getting offended by his actions. That's when I thought, "man what is this world coming to and who hires these people".

To make the story short, the kissing idiot ended up shooting himself in the foot with his own pistol. He had made a couple of rude racist remarks in the shuttle van about Spanish speaking people even thou myself, the First officer and the van driver were Hispanic. So I got him on that and they suspended him for a few weeks for his racial slur insubordination.

On another flight from Vegas to Washington DC and about 45 minutes from landing, I got a call from the Lead FA. She said there was a sick lady and that she was getting worse. She had properly followed procedures and a Doctor on board was looking over her. She was going unconscious again and this is when I heard about it. About one hour later.

Apparently she'd had a stomach reduction operation and was still very weak. It was too late to get the Med Link people on the radio because we were starting our descent shortly and our workload was increasing. So I requested a speedy approach to the Washington Airport and a Med Evac van was waiting at the gate when we pulled in. As the two big overweight men from the Med Evac were trying to move her to the wheel chair, they dropped her, I couldn't believe what I was seeing.

The poor woman was still conscious and I clearly remember how as they reeled her out she looked at me and smiled as if to thank me. I could tell from her eyes that she was grateful to have made it, at least to the airport she did.

I was happy to see her alive and thought it would be all okay but once at the Hotel I got a call from our station Manager that the lady had passed away in the Evac van on the way to the Hospital. I was so sad to hear these news that even now when I write about this I get a lump in my throat. Later that night, the Lead FA called me on the phone crying, saying she was so sorry and that she did all she could. I tried to calm her down and didn't want to make her anymore guilty than she already felt. I think she knew that if she had called me as soon as the Lady passenger started developing problems, then maybe we would have had more time to plan and divert to a closest Airport, and maybe it would have saved her life, we'll never know.

Sometimes there is only so much you can do and you have to use your best judgment, in the old days, the Captain had a lot of Authority in the Airplane and while on the ground.

Nowadays, the station Managers have the control of the Aircraft on the ground, but once those aircraft doors are shut it's the Captain's Airplane.

Sometimes, the station managers or other ground personnel are very inexperienced and when given such positions as controlling who gets on board and who doesn't during oversold situations, they tend to take preference over friends or family members trying to get onboard. This happened once on one of my flights.

On a flight from Vegas to New York JFK I was trying to bring along my 13 year old son who was visiting me from Germany for the summer. The flight was oversold but there were a few no shows and the standby list was short. The Ticket agent at the moment said it looked like my son would be able to get aboard because he was number one on the list. That changed when the Supervisor showed up, an inexperienced young flamer (not kidding) with an arrogant and resentful attitude towards Flight crew because he didn't get hired as a Flight Attendant probably due to his weight and sloppy appearance. A few minutes later I walked out of the Airplane to check on the status of my son's position. I was worried because I couldn't leave him alone in Vegas. I explained to the Supervisor my predicament and explained to him how important it was for my son to get on board. He didn't show much interest and even referred to me as " this guy's son won't make it on board", what an asshole, I was the Captain of the flight.

He wouldn't look me in the eye when he said my son was on the bottom of the standby list. I added that if my son could not get on board, I might have to delay the flight even more.

He thought he had control of the situation but he didn't. He tried to cheat to get his friend's parents on board first, and in First class. This was right after he told me the flight was full and no Standby passenger was getting on board. They were an older couple who weren't supposed to make the top of the standby list.

I found out when I walked back into the airplane and saw the older couple already pre-boarded in First class, totally out of Company rules.

I walked back to the gate and inquired at the desk about the status of that couple on board, the other agent told me that the Supervisor had taken a paying passenger off First class to make two seats available for his friend's (probably his pillow biter) parents who were also on Standby but should have been below my son on the standby list. The bloody puffer really pissed me off. I called him to the airplane and told him to remove those passengers now, to put back the paying passenger in his seat and to put my son in the remaining open seat, NOW.

He had no other way to look, I stood next to him as he politely asked his friend's parents off the Airplane, I even apologized to them for the inconvenience as they walked out. Then my son boarded and off we went, he looked at me with hate in his eyes and I knew he was going to try to report me. And he did.

But he didn't have a case, he was cheating the system and acting contrary to company rules. I wrote my report too and explained to my Chief Pilot what he did. He tried to report me for abusing my Authority but nothing came of it because I acted in favor of the company to get a paying passenger back in his seat. I didn't hear a thing after that and I never saw that guy again, I think they removed him from his position.

The case of seafood buffet by the pool: At my fifth Airline we were overnighting at a crew Beach Front Hotel in North Miami for up to 48 hours. There were some wild parties there and it was common for European crews to be laying around topless by the pool or the beach. On one particular long layover, the crew had been partying until late night and decided to all go skinny dipping in the ocean. There were the Flight crew and a few Flight attendants. One of them thought it would be funny to take their swimming gear away and hide them by the pool so they would have to walk back naked to the pool area, it was around midnight and nobody seemed to be bothered by it.

However, while they hung out at the pool naked, things started getting steamy and someone later reported to the Company that one of the Pilots had been having oral sex with one of the girl flight attendants sitting at the edge of the pool. The person snitching or reporting them was a gay flight attendant who thought it was "dishgusthiinn" and offensive. So naturally the Flight attendant denied it all and the Pilot being an honest guy replied "I don't remember, I was too drunk at the time". That didn't fly too well with the Chief Pilot and he was sent to AA for treatment. However, that story circulated around flight crews and everyone staying at that Cherry Frontanac hotel wanted to meet our flight attendants, they sometimes referred to them as Seafood Buffet by the Pool.

One last case, "The day I got picked up by a Stripper". I was flying a round trip from Vegas to San Francisco. While we waited at the San Francisco Terminal I noticed an attractive lady wearing all jeans up to her cap and I noticed she was staring at me. We sort of made eye contact, exchanged smiles and then I boarded to get the Flight deck ready for Departure.

Later during the flight one of my Flight Attendants told me there was a Lady that was interested in meeting the Captain. I asked her if it was the Lady in Jeans and she said she was. Since I couldn't invite her to the Flight Deck anymore, I told the FA to tell her to wait for me at the end of deplaning once we land. Sure enough, after I shutdown, finished all of the Checklists, I walked out and saw her waiting by the counter. We introduced ourselves and then she said in a flirty way, "Sorry for being so bold and direct, I normally don't do this".

I don't remember if I had been picked up like this before by an attractive Lady while I was operating a flight so I was flattered. We went and had a coffee at a Starbucks and then we made plans for that evening. Later on she picked me up at my Hotel and showed me around Vegas. We had dinner, drinks and then she asked if I wanted to see her place. I couldn't say no, first of all she was attractive, big breasted, nicely tanned, fun to talk to and hang out, and I knew what was going to happen next. It turns out she was very religious and wanted instant marriage.

No, just kidding.

Actually, what really happened was what I expected to happen. We got to her nice place and ended up having sex pretty much all night. She said she worked as a Manicurist and Stylist now but admitted she had been a Stripper, or better said, Exotic Dancer. She had a great firm body and was only in her mid thirties. We met up a couple of more times after that and she started taking me to wilder clubs and sort of underground secret clubs in the city. She was a very open minded girl and was willing to show me a good time. Eventually I moved back to San Diego and couldn't see her anymore, bummer because it was great while it lasted.

The good old days of Aviation are almost gone, gone are the days when I could take my Son, Wife or girlfriend in the Cockpit. Yes, thanks to Bin Laden everyone will say, but I would say, thanks to the CIA for training Bin Laden, pissing him off and letting his buddies into the country to take flight lessons.

Things have changed now, now all we need at the Cockpit door is the sign I mentioned before, "Do not feed the animals". Because we're locked in from boarding until de-boarding, except when we need to use the bathroom.

At my present Asian Airline, we the Flight Crew don't have any control or supervision as to who gets on board or who doesn't. Courtesy and politeness is such that even a terrorist with a bomb under his turban or a wrapped-around car-cleaning towel on his head would be welcomed in. On the B747 you sit in the cockpit on the upper deck and you can't really see who is boarding unless the jet bridge has glass panels.

Yes, security measures are always in effect especially in the States, overly exaggerated but they make the public feel safer when flying. What they don't know is that dozens of individuals of all types, nationalities, backgrounds and religious beliefs have boarded the airplane before the passengers. To clean, take away the trash and supply the Aircraft with food and water. Some of these employees are subcontracted by budget companies who have made minimum back ground checks on these people, or are in the process of checking their past while they're given some security clearance into some Airports. I'm not kidding, some of these people are from troubling countries that breed or sponsor terrorists. So, does that make you feel any safer?

Don't worry, if your airplane doesn't blow up in mid-air, you're most likely to croak of food poisoning from airplane food. Or from getting run over by a turboed taxi driver at the airport.

Food poisoning is common on airplanes, you just don't hear from it as much because it's hard to pinpoint where the bad food was consumed. Myself and a few other Crew members I know have had food poisoning from airplane food. Imagine all Flight deck crew getting sick from food poisoning in flight at the same time. That would be chaotic on a long International flight, having to divert to an Emergency airport in the middle of the Pacific so the Pilots can poop their guts out.

Well, we're not supposed to eat the same meals according to Company rules, that way one guy gets the mad cow steak or chemically infected pork, the other guy gets the mercury poisoned fish and the third guy gets the birded-flu chicken. How about that, it's all about safety isn't it. Oh yeah, and did I mention that the pork or chicken probably came from China?

Incredibly, the crew menu never changes, it's always: feather, leather or gills, (chicken, steak or fish). No thanks, I'll have my PBJ sandwich instead. (peanut butter jelly).

At least we can still get fresh brewed coffee if we request it from the Flight Attendants, we also get Oshiboris, hot wet towels to clean our face and hands with them. Of course I'm sure many of the major US Airline crews don't get that anymore, "go get it yourself chum" is probably what they tell them if they would ask for Oshiboris and fresh brewed coffee.

I used to have a saying that I would share with my comrades in flight, that is my rule of three.

According to me, at least three things in life have to be fresh. Coffee one of them, the second one being seafood, and the third, well, you figure it out, if it smells like the second one it ain't fresh, and vice versa. Oh yeah, the little pleasures of life are the ones that count.

Speaking of safety, have you noticed how airport security rules have become stricter? Now you can't even carry your toothpaste with you, or expensive cologne, etc.

Not even you're little bottle of Tabasco sauce to kill the bugs in your airplane food. Oh yeah, and now you have to pay for your own food and drinks on most flights. Shouldn't they be paying us to eat those crappy meals they sell?

Also, recently there was a case of a Mother and an autistic toddler getting kicked out of a commuter flight in the States. What's the deal here, now even toddlers are considered terrorists? Apparently the Fright Attendant frightened the screaming child and the situation got worse, then the Mother was upset and the young and inexperienced Captain Mayhem decided to divert and drop them off. Wouldn't it have been easier to continue to destination to accommodate the rest of the passengers? Why do some Flight attendants have to act like Air Police? Why do people panic over a screaming child? The airplane will not fall out of the sky with a crying baby you know. So much for Constitutional Rights these days.

Okay, enough of the pleasures of flying, I personally don't like to fly as a paying passenger but I love to fly the airplane, which is totally different.

I still wouldn't want to do anything else, okay, except maybe be a Professional surfer or a Rock Star. So I still do love flying, I just don't like what bean counter accountants, overly ambitious (greedy) managers and CEOs have done with aviation and how the FAA has taken the liberty and fun out of it.

BACK TO THE EIGHTIES. THE WAY TO MY DREAM OF FLYING.

After I had my first Flights in Mr. Brannen's Cessna-172 in San Diego, I took a couple of years break while I traveled and lived in Europe. I had intended to return in three months to resume my Education so I could eventually join the Air Force for free Flight Training, but I changed my mind because the Air Force ROTC didn't guarantee a flight slot, they said I could end up driving a truck. So that was it for the Air Force interest.

When I returned to San Diego in November 1986, I started inquiring on other ways of getting Flight Training privately. I only had around $7,000 dollars that I saved while working in Germany (I worked as a Civilian at the US Air Force and Army bases as a Gymnasium attendant and later as a Waiter and an Inventory clerk at the Mainz Kastel casserne). it wasn't even enough to get started so I almost gave up my dream, except for the fact that every day there were jet planes flying overhead Ocean Beach which kept my dream alive. Every time one flew overhead I got a sad feeling, it made me sad to think that I would end up as a Carpenter all my life and not fulfill my dream. So I promised myself I would pursue my dream and find a way to pay for my Flight training.

I met an angel when I walked into National University one morning. There I met a counselor whose name was Kimberly Sanders, she was an intelligent and attractive blonde who also was a Commercial Pilot working on her ratings while working there. She oriented me in the best direction, guided me and coached me on how to apply for every Grant and Scholarship possible.

My friend Gary Silva also worked there at the time while working for his ratings too. I registered for the first Semester with only 20 dollars. She said not to worry and that I should try to get ahead as much as I could with my Flight Training. I also applied for student loans to continue the expensive flight training costs. I did manage to get a few Scholarships and Grants fortunately and that covered for 80% of my Bachelor Degree, in Airway Science with Emphasis in Advanced Aircraft Systems.

I also got my Commercial Pilot License with an Instrument and Multi Engine Rating within two years. Then as I was running out of money I got some extra money from an insurance settlement after someone rammed my car from behind and gave me a whiplash back injury .Then within a few months as I was riding my motorcycle to school, someone opened his door at the red light as I was passing in between cars. I flew like Superman over the door and landed in a Judo fall in front of the car, I was almost unhurt (I couldn't work for six weeks due to my leg being strained thou) but my bike was a little crooked. I almost got a big settlement from that but one of the kids in that car saw me surfing by the pier a week later and told their attorney, she then argued that I could work and therefore wasn't entitled to the full settlement. I couldn't work because I couldn't rely on my weak knee while walking on roofs carrying tools above two stories high. But I could surf while being careful.

A few years back I could have died in another motorcycle incident. I had been working graveyard shifts and was usually sleeping by day. One Saturday morning I didn't sleep after work and went surfing instead, then stayed up all afternoon at a beach party. By night fall I knew I had to get home and I decided to drive my Honda 900 bike home. It was a cool night and I decided not to wear my helmet so I could stay more awake with the cool air on my face.

I was on freeway I-5 south going at about 80mph and kept wanting to dose off but I kept fighting it and even sang aloud and slapped my own face. Suddenly like in a dream I felt myself bouncing in rough terrain, that woke me up. When I opened my eyes I was still sitting straight while my subconscious mind drove my bike straight but I had veered off the concrete and now was on the grass, I was headed straight into a concrete wall supporting a bridge. The shock of waking up to a near death was such that I felt a jolt in my heart like being stuck with a pin. I immediately geared down and veered back to the concrete while skidding away from the wall. Phew, another cat's life gone.

Thanks to both of my accidents and the attractive cash settlement, I was able to finish my other three last Ratings, Flight Instructor, Instrument Instructor and Multi-Engine Instructor. Of course all those mentioned physical accidents have taken a toll on my poor body and sometimes I feel the effects of it. No pain no gain right, it's so true. A few years later I got my ATP, Airline Transport Pilot License.

DEATH OF A PILOT FRIEND.

Around 1988 I started Flight Instructing out of Montgomery Airport at California Wings initially, sort of free-lancing while I was also flying TV reporters over the freeways to report traffic conditions. On a little Tiger Grumman two seater I would take a channel 8 reporter in the mornings and late afternoons sometimes to do his traffic reports live over the city. There were two of us doing this at the time, Doug (rest in peace) and I. Normally Doug Hayden had the evening runs and I the morning runs. I was also still working as a carpenter sheeter building the roof of new homes,(I did this for four years while going to University and Flight Training).

On this particular morning Doug had asked me to change with him because he had an important function that evening. (I believe it was to be his one year Marriage Anniversary celebration). So he asked to do my morning flight in exchange for the evening one. I happily agreed to help him out and approved of the change with Flight Dispatch. I was also working at another Flight school occasionally and that morning as I was headed to the airport I heard it on the radio news.

A small aircraft had crashed on the freeway 5 junction with the other freeway that goes to Escondido, they described how two people on board had been killed and mentioned the aircraft as belonging to California Wings.

I got goose bumps inmediately so I stopped driving and pulled over for a few minutes. I knew it was Doug and I was so sad for him and his wife because they had just been married for one year, he was the nicest guy too. I really mean it, he was the nicest guy in that Flight School. Very easy going and friendly. We had helped each other often with flight changes and I knew quite a bit about him. He had been in the ROTC Air Force training and just as he was going thru jet training, the program got cancelled and he was back in the civilian world earlier than planned. So like me, he was trying to get flight hour experience in order to eventually make it to the big Airlines someday.

I knew the reporter too, well enough to know that he could be a bit impulsive. On a couple of flights with me he asked me if he could fly the airplane. On occasions I let him because he had a bit of experience although barely enough for straight and level flight or shallow turns. Sometimes he would get pushy when he wanted to continue to fly at lower altitudes with steep turns to over look at traffic below, but I wouldn't let him because I didn't trust him that much.

The Tiger Grumman had a very short wing span and couldn't handle steep turns for two long, even at full power it would start wanting to stall or fall out of the sky, so you had to be very careful at low altitudes because it's almost impossible to recover from a stall at low altitudes.

That's exactly what happened to Doug and the Reporter. Later the FAA interviewed me and I got from them the gory details. Both their hands were found tight around the controls, with their bodies heavily damaged and dismembered. Apparently, the reporter was trying to fly, or had been flying when Doug tried to take the controls back but the Reporter never let them go.

In other words, here's what I think happened. The reporter asked to fly, Doug being a nice guy let him, they got low, around 1,000 feet or lower (they were reported to have been low over a ridge under the cloud bank) There was a big car accident close to the I-5 and 78 junction and the reporter wanted to fly circles over it to have a closer look. He probably over banked the airplane and when he felt it stall, he pulled up on the controls in panic while overriding Doug's effort to recover.

Normally all you have to do is level the wings, add more power and drop the nose slightly to get some airspeed back, but with no altitude that's almost impossible. To aggravate matters more, it seems that the reporter panicked, pulled up and aggravated the stall into a spin, nose down they went inverted into a little hill by the ridge to which an explosion followed.

Phew, I wondered if that could have been me, I don't think I would have let the other guy fly at low altitudes. Later that week Channel 8 had an interview with me, incognito at my home, they made big news of this story because of their reporter involved.

Shortly thereafter I went to work for San Diego Flight Training, a more prestigious and Professional Flight School with newer airplanes. Rick the owner and manager was pretty cool and nice to work for. I got a lot of multi engine hours thanks to a wealthy student who insisted on getting all his ratings on a multi engine aircraft, that was great because when you're starting out you need to get multi engine hours as soon as you can to qualify for most jobs.

My student Dave was very bright but he lacked guts and self security. Well, that fear of flying of his, saved us one day in flight. He was flying under the hood (his view blocked from the outside and only on instruments) on an instrument approach into Montgomery Field and in visual conditions. He usually would ask over and over again for me to keep a continuous look outside for other airplanes, which I always did. On this particular flight he suddenly looked outside and asked again, " are you looking outside? Is there any traffic coming our way?". "Of course not", I said while looking to my right and left. Then my eye caught a glimpse of something in my blind spot behind the wing strut, coming our way, on a collision course at the same altitude.

I suddenly took over the controls and took evasive action to avoid the incoming airplane who should not have been there at that altitude. It was probably some bloody lawyer in a Bonanza. Anyway, Dave's fear of flying probably saved us that day , the problem was that he couldn't relax and consequently ended up failing his final flight exam for his Commercial rating. He was pretty good at flying the airplane and he was a pretty smart guy as well, but unfortunately he couldn't get himself to take it easier and enjoy the flight.

He was also a super nice guy but I don't think he was cut for the real Aviation world. In the real world in Aviation, you have to be a little on the tougher side, not totally ego driven but you do need a bit of ego, self assured and courageous. Not to the point of arrogant ignorance and disregard like some pilots from the old school days.

In the old days, the Captain was the supreme authority on the aircraft, he could do anything he pleased and get away with it. Not anymore, after a few accident investigations they have implemented what they call CRM, Cockpit or Crew Resource Management.

PF, Pilot Flying and PM Pilot Monitoring terms have been implemented, although not disregarding the Captain Authority if needed, sometimes it is not fully used when necessary. Example, the AA flight out of New York a few months after the 9/11 events that crashed after takeoff on climb out. They encountered wake turbulence from another heavy aircraft in front of them. Their aircraft was an Airbus older version. The Co pilot flying apparently over controlled the rudder in a very rough manner with his feet and ripped the tail right off. Composite plastics don't do very well after a few years and when subject to such stress it cracked the rudder out of it's place. The vibrations were so strong that it also physically lost an engine and plunged to the ground, killing everyone on board and on the ground in it's path.

The recordings from the CVR (Cockpit Voice Recorder) showed that the Captain was coaching or telling the Co Pilot to recover, to come out of it.

In my opinion, the Captain should have taken over inmediately. The procedure used for recovery was apparently partly correct but overly exaggerated and over controlled. Pushing the rudders left and right to their mechanical limits continuously with much force is like swerving your car full left and right during a skidding turn on the freeway, but if you let the wheel go, it might stabilize itself.

In cases like that, Captain Authority should not be doubted. At my present Company, Captains have more Authority and there are many occasions or conditions when we're not supposed to let the Co Pilot fly. It's not to degrade the Co pilot skills or experience but for Safety regulations or Insurance reasons.

Life has been good to me, I 'm still healthy, young enough to have fun and still enjoy it. I have flown around the world almost twice. As a Boeing 747 Captain, the salary is decent, compatible and the responsibility is the same as for any other aircraft. One life, ten, one hundred or five hundred makes no difference, you're still responsible either way, besides, my life is the most important one because if I stay alive, everybody else will survive. Life as an International Pilot can have a toll on you thou, the jet lag, the plane food, the all night flying thru different time zones, the occasional stress from training or from high workload approaches and landings in bad weather. Not to mention the occasional parties and flight attendant chasing that goes on sometimes, smoking and drinking makes that worse so you do want to keep that under control.

Everything eventually gets old and sooner or later you start longing for something more fulfilling, such as a stable relationship, and a stable balanced life. What I mean by balanced is, spiritually, physically and mentally balanced. I think I'm almost not there yet but not quite so near, or maybe pretty far but closer than I think, (hmmmm?) the point is, I'm working on it. Well, we will always be searching and learning until the day we die so it is a continuous journey of self discovery, in fact it's like an adventure.

BACK TO THE PAST, HITCHIKING ACROSS EX-COMMUNIST GERMANY.

And speaking of adventure, let's go back to just that. So back to the 1980s. I decided to stay in Germany a little longer and accepted my friend Karl's invitation to work the grape picking and wine making at his parents farm. I was in touch with a few of the girls I had met in the South of Europe and had been invited to visit them. Jette from Denmark, Hanna from Sweden and Marit from Oslo. Also another Brita from Stavanger, and Ayla from Berlin, plus Anna and her sexy friend Vipsy in Oslo, I think that's all. So after working a couple weeks in Mainz, I started to hitchhike for Berlin. It was pretty easy at the time but it was somewhat dangerous to hitchhike across the previous East German territory dividing West Berlin. There used to be a large sign in three languages, German, French and English, warning people about how dangerous it was to hitchhike across East Germany, it noted how many people had disappeared, killed and raped , etc. Gulp, but I did it a few times anyway. I felt I could handle any situation, I had been practicing Judo, Shotokan and Aikido the past couple of years and also carried a small knife in my boot just in case.

There in Berlin I was introduced to open minded lifestyles and open air nudity. People were so carefree and easygoing. Ayla who I met in Ireland and her roommates used to get up naked every morning and have coffee and toast in their birthday suits, It was a good way for me to come out of my shell some more. Free love was practiced casually and at least once, I woke up with one of her naked girlfriends and she didn't seem to mind.

I hung out at Ayla's and her friends for a week or so and after a wild party on Saturday night I started hitchhiking out of Berlin the following morning. It was good timing because that morning I woke up with her male roommate's wife naked in my bed. She had actually jumped my bones the night before already at her apartment and I thought she would be discreet about it, but this morning she wasn't. Her husband or ex she said didn't care, he had a couple of girlfriends and didn't care about her anymore.

What really grossed me out was that as I was walking towards the bathroom, I caught that girl's husband kissing a guy in the kitchen, obviously he was bisexual too. That later gave me a terrible AIDS scare that I never forgot about.

I returned to Berlin the winter there after but this time I was driving in my own car with US Europe license plates since I was employed as a US Civilian. Two German and one Italian girl friend were riding with me (Karl, Ingo and Santina). It was a cold winter night when we arrived at the Checkpoint to the East German gateway. The Germans directed us to the Russian checkpoint because the US had diplomatic arrangements with the Ruskies to look after US Personnel crossing into Communist German territory to get to West Berlin.

When we pulled alongside the Russian guard, we all smiled at him and said Merry Christmas but he didn't smile back. Instead he clenched his weapon even tighter. We all started laughing nervously and he clenched his weapon even tighter. I showed him my government clearance papers that allowed me to enter and he signaled me to return and drop my German friends off at the German gateway. Then he asked me to trade a US Dollar for a ten Russian bill piece in his broken English, so I did.

Later I understood why I had to drop my friends off at the German entry and why they couldn't drive with me in my car thru the US/Russian gate. That was a bummer because it was pretty damned cold and I didn't want to drive alone for the next two and a half hours at midnight across enemy territory. My friends weren't that excited either with hitchhiking on their own at midnight in zero degree temperatures but I had no choice but to drop them off. Neither one of us knew this was going to happen, otherwise we would have used other traveling means.

So now I had to go back to the Russian young guard who was dressed in his best military attire and now seemed a little friendlier to me. There he directed me to park my car and walk over to the US Army checkpoint office to get my clearance papers stamped by US

Military personnel. He then saluted me with a firm military salute and I responded likewise, it felt pretty cool. I was sporting long curly hair to my shoulders, a full beard, and dressed in jeans all over so when the US Army guy saw me approach his counter, he frowned in an unpleasant way. (He probably thought I was Charlie Manson.)

He said to me, "Son, before I stamp your papers, I'm gonna ask you to go to that bathroom and shave your beard off, and maybe cut your hair shorter while you're at it, we don't want to give the Russians and East Germans a bad impression." I looked at him in disbelief and responded, "Sir, with all due respect but, I am not in the Army, I'm a US Civilian and I don't have to shave or cut my hair, I have clearance authorization documents to allow me to cross to West Berlin, so do you mind?" Incredibly he nodded and agreed, stamped the damned papers and sent me on my way.

But not before terrifying me about what could happen in those two hours and a half of driving across East German territory in the middle of the night. He gave me a large typed instruction folder with German and Russian sentences and said that if I would be intercepted by East German military or police, I should stomp on the gas pedal and haul ass as soon as I could. And if they would block my car, I should lock my doors and show them the folder in German, where it explained that I demanded to speak to a Russian Official. He said that the East Germans didn't have any Diplomatic relations with the US and therefore could do anything possible to interrogate US personnel, even torture or disappear them.

It all sounded like a joke because all they would get out of me would be on how to make a killer cappuccino. As a waiter at the Wiesbaden Officers Club I didn't have a lot of top secret information except maybe on the no tipping techniques from cheap Military Pilots.

I didn't like what he said and I must admit I was a little scared and excited at the same time. I sort of felt like I was James Bond driving across Enemy territory in the middle of the night. So I said "Thank you Sir" and disappeared into the night.

I was really tired while driving and I could feel myself starting to drift away almost to the point of falling sleep so I started to slap my face, sing and scream to try to stay awake. Eventually, against all instructions given to me by the US Sergeant, I stopped the car in the quiet of the pitch black night. I stepped out while listening very careful and proceeded to take a much needed leak. The night was cold and dark and I couldn't see more than a few feet in front of me. It was pretty eerie and silent and I could even hear my own heartbeat pounding like a rabbit's heart. The other noise came from taking a leak and it sounded like a storm shower, pretty soon I started getting goose bumps.

No, I didn't cry for my Mommy but I could hear my heart beat accelerating. So I got back in and took off in a hurry on my way to West Berlin. I made it within the time frame of two and a half hours and life was good again once I crossed over to the civilized side. My friends did make it pretty quick too since they got picked up in a van right after I dropped them off at the border.

A few days later I had to return the way I came so I made sure I would cross by day this time. So I started out after having breakfast. The same routine of stopping by the Russian guards first and getting my paperwork stamped by the Army personnel, except this time they didn't hint anything about my hair and beard.

However, this time the East Germans did try to intercept me. They had a checkpoint about 20 minutes before reaching the West German gate and when I saw it I felt my nuts crawl up to my throat. I remembered what they had briefed me about at the US Army checkpoint and I knew I wasn't gonna stop. I pretended to slow down while a couple of Police and Military vehicles sat on both sides of the road and the Officers signaled me to pull over. As Soon as I passed in between them I stomped the gas pedal and accelerated my little Opel as fast as it could go. The East Germans didn't expect it and by the time they got in their vehicles to give me chase I had a good lead over them. I was watching them on my rear view mirror and they still looked quite far behind me.

I hooted and screamed in excitement as I saw the West German gate ahead, I knew I had made it and outran the East Germans. When I made it to Wiesbaden where I lived, I told my roommates the story and they thought I was crazy because they said that those dudes wouldn't have hesitated to shoot at me.

GRASS FOR BREAKFAST WITH FRIENDLY GERMAN COWS.

Back to the 80s summer in West Berlin, I was getting ready to hitchhike out of there for the West German side but had forgotten to cash some money before I left. So I waited for a ride at an intersection of the autobahn, after standing at the West Berlin gates of freedom with a cardboard sing that read, WEST GERMANY (on West German territory but in an island in the middle of Communist East Germany). I started regretting my lack of planning, I was hungry, thirsty and had a bad hangover. Fortunately, I got a quick ride out of Communist German territory but got dropped off in the middle of two intersections with nothing around except cows grazing behind their fences. So as I watched how the cows were happily chewing on tall fresh green grass I had an idea.

The grass really looked refreshing and tasty to the cows so I decided to join them for breakfast. The grass tasted great, moist and refreshing. Needless to say, my headache went away, I was no longer hungry or thirsty and I felt energized, thanks to the German cows invitation for breakfast.

When I made it to Copenhagen the next day, Jette met me at the train station, we then stayed at her Mom's apartment and met up with Hanna. Jette was so cool she let me stay alone at the apartment with Hanna for a whole day, it was a secret affair I was having with Hanna since she was still somehow together with her boyfriend, we knew we couldn't do that for much longer so we enjoyed the moments of love and sex, she was a beautiful girl, great sense of humor and a great lover.

I guess I fulfilled in her something she hadn't felt before and had fallen in love with me since we met in Anttibes. I remember the last day we spent together, alone, just her and I in the apartment, naked all day, eating peanut butter of our nipples, making love and sleeping in each other's arms. We parted and were sure we'd see each other again, and we almost did later.

It was the end of summer so the weather was still good enough to travel. I visited around Germany, mainly people I had met, musicians, adventurers like me and girls. I ran out of money and played music with other musicians on the streets when needed.

So I eventually returned to Mainz and took a job as a Gymnasium attendant at the Army Barracks where I worked until December or so. By then I had resolved to accept the Scandinavian girls' invitations that winter, plus, I was getting bored in Mainz and I felt I was overstaying my welcome, even thou my friends in Mainz, Karl and his group of friends had somehow adopted me and provided their homes when I wanted to. Their parents were always very nice to me too.

LIVING WITH MY FRIENDS FROM MAINZ.

There was Karl, Volker, Thomas, Andrea, Hubsy, Petra, Ute, Peter, Christina 1 and 2, Klaus, Ruby and a few others. It was a great time of my life in that year of 1980 something. I worked and shared a nice flat after that on Moritstrasse 47 in Wiesbaden with Karl, Ingo and another guy called Ralph. I was seeing various girls, including a soldiers lonely lovely wife, beautiful girl from California. She had a gorgeous figure and a very pretty face, but I'll tell you about her later. Nevertheless, I still felt empty and unsatisfied, not to mention very lonely.

One night in the beginning of Winter, alone in the apartment while listening to the Dark Side of the Moon from Pink Floyd, I felt so alone and depressed that I swore I would hitchhike out of Wiesbaden the very next morning. I packed my back pack once again, said good-bye to my friends and headed for the Autobahn North ramp the next day. This time I was visiting Marit from Oslo, Hanna and a couple of other Norwegian girls that had already invited me.

I started hitchhiking towards Denmark, one of the rides I got from Germany was with an old man towing something with his old truck, he said he was going into Denmark so I relaxed and fell sleep. When we got to the Danish border the Border Agents wouldn't let him thru due to insufficient paperwork so I said thank you and goodbye and crossed the border on foot.

HITCHHIKING IN WINTER ACROSS SCANDINAVIA.

The next nearest town was around 6 kilometers away and it was freezing windy and cold. I kept walking until I reached the town, it was late and dark so I thought it was around five o' clock in the morning because I lost track of time when I fell sleep. I thought I had slept all night in the guy's truck. So when I reached the town and saw kids on the street I really thought these were early bird kind of people. I still thought it was Monday early morning so I walked to the nearest Truck rest area to try to hitch a ride. When I got there the gates were closed and all the trucks were locked up.

So I asked someone walking by when the trucks would be allowed to drive away and he said that tomorrow morning at 6 am. I was shocked to find out it was only Sunday late afternoon. Now I had to look for a warm place to sleep. There were no Youth Hostels nearby and I couldn't afford a Hotel so I looked for other options. One of them was visiting all my fictitious friends in the nearby apartment building. So I kept ringing a few bells at the main entrance until finally someone opened the door. I sneaked in and slept downstairs near the main heaters where I laid on my sleeping bag and a few cardboard boxes flattened out. Looking at my recent photos from my Summer adventures in France and Portugal, with a small flashlight in the dark but warm attic was my little world and I sort of enjoyed it. I felt homeless, unattached, free, a little alone but gratified to be living one day at a time like this. As long as I was traveling and headed somewhere I didn't feel lonely anymore.

In the morning I hitched a ride with a truck driver to Copenhagen, I continued from there after taking a two day break in the Copenhagen Youth Hostel, it was now full on Winter and it was so bloody cold and windy in Denmark. I got dropped off on the Swedish side of the port at night by another truck driver who parked his truck and wouldn't be driving until the morning. Now I was left out in the cold at night, it was windy and really cold, snowing and I felt pretty miserable and hungry. I marched up and down near the Customs gates to stay warm and hoped a car would show up. I was a little worried because there was nowhere warm to sleep so I knew I had to stay awake and constantly moving to stay warm. The Custom Officers stared at me with mistrust so I didn't think they'd offer their warm offices for me to camp out in my sleeping bag.

Then I got lucky and caught a great ride all the way from the Port Ferry town of Helsingborg on the Swedish side to Oslo Norway. At first when he rolled down his window and asked me where I was headed I felt suspicious, he was a big guy and I was worried he could be a serial killer or something. But I was freezing, hungry and desperately needed a ride to Norway so I said I was headed to Oslo, he smiled and said, "Great, that's were I'm headed, can you drive in the snow?" "Of course I can" I said, even thou I'd never seen snow in my life until this night. I volunteered to drive because I needed a ride and was freezing my ass off.

We stopped at a rest area and he bought coffee and sandwiches for both. I fished tailed that car on the snowy road most of the night thru the Swedish forest on the way to Norway, I felt elated, full of life and happy. Happy to be inside a warm car and drinking a delicious hot coffee with a sandwich. Life was great when you could enjoy the little things in life when that's all you have at that moment.

We arrived in the wee hours of the morning to Oslo, I thanked him very much and then I took a short train ride to Marit's town which was about an hour East of Oslo where she was waiting for me with her Mom. I couldn't believe how lucky I had been to be invited and treated so nicely by all these people I had met in Europe in the summertime. Her Mom was a very nice lady but her Dad almost had a shock when he saw me on the couch when he got home, I guess he had expected a blonde person. You could tell he wasn't that excited to see me. Well it's understandable because I guess he was protecting his little girl.

NORWEGIAN WOOD AND LOVE.

(I, ONCE HAD A GIRL, OR SHOULD I SAY, SHE ONCE HAD ME)

Marit and I fell deeply in love while I was at her house, I had never felt this kind of love before so I thought I was in heaven. No one before had told me that they loved me so I was elated to hear Marit tell me that. We were keeping it a secret for fear of her father. One night he almost caught us smooching in the attic where I slept, she still had her top and skirt on when her Dad suddenly busted the door open. I heard the creaking of the wooden stairs as he was tip toeing quietly to peek on us and that's when I suddenly threw myself into the carpet and rolled a few times to my sleeping bag, where I pretended to be sleep.

He asked her what she was doing there and that she should be in bed by now. She said she had fallen sleep and was leaving and that he should leave first, but he insisted for her to go back to her room right at that moment. I was terrified he would notice something might be missing if he looked up her legs on her way up the stairs, but the smart Girl rolled the blanket around her hips on the way up.

So I lived another day because I didn't get shot by her Dad. Marit had had a very hard time after her twin brother died a year before I met her. He was on a motorbike with a friend driving at night in the snow when they ran into a driving car. He could have survived if the car had stopped but it kept going and he eventually bled to death internally when he got to the Hospital. Her Mom was the nicest lady and she treated me like a son, probably the son she lost. I think I helped Marit get over her grief when she met me because she admitted to it when she told me she loved me. She had an older and a little sister who were also very nice.

The next morning as I was saying my goodbyes to the family, her Dad was at the door and as I said my "Thank you for everything" line, I tried to shake his hand but he didn't extend it. He just wished me a good trip and walked back inside. I think he suspected something and was afraid his daughter would fall in love with me. It could have been worse if he had decided to throw me out of the house into the cold in the middle of the night. (he could sense something going on between us).

Marit had arranged for me to stay at her girlfriend's house for another week, which was very nice of her and her friend besides being practical because it was close to her school and she would stop by afterwards to spend some time with me. There we made love in the attic alone in our romantic surroundings of the cozy and warm attic. Thereafter I visited my friend Anna for about three days while Vipsy and her showed me around Oslo a bit. After that I went to the Oslo Youth Hostel where I worked a couple of hours a day for a free room and breakfast.

A friend I met there, Rudiger from Austria and I played our guitars in the Oslo subway to supplement our expenses. While I was there Marit would come and stay with me on the weekends, of course her Father didn't know it at the time. There I met other friends as well, my good friends Carlos and Odette from Calexico who were newly wed at the time and are still close friends of mine. We all celebrated Christmas, the pair from Calexico, a couple of Canadians, Karl from Germany who joined me there for a couple of days, and Rudiger the kitchen help.

One day Karl was in one of his terrible moods, he was pissed off because he had hitchhiked to Stavanger to meet me there where he thought I was going to be with another Norwegian chick called Brita. I decided not to go because I wanted to stay close to Marit, but there was no way of me telling him my change of plans so he spent a couple of days freezing his ass off hitchhiking there and back to the Oslo Youth hostel. I remember as we were having a hot drink in the room he started getting pissed off because I was slurping sipping my drink. He said he would kick my ass if I did it again so I did it again just to challenge him. He had been a cop and he thought he was tough and could antagonize me with his bullying. I purposely slurped my drink again and suddenly he pounced at me like a mountain lion, but I caught him in a Judo throw and he landed on the bed where I put him in a shoulder lock. He wasn't expecting it and he gave up and we made peace. We fought like brothers sometimes even thou we were best friends.

On Christmas night we borrowed some trays from the kitchen and used them as sleds, we started from the top of the hill (where the Youth Hostel was) all the way to the bottom, we were happy and excited by the Christmas spirit and by the effects of the hot Rum we drank so we snowballed each other as we rode down the hill on kitchen trays. It was one of my best Christmas'.

Then one weekend that Marit was with me in Oslo, her Mom found out the truth because of an avalanche that had occurred at a ski resort where she was supposed to have been with her friends. She had to tell her Mom the truth and she accepted our situation and kept it a secret from her Dad.

So now I was out of money and needed to go back to work in Germany, it had been almost three months and I stayed there in Oslo the whole time because of Marit, I didn't care about anybody else anymore. I Actually cancelled my other refueling stops, what I mean is, girlfriends on my list to visit, in the city of Stavanger and near Oslo.

Marit bought my ferry ticket to Copenhagen and packed me a two day lunch, she cried and we hugged and kissed goodbye, she promised to visit me in Germany but I didn't believe it at the time. I was sad and lonely again, like a dog with no home, well I kind of had a temporary home with my friends in Mainz and Wiesbaden, I also got my job back thanks to my nice friend in the hiring department. On the way back thru Copenhagen I tried to reach Hanna on the phone, she was supposed to expect me that week. I didn't know how I would feel about her now but I wanted to see her anyway. It was probably for the best she wasn't there anymore, she hadn't heard from me so she left to Sweden for the weekend.

I ended up waiting at the Copenhagen train station for a better weather window to hitchhike in. I was hoping Hanna would arrive in the meantime so I could have a warm couch to sleep in and maybe a warm meal. I was really out of money now and I had already eaten all of the lunch Marit had packed for me. I started getting worried because I was cold, hungry and feeling a little desperate. I considered playing my broken guitar inside the station to raise up some change but I was demoralized and tired, I also missed Marit greatly.

So while at the train station, looking hungry and tired, I guess I caused pity to a nice gentleman who offered to buy me lunch and said to keep the change. I was happy to have a warm meal in my stomach again and some change jingling in my pocket too. The man offered his apartment if I didn't' have where to stay, but I didn't feel I could trust him so I thanked him and said I had somewhere to stay that night.

I decided to walk about ten blocks to Hanna's apartment building and see if she had already gotten there. It was cold, wet and dark by then so I just rang the bell until someone opened the front door, one of her neighbors who knew her let me in and said I could sleep on the couch in the community living room. I was so happy to have a sleeping couch inside a warm house and I went into a deep sleep content like a baby with a stomach full of warm milk. In the morning I thanked her friend greatly and parted. But not before another drunk neighbor bar-girl woke me up with an invitation to her room for a drink, I declined the drink and instead hinted for coffee and toast while hoping for the best. She declined and said "a drink or nothing". I said "no thanks" and left.

It was now a beautiful sunny morning, with fresh snow everywhere and warmer temperatures. I had some change from the previous day so I could buy myself a coffee and some toast. Life was good and I was happy to get going once again. It's amazing how you can be happy with so little, such as a hot cup of coffee and one piece of toast when that's all you can afford. So now I walked to the nearest Highway ramp entrance headed South. Stuck my favorite thumb out, showed a smile on my face and hoped for the fastest hitchhiking to Germany. I did make it to Mainz very late at night but in one day fortunately.

BACK IN GERMANY.

So now I was back in Wiesbaden again, with my friends Karl and the gang. It was a cold and lonely winter and I longed for Marit but I didn't know when I would be able to see her.

I had to work at the Army base to raise some more cash so I couldn't travel anymore for the moment. Then in March Marit came to see me, she also came in April for a week against her Father's word. We were so happy to be together again and every day was a bliss because we were in Love.

Right before she arrived, Ingo and Karl were going on spring vacation to the south of Europe and Ralph would be staying with his parents. Then Ingo acted very strange and it was something I never forgot about, he said I would have to stay somewhere else because the landlord wouldn't recognize me and they might have problems with him because of me. I asked him where should I stay with Marit coming in a few days and he responded, "That is your problem". This didn't sound like Ingo but he was serious about it because he was afraid he would loose the apartment. Karl and I thought he was overreacting. I said not to worry about it and that I understood but later on Karl handed me his key and said not to say anything and that I should just stay there and not worry about Ingo. Of course I stayed and had the place to myself with Marit but I never forgot about Ingo's poor ethics and attitude. A few years later when he visited me in California I reminded him of that and let him know that what he did was cruel.

Germany had been good to me, I loved it there and all my German friends as well. Before I left Germany I had a couple of other Girlfriends, Angi, Ute, Barbie, Andrea and Bee. Angi was a sweet partly redhead sister of a friend of mine, we had an open thing with her, she was very open minded and seemed to be experimenting with both sexes. Then with Bee who had been Karl's lover at first, we got engaged in a hot crazy sex kind of thing, I guess she was heartbroken thereafter because she cried to Karl my friend that I used her. Karl was pissed off at me even after he assured me he no longer had interest in her. She was a hottie, nice little tight body with big breasts and a pretty face, naughty and passionate girl.

One day she caught me red-handed when she just showed up at the beat up apartment I was staying at with Karl's brother Horst (This happened later the next year). She said she missed her last bus home and would sleep on the couch, well she had no choice because another girl, Barbie was occupying the bed with me. Of course she was furious but she contained it until the morning. To make matters worse, Horst showed up and I was occupying his bed with Barbie, and Beena was occupying his couch. So he didn't mind as long as she would let him into her panties. She kicked and shoved him away all night and he was ready to kill me in the morning. I guess they also heard our panting from the other side of the Studio. In the morning she was gone, but she left a goodbye note on a page on the table. She was a good artist so she drew a hand with a big middle finger sticking out, it said, Fur Dich. Only for you. I did feel sorry about that so I apologized later to her. She apologized in return and we remained shagging friends for a while.

The soldiers ex-wife was Dee, she was a gorgeous blonde with a beautiful figure, she was really into sports. I liked her but I didn't think she'd be interested in me because of her recent divorce. Then one day after work she invited me for dinner at her house with a couple of other people. After everyone left, we had a few rum and cokes and it started getting late so she told me to wait a while longer and that she'd give me a ride home.

Then she suggested I stay overnight because it was late and she was a little tipsy to drive. I couldn't believe what was happening because I really did dig her and had in fact secretly fallen in love with her body and face. So pretty soon as I was caressing her shaggy cat, (she did have a shaggy cat) she crouched next to me and started petting her cat too. Then we started kissing and my caressing went from her cat to her other pussycat. She wasn't wearing undies or anything under her skirt so I figured she had volunteered as my dessert. It was a great night but I had nightmares that her ex-old man would show up and empty his M-16 on me.

One day he did show up at the Army Gym where I worked, in full Army fatigues. I really thought he was there to shoot me with his M-16 on his shoulder and when he said, "Hey, Dee told me all about you" my heart freaking stopped. But he only meant she told him she knew me and that I worked there at the Gym, fortunately this time, he was just there to work out. Phew, I cheated death once again.

There where a couple other girls but I 'll only mention the most significant ones in my life.

ONCE AGAIN, BACK TO GOOD OLD CALIFORNIA.

Now it was time to go back to California, it was March or April and I'd over stayed for around nine months, I'm not sure. I didn't want to go back but I had some legal matters to attend. (remember my old 69 convertible Mustang with the good shocks?) It had gotten stolen, literally, by the Italian crook owner of the Sav-On storage place on Main Street in Chula Vista California. He just decided to keep it by forging paperwork to get authorization from DMV (Dept. Motor Vehicles) to grant him the title of my so beloved Mustang with the good shocks. I did take him to court and settled after my Lawyer, who turned out to be his Lawyer's friend betrayed me and insisted I accept his first poor offer, it wasn't even enough to cover for all my belongings and car but I took it. Now you can understand my disgust for lawyers.

Marit promised to come and visit me in San Diego that summer and she did. So did my friends Karl and a few others. At first I lived with my brother Joe in Chula Vista until I got settled with a job and after that I shared a house in Imperial Beach with two Navy sailors who were pretty cool, two blocks from the beach pier.

I also got a night job at a Brand Paints store and tried to continue going to College but it wasn't easy to concentrate because there were so many things going thru my head. Besides, it was very difficult staying awake in class after working all night.

I had wheels by know, a Kawasaki 650 Honda motorcycle so I could show Marit all over town. I went to see her after that to Portland Oregon after she started College there. I rode my motorcycle in October and almost froze my nuts off while driving over the mountain pass, so I stopped in Santa Cruz at my friend Carol's house to thaw out in the bathtub and then continued the next morning. It was still wet and cold so I had to abandon the bike in San Francisco and rode the rest of the way by Greyhound. This visiting back and forth went on for about a year until it was time for her to go back, we wanted to get married but I didn't want to give up my dreams of becoming a pilot and move to Norway so we decided to wait.

I was disappointed because she changed her mind at the last minute and said she could only come and visit me for only one week, instead of the whole summer as she had promised. Apparently she wanted to tour the US with her College friends (or new boyfriend) first. So in a moment of rage which I later regretted I told her not to come at all. I lamented that greatly because I went to Mexico instead and didn't know if she would try to come anyway. I suffered my own consequences because I didn't see her again, ever. I was upset for a while because I thought I still loved her. We stayed in touch but I was never able to go see her again to Norway and she never came back to the States, so we remained friends and maintained contact for many years after that. The last I heard of her was, when she moved in with a boyfriend and became a TV reporter in Oslo. (It had to be this way because I wasn't really willing to give up my flying dreams and besides I would have missed out on the sexier girls that came in my life afterwards).

BEACH BUM IN OCEAN BEACH.

After she left, I just sort of lived and enjoyed life day by day, surfed, rode my motorcycle around, played guitar on the beach and of course worked for a living at Standard Brand Paints. Occasionally I met beach girls on the Beach. One of them was a pretty redhead stripper who I met while rolling a Drum Tabak cigarette at Imperial Beach. She thought it was a joint and just came over with a friendly attitude, I did tell her it was only tobacco and shared it with her anyway. Then I said, "hey, let's go for a bike ride". So we cruised to Coronado and started making out at the beach, we almost had sex there but then she suggested we go to her friends apartment because she was house sitting it. We went there and she pulled out a sex game, somehow we ended up in strange compromising positions and partly naked after loosing garments one at a time, then we had to kiss or lick certain parts of the body because it was part of the game. We eventually fell sleep exhausted after changing the game rules so we could have sex on the carpet.

The next day I went to see her dance at the Dirty Dan's strip club. She was hot at it and she danced mostly for me. She did have a drug problem and I kind of felt sorry for her. I realized I couldn't help her so I stopped seeing her. I remember how she used to brag that she was going to get her pretty face on the cover of Cosmopolitan magazine, but I couldn't help thinking that maybe if she fixed up her teeth and gave up drugs she could be a model since she had a very pretty face and a hot body.

I tried to continue my education while working graveyard shifts at the Paint store and living in Chula Vista with a good friend and on weekends in Ocean Beach. I lived with George, (Gogi) his Mom Lucy who was very nice to me and his little brother Fermin. My buddy George and I worked together and had a nice group of friends from the Paint store, they were all a good bunch of hard working guys but they all had drug problems with crystal Meth. They worked hard all night and sniffed Meth to stay awake but because I was the only one who didn't do that, they continuously tried to convince me to do it.

On weekends we would stay at George's brother Charlie's place in Ocean Beach on Santa Monica Avenue. Usually one of us would end up sleeping on the couch but we had an agreement that if one of us had a girl we could claim the bedroom and queen size bed. Charlie and his room mate Joe were pretty cool with that and if it meant bringing in girls for them to meet, then they were okay with it. I usually kept my surfboard there with them so I took every chance of surfing the pier or Sunset Cliffs.

One late afternoon as I was surfing from the left side, under and to the right side of the pier (looking at it from shore), I noticed a cute blonde staring and smiling at me, she turned out to be from Phoenix. I looked up to where she was and asked her how she was doing and what she was up to. I then suggested to maybe get a pizza or something and she agreed. Easy pick up, considering I was still in the water sitting on my surfboard while she stood above me on the pier. So we had a pizza and then I invited her to my apartment for a beer (and it wasn't even my apartment). When we arrived to the apartment which was all within one block, Charlie's room was occupied by him with a girl.

So I went to plan B, we also had an understanding with their neighbor Don, a pretty easy going dude from Iowa who also liked the community agreement we had as long as we brought chicks to their apartments.

Nobody was at his apartment but the doors where always open, only Deuce the dog was there, (a shaggy cute Maltese) and he wagged his tail when he saw me, he was sporting a new hankie around his neck. So with Deuce's approval, we went into the spare room, started smooching and undressing and then the cute blonde proceeded to practice on me her deep breathing techniques with my breathing tube, she was pretty young and had a tight beautiful body too. She only stayed a couple of hours because her parents where waiting for her at the Hotel in front of the pier. Deuce in the meantime, guarded the door for me cheerfully. An advise to parents, don't let your young teenage daughter disappear from your sight when on vacation.

On another occasion, I brought a Finnish girl that I met thru another French girl to Charlie's room while one of the girls we knew laid there kind of drunk. We just rolled in the big bed and ignored the fact that there was Charlie's friend sleeping there, she ignored us and kept sleeping. Another night me and the Finnish girl ended up in Don's bed, the Finnish girl and I just jumped in the bed and started smooching and undressing for sex, without taking notice that Danielle the Dutch girl was sleeping in it because we figured it was big enough. But she couldn't sleep with all the commotion, moaning and deep breathing so she got up and left us alone.

All these European girls we had met thru a French girl called Marie Claude, who was an Au-pair baby sitter and she had many other European girlfriends that we eventually met. We called them the sexy babysitters.

Then one night on my Birthday they all organized a little party for me. We had the usual Party signs hanging over the sidewalk, a huge red plastic rocket, a maniquee with crotchless panties and a pirate flag. It was all easy to see because our apartment was not far behind the Lifeguard Tower on Santa Monica St, almost corner with Abbott st. next to the beach. That night they all organized a present for me, Denielle (not the Dutch Danielle) was my present, she was an exotic cute dancer and wild thing that we met roller skating in her skimpy bikini, and she was waiting for me in Charlie's room in her sexy negligee. She kept whispering the Happy Birthday song in my ear as she made wild love to me. After it was all over it was sort of embarrassing to come out of the bedroom and have my friends hoot and clap.

Life in Ocean Beach was great at the time, before all the Real State Mongols moved into town and converted it into another Real State gold mine. It had been a Hippie and Biker town for a few decades. The main street, Newport avenue still has all kinds of antique shops, restaurants and lots of bars. It was really and still is a cool beach town with a 1960s atmosphere. At the time it also had a movie theater were they usually showed classic surf movies. I saw there the first time Big Wednesday. There were the usual bar fights but also stabbings and shootings due to drug deals gone bad amongst bikers. The Police eventually cleaned it up a bit and it's now a nice beach town to live in, although much more expensive.

I was a beach bum at the time without a worry and just living day by day. Surfing up to four hours on some days and hanging out at the beach or bars was the common thing to do. I had a Honda CB 900 and had long curly hair down below my shoulders so I probably looked like a hippie beach bum but I wasn't. I knew I had to keep myself clean because I didn't want to end up like the rest of the people I knew.

I had dreams and knew that eventually I would find a way to accomplish them. I saw how my friends started to deteriorate from partying and doing drugs too often and even my brother was being affected by this. My buddy George and his brother were also feeling the effects of it. Eventually Charlie lost his apartment and George had to move back in with his Mom. I on the other hand decided to go traveling and find new horizons.

I wasn't over Marit and my traveling spirit was still very much alive so I thought I needed to hit the road some more and get away from my current wild situation. So after a few drinks one evening I accepted an invitation from my cute friend Inky, and joined her and a Finnish girl that I used to 'finish' with, you know what I mean. So I sold my bike again, packed my old back pack once again and off we went on a drive across America.

Inky was my new best friend, she was a pretty attractive blonde from near Amsterdam, I got along with her great and we hung out together pretty often. Every one else thought we had something going but I held back at first because she had a little bit of a bossy attitude at times. I think we did have a mutual attraction and only a couple of times did we get close to getting sexually acquainted. I knew deep inside it was better to stay platonic friends with her because of our characters and personalities. One day after swimming she told me we could share the shower which would be normal to do in Holland. I took it as an invitation to help her get soaped up and out of her bikini but she panicked and ran out in a hurry. After that I never tried again, she hinted at me with interest much later when we were both single again but I didn't want to anymore. We actually slept in the same bed a couple of times but that was it.

Anyway, we were to deliver a Company Business car to New York City and from there Inky invited me to join her to Holland. She said we could get cheap one hundred dollar tickets from New York to Amsterdam with a new Airline called People Express. So off we went, Inky, the Finnish chick and myself.

I hadn't asked Inky for her approval if Finny joined us to pitch in money for fuel up to Denver where she would stay, partly because I thought she'd agreed since it would reduce our share of expenses. Later I found out she wasn't very happy about the company of this girl, I think she suspected I was involved with her and it bothered her. We made a technical stop (refueling stop) in Phoenix to visit the pretty blonde I had met in Ocean Beach that summer and then dropped the Finnish girl off in Denver, (they didn't get along, jealousy or something). Inky and Finny were pissed off because they had to put up with each other for a few hours while I was gone a couple of blocks away with my Phoenix Blondie at her house in her parents camper. I guess it wasn't cool having left them waiting at a Community park nearby.

When I got back before midnight they were both ready to claw my face off but I diffused the situation by inviting them to have a few drinks nearby. Then we returned to the park to camp out and I decided to be a total gentleman. So I let them sleep in the car and I rolled out my sleeping bag on the grass nearby. In the morning my upper lip was swollen from a spider bite and they said I deserved it for abandoning them like that. Karma in action again.

After stopping in Denver, my friend Inky Dutch and I continued to drop the car off in New York. We had been given instructions on where to drop it off but since it was pretty close to Harlem, we ended up accidentally driving right thru it. Inky was terrified so she put a towel over her blonde head while we asked for directions out of there. Then we caught our flight that same evening to Amsterdam and I stayed at her parents nice home for a week before starting my hitchhiking adventures once again.

They lived next to the railroad tracks in a small town and their back yard had a gate that opened to the tracks behind the house. One day I was exploring around and I decided to check out the tracks and trains go by. However, when a train was approaching it suddenly slowed down when it saw me standing by the tracks. I wondered why it wouldn't continue but it didn't move on until I walked back behind the fence. When I told Inky's parents about the experience, they said that because of the suicide rate amongst teenagers jumping in front of trains, the train operators were instructed to stop whenever they saw young people near the tracks. That operator actually thought I was trying to end up like a bug spread on his windshield. He was so wrong because I loved life so much.

Inky and I also went horse back riding, the English way, which was totally weird to me since I could only ride Western or Indian style. My back was already in bad shape and now it was even worse. I was in pain and Inky said she'd give me a massage. So that evening as we all said our "goodnights", Inky came to my room and sat on the back of my upper legs to give me a back rub. The door was partly open and when her Mom walked by the hall way she happened to see us and she let out a sound of astonishment, she probably thought we were "doing it" totally the wrong way and Inky and I just rolled in laughter. I think she explained to her Mom the next day what was really going on. I left for my hitchhiking travels the next afternoon, Inky dropped me off at a Hi-way intersection going South and we said our good byes with lot of hugs, I really had a great time traveling with her and it was kind of sad to part our own ways now. Besides, I still hadn't decided where I was really going, I thought about going North to visit Marit in Norway but common sense told me not to. So instead, I headed East back to Germany to visit my old friends again.

BACK IN GERMANY.

I stopped over in Mainz where my friends lived but it was cold and wet and Karl had arranged for me to stay at his brother's flat, an abandoned flat were only bums and a couple junkies lived. One night a couple of junkies kicked the door down and were threatening to beat up his brother, apparently he was still shooting up heroin and none of us new it. They threatened him if he didn't pay after roughing him up a bit, while they ignored me on the couch and eventually left. That experience convinced me it was time to hit the road. I did stay in Mainz a week or so but my money was going fast and I wasn't doing anything productive. It was good to see all my old friends again but I felt I had to go south where I could make my money last longer. Besides, I had started something with one of my old flames and didn't want to get tied down, so I started hitchhiking again except this time I headed South.

TRAVELLING ACROSS MOROCCO.

I bought a nice pair of warm hiking boots (which later got stolen in Morocco while I slept on the beach) and hit the road to warmer latitudes, towards the tip of Spain and Gibraltar. Within the next few days I was traveling along the Mediterranean coast bound for the North African Coast. While hitchhiking across France I had a couple of good and bad experiences. The great one was when the free spirited Community Hippies picked me up in their van. The owner was a super nice guy who took me to meet his other bros and wife with baby. They were all a cool group. They were remodeling a house they lived in and that's what they did for a living. They were self sufficient and had made this as their own business. They obviously didn't have much money because their house was lightly furnished, but yet, the owner offered me his last food in the fridge, a yogurt and a piece of bread.

I didn't want to accept it but he insisted and said they were going shopping for more food. I really appreciated his generosity because that night they didn't let me hit the road, they insisted I stay and assured me they would drop me off by the Highway the next morning.

So we all had sort of a little evening meal with wine and good tobacco. We made music and sang along to Neil Young songs thru out most of the night. The next morning they dropped me off by the ON ramp to the Highway where I stood and waited for a long time. Obviously most French were wary of Arab or Latin looking long haired handsome (lol) gentlemen like myself at the time. About an hour later the Gendarmerie showed up and started harassing me for Papier, that is, Documents, legal Documents. Apparently they thought I was an illegal Arab. Then once they checked my passport they ushered me away from the Highway and said if they would see me there again they would arrest me.

So I decided to walk a couple of kilometers to the Gas Station on the side of the Highway. There I could personally ask drivers for a ride as they were stopping for gas. I would approach them and politely ask them if they were headed in my direction South towards Spain.

I hadn't been there longer than ten minutes when the Station Assistant- Cashier walked out with a broom in his hand and motioned me rudely to move away from his station, saying that I was scaring his clientele.

I politely told him to fox off and pretended to walk towards the freeway but instead I stood behind the wall of his little miserable insignificant concrete world and from there I asked the people as they were walking out of his Mini Mart after paying for their gas.

Pretty soon a nice gentleman said he'd take me. But as I was boarding the car the cashier guard dog noticed me and rushed out to bark at me again, I was already closing my door and as we drove away I flipped him off the middle finger. In France it means have a nice day, I think.

Hitchhiking wasn't that easy in Spain but truck drivers and traveling businessmen were happy to take me along and talk and talk. Sometimes they invited me for lunch and insisted on paying which was great because it helped me make my money last longer. Especially with the French, they always bragged about how cool they were while giving themselves a thumbs up after they bought me lunch or dinner.

There was the occasional pervert who would hint or try to hit on me, but I was ready for defensive action just in case with a little pocket knife hidden in my boot. There was never the need because I made it clear to them that I wasn't going to tolerate their actions. I guess I looked serious enough and at the worst they'd tell me to get out of the car.

I caught a ride with a strange Tunisian who had a van full of furniture because he said he was getting married soon, what, didn't they have furniture in his country?

He kept asking me why I hitchhiked and if I had money so I was acting very wary of him. I guess he was trying to see if I could pitch in money for gas. That night we camped by the side of a Gas station but in the morning he pretended he'd lost his wallet and he didn't have any more money for gas. I said we should drive back to the spot where he had stopped for a leak the day before, so we did but he didn't find his wallet. Then he pulled into another gas station and said he would wait there for a phone call and that I shouldn't wait for him. So I said thanks for the ride and I kept walking towards the road to hitchhike.

A few minutes later I saw him drive away in a hurry, the bloody liar. I was hitchhiking remember, not ridesharing dude. I also met a nice teacher who was vacationing by herself on the Mediterranean coast in a small town. She picked me up and said she was only driving about two hours South and that was good enough for me. When we got to her town she asked me if I wanted to join her for dinner and I accepted. She talked to me about her little sister who had ended as a junky prostitute since she was 15 years old. She had started doing drugs early and had gotten addicted to heroin, then prostituted herself, her Father was devastated but couldn't help her much.

I noticed all around Europe there was a big drug problem during the 1980s, young kids, teenagers high on LSD or trips as they called it, I also knew a couple of young pretty girls willing to runaway from home and go with me hitchhiking, but I didn't want trouble so I always traveled alone. The French teacher said I could stay the night in her cottage and of course I thought I would get some action. But that night after we had dinner and some red wine, the French teacher turned off the lights, undressed down to her panties and crawled into her sleeping bag. I tried briefly to get an invitation for some dessert in her sleeping bag but she made it clear she didn't want to by saying, "non, non, non, pas du tout". (Not at all). Women, can never figure them out. The next morning we had coffee with the cold Mademoiselle, no sex, and a croissant. I thanked her greatly for her generosity and continued on my way South, to Africa. Of course the Spanish security guy at the entrance wanted to know if I had shagged her, he had a big smirk on his face when I told him I hadn't because he assumed I had and didn't want to admit it.

Hitchhiking in Europe was fairly easy and safe back then and it allowed me to meet the real people from different parts of the countries. Truck drivers specially had some good stories to tell. One of them told me he had just gotten out of prison after twelve years in the can for armed robbery, that worried me a little bit but he was cool and didn't do anything abnormal. Another guy told me that he was driving across the Arabian dessert when a camel suddenly jumped in front of him in a suicide gesture (I guess it preferred to be killed rather than to be proposed romantically). Well, that camel belonged to a wealthy Maharajah in the area and when the police finally showed up they arrested him. He was held there against his will until his Company paid a hefty fine for killing the bloody camel.

AFRICA, TRUE ADVENTURE.

On the ferry from Gibraltar I met a group of French Surfers on a Ford blue van with all their surfing equipment, then once we were on the North African continent at Tangier, I started sticking my thumb out only with European looking cars. Hitchhiking was dangerous in Morocco so I was wary of trying it with the locals. I'd heard enough stories of someone getting picked up, beat up or knifed and abandoned on the side of the road without their back pack.

Then I saw the blue van full of French surfers I had met at the ferry. At first they thought I was a local Moroccan that might have some smoke to sell them, but after talking about surfing, they gave me a ride and allowed me to hang out with them for about two weeks. That was really an adventure that could have ended up sour.

They would pull into the towns and buy hash to smoke along the way, I wasn't a smoker but I didn't mind people smoking it. Then one day a deal went sour in Casa Blanca because a couple of Moroccans wanted to rip them off. They had originally invited two of the French dudes and me to a local Café', then while drinking mint tea they offered us what they really sold, sweet tasting tobacco so I thought. They reached an agreement and a place to meet and off we went.

This is when I should have split on my own but I needed to go back to the van to get my backpack first. While we waited for the other French guys to arrive so I could bid my farewells and Merci's, the Moroccans showed up. They wanted to close the deal which had been for a few grams in exchange for a pair of sneakers, T shirt and 100 Francs.

Well, now there were two other big dudes with the little dude that had invited us originally, two of them entered the van and gave the French guy the stuff, it looked pale and underweight so he questioned it's weight and texture but the Moroccan promptly responded in an aggressive way that it was the correct type and weight.

I opened my big mouth and pulled out my little key holder scale that I had from Germany and said, "Hey, let's weigh it with this", but just then the Moroccan snapped it from my hand and slammed it on the floor and said that my little scale was no good. So I picked it up, put a half a gram coin on it and said, "Let's test it first" and of course it was exact so my French friend proceeded to weight the "stuff". They started to yell at us and cuss us out and show their knives before we announced that it was indeed only half of the weight.

It got scary but fortunately the other French guys showed up, there were five of them remember? When they saw themselves surrounded and outnumbered by five very fit and buffed up French men and myself, a semi marginally buffed up Latino, they lowered their knives and calmed down, then they accepted a T shirt and 50 francs only and left. We hauled ass out of there because we had heard stories of them ratting you out to the cops after a deal.

And off we went South, along our way towards the Great Sahara Mauritanian desert, the Western Sahara. I figured it didn't matter to stay now, since I would be a target alone if those Moroccans would see me again in town, so I remained with the French guys. Besides, I wanted more adventure outside of the cities and into the Saharan Desert and that's where the French were headed.

Other than that experience, Morocco was a beautiful magical adventurous place, I actually enjoyed it more than Europe. Warm, cheap, wild and unpredictable. You could be in a modern city like Casa Blanca and then a couple of hours later out in the bush or desert and back in time hundreds of years. Away from civilization we traded stuff, tee shirts, sneakers for fish and other stuff, surfed and rolled in the sand dunes.

There was a picturesque town next to a great bay where we had stopped to have dinner (homemade Kus-kus) at a local Restaurant owner's house. His friends joined us for dinner and wine and we all were like a big happy family. That night the owner offered his yard for us to camp and it was on top of the cliff where we had the view of the bay and the coast, really beautiful.

In the morning we all drove down to the beach so my French friends could windsurf. The session didn't last very long because one of the guys lost his sail out beyond the breakers and he couldn't retrieve it. So we hunted up and down the beach but to no avail.

When we returned to the Restaurant owner's house and explained to him what had happened, he said, "Pas problem" His fishermen friends would probably find it and would bring it to him. Well, it turns out, that one of his friends that had joined us for dinner the night before, heard the conversation and went out and investigated who had found it. He then negotiated a deal with the fisherman and said he would take care of the sail.

That afternoon we heard the great news that a friend of his had found it and would bring it to us. But before he brought it back he demanded a fee of 2,000 French Francs, (approx. 300 US dollars of those days) he said it would cover the gas and boat fee it cost him to retrieve it. The owner of the Sail reminded him that just the night before he had called us his friends, and now he wanted to take advantage of us. The Moroccan replied, "Friends are friends, but business is business my friend".

He really was serious, I think he dropped the price down to 1,500 Fr. We were a bit disappointed but that's how it is sometimes in countries like this.

There was a lot of surf to be found down there, specially the further south we went. One great surf spot was Taghazoute, it had a powerful right break off a rocky point (I think it was called Anchor Point) and it just went on for ever right after right. It was up to double overhead and held that way for two days. I almost got slammed into the rocks on one particular wave after I got hit by the lip, I thought I would feel the impact any time while I was being churned under water, but I made it out without any scratches, it was really worth surfing the place, a powerful wave it was.

We camped along other surfers from Europe and shared the waves in brotherly fashion, unlike California, there was one surfer dude from La Jolla there too. We went further south of Sidi Ifni, a small town called Laayoune and further South, thou we knew we weren't' supposed to be there because it was considered war territory with Mauritania, but we didn't care.

It was a beautiful contrast to have the Sahara Desert on one side and the vast Atlantic on the other, like day and night. The nights were so beautiful specially with a full moon, countless stars blanketed the night sky and the glow of the white water in the crushing waves orchestrating the night was enchanting. We were camping near some fishermen huts who spent Winter fishing the beach with nets and sleeping in their mud huts on top of a Cliff.

CHRISTMAS EXPERIENCE.

Then Christmas night, after having dinner with my French friends who were smoking and having red wine to celebrate I had an idea. I told them I was going to walk to the fishermen's huts to negotiate a fish for supper. So there I went walking into the dark night along the beach, just using the fire light emanating from their hut as a directional beacon. After twenty minutes or so I got there after climbing up the cliff to one of their huts. I knocked on the door and caught them by surprise because they didn't expect anybody that night. They were very courteous and asked me to join them. I asked them if they had some leftover fish they might want to trade or sell. They said they were just going to pull in the fishing nets in an hour or so, so they first invited me to join them for a smoke, a drink and some fish vegetable soup. We all sat around the fire and passed everything around, the bread, the wine and the peace pipe, or big joint (I just passed it to them). Then by 10 pm or so we descended to the beach to pull the nets in.

We all rolled our pants up and entered the cold water to our upper legs to start pulling the nets in, there were around eight of us all together. I felt so elated doing this on Christmas night with strangers who took me in and shared their little supplies and company, it made me feel like a true fishermen although I had never done this before. Finally after an hour or so we had all the nets on shore and there was nothing in them, only a baby shark which they threw back in.

The Fishermen said, "Desolee mon frere" (sorry brother) and I thanked them greatly for everything, the whole experience had been far better than any fish. It was a great Christmas nevertheless. I walked back to our beach camp for about two kilometers in the pitch black night, along the soft sand with only the sound of the waves and the reflection of the stars, thousands of them. I felt elated, alive, complete, and I wanted to walk all night but soon I made it to were my French friends were, sleep and stoned by then.

ALMOST DIED SURFING.

The next morning I checked out the surf, it was a little choppy and rough I thought, but it was Christmas morning and I was determined to go surfing. My friends thought it was too rough for them, pussys I thought, so I went by myself with only a spring wetsuit on and one of their boards with an old leash.

I should have observed the rip current, but I just jumped in and started paddling out and duck diving thru the breaking waves for a few moments until I made it to the lineup . I was pretty far out there, it was breaking a few feet overhead and I was getting cold already. I caught the first wave, wiped out on the second one and lost my board, when I popped up for air I got hit and pummeled by the next set. Now I was in the churning water, like a cat in a dryer, tumbling and rolling. I started panicking and started swimming for what I thought was the top, but instead I hit the bottom. Shit, now I was worried, running out of air and without a board, I was also getting pushed out to sea by the rip current.

I really thought I was going to drown while I was getting thrown around under the white water, I almost couldn't hold my breath but I remembered to keep my cool and almost saw my life flash by in a matter of seconds. I thought about my parents, who by the way didn't know where I had been or where I was since a year ago. I was still re-belling from them and disappearing like this was my reaction for some childhood resentments I still kept.

The thought of dying where nobody knew me scared me more than actually dying. I'm sure the French dudes would have just burnt all my belongings and said nothing to the authorities for fear of being questioned. So I knew I had to keep calm and hold my breath a little longer, and I did. It's amazing what a difference it makes by remaining calm. I observed for bubbles and figured out the correct direction to swim up, caught air and dodged some more white water. By now I was way outside beyond the breakers, alone, without a board and getting hypothermia.

I really started praying to God for help, I knew I was a goner because I couldn't swim against the strong current anymore, my arms felt like spaghetti and I could only float on my back. My next big fear where the brothers in gray suits with fins and sharp teeth, there's many of those in the cold Atlantic.

I was trying to swim at an angle to the current but with little advance. I couldn't see the French on the beach and they hadn't noticed I was in trouble. Then, like by an act of miracle, my board appeared, the current I guess pushed it over to me like by a miracle. I was so happy to see it I felt like kissing and hugging it and so I hung on to it and rode the white water in. The French had not even noticed my predicament. They just said, " salut, we saw you in di water waviing' at us, did you hev a fiu gud waves Henri (Anriii)?". They actually thought I was waving hello at them when I was trying to get their attention before I drowned or got chomped by a shark.

Then we drove to Marrakech for New Year's but we couldn't find anything open where to celebrate, so we traded a watch for a cake and a bottle of champagne and we celebrated just us six in the van. It was a freezing cold night and we all slept in our sleeping bags inside the van, like sardines in a can. I eventually left the group when they started hinting that I should pitch in money for gas, I did pitch in a few bucks and even then one of them ripped off my nice Pink Floyd, The Wall T-shirt, I found out later.

They eventually dropped me off past Barcelona, actually into French territory, it was about 10:pm, snowing and as cold as hell, I was worried I was going to freeze overnight so I just walked and walked towards the Freeway entrance at the Toll Booth. There I made a sign on a piece of cardboard that said Limoge, and waited.

Shortly, a guy on a Citroen stopped and said he was going to the nearby town, I guess he felt sorry for me. It's actually easier to hitchhike when it's shitty and cold outside because people tend to have pity on you. We stopped somewhere along the way at around midnight and my private driver stopped at a bar café' for a baguette and wine. Oh, that must have been the best baguette with wine I'd had in a long time.

These French people I met on the road where true gentlemen and goodhearted people. The French dude was cool because he offered to pay, there where a couple of prostitutes inside that café' trying to stay warm in their mini-skirts and I pitied them. They probably pitied me because to them I looked like a bum, skinny and very tanned, with long curly scraggly hair, with my old empty backpack because I was wearing all my belongings to stay warm. I had my guitar and was wearing babooshes on my feet with four pairs of socks, (basically, slippers made out of leather with car tire soles). I bought those in Morocco after they stole my nice hiking boots at the beach while I was surfing or sleep, I don't exactly remember. They were slippery and I fell down a couple of times and broke my guitar.

Actually I had already broken another guitar when I was in Norway in the winter. It happened while I was trying to catch the coming train that was approaching the station. I had to cross the tracks so I did it with my back pack on my back and my guitar attached to it in it's soft case. I hit a slippery spot on the tracks and my legs flew off towards were my head was. I landed on my back or better said on my guitar and I heard a loud crack on my back. I could see my guitar with it's neck hanging down like a dead goose but I grabbed it as it was and boarded the train. Every one inside obviously saw what happened but just pretended nothing happened. My face must have been red in shame but the nice Norwegian people just ignored what happened. I guess that happens often there in the winter.

Very early the next morning my driver dropped me off at a nearby town not far from Limoge, it was the town train station and he said I could enter the waiting lounge and wait there for the next train. So I thanked him greatly and picked the next bench to sleep in. It was around 2 am and I was super exhausted. I pulled out my sleeping bag and slept a couple of hours until the cleaners arrived and politely woke me up. I was very thirsty so I walked up to the station restaurant and brushed my teeth and combed, as close as combing could go because my curls had turned to dreadlocks by now, exposed to much ocean water and sun in Morocco.

So I very politely asked the male attendant if I could please have a glass of water. The sonofabeach denied me the glass of water and pointed to the bathroom, indicating I should drink out of the faucet. I had never before been denied a glass of water and I was upset so I told him in English my opinion about him. Then I proceeded to catch the next train to Limoge to see my brother.

ANOTHER CLOSE CALL, PREMONITION SAVED ME.

Well to make the story short, I returned to Mainz after making a brief stop in Limoge France. My brother Joe was staying there with Momo (This guy was the most vane guy I have ever known, every time he would see a mirror anywhere he would stop to check himself out and sometimes he even jumped up with comb in hand if the mirror was at a higher level. He took us on a drive in the snow while he practiced his Starsky and Hutch skidding and drifting with his car), he was a friend of Marie Claude, the girl that invited my brother to France. We celebrated New Year again just my bro and I drinking red wine and walking in the snow till the middle of the night. It was one of the best get togethers I've had with my Brother. Eventually I made it back to Mainz and got a job at the U.S. Army casernes as a waiter at the Wiesbaden Officers Club.

I almost never made it because as I had left Limoge hitchhiking North bound towards Paris and then Frankfurt, I got stuck in a little village where two cross roads met. I had spent at least three hours with no luck. The ground was covered in snow and the sun was shining. It was a beautiful day but I knew I had to get a ride before night struck. So I stood on the middle aisle in between two roads with my sign on a cardboard that said 'Paris'. Then I heard a truck approaching, then there was another one from the other direction. I saw them approaching and wondered if they weren't going too fast for that intersection.

One of them was headed West or into the sun and the other one South. The one headed West was also going pretty fast. Then suddenly as if instructed by my inner voice, I felt an urge to move off that aisle I was standing on, just in case. Maybe a premonition, I don't know but I moved to the other side of the road. Just then, as they both approached the light at the intersection at the same time, one of them didn't see his red street light because of the sun blindness effect and slammed side ways into the other truck who had the right off way. They both skidded right over the aisle with a loud bang, exactly where I had been standing seconds before. It was such a spectacular live show of what my last seconds would have been like, slammed and smeared on the pavement like butter, they then slammed into a house on the corner and knocked the wall down. Incredibly, both drivers were unhurt, they crawled out of their Lorry trucks and almost jumped into a fistfight. It was like watching a 3D movie, live.

I did eventually make it to the outskirts of Paris at a Rest stop Gas station but I got stuck in that place for two whole days. Fortunately, the restaurant manager had pity on me and let me roll out my sleeping bag in the lounge at night because it was so cold outside. Winter of 1985 had been the coldest with the most snow fall in Europe in decades. All the roads were blocked by excess snow and my chances of getting out of there were slim. Finally on the third day a big 18 wheel truck arrived, I approached the German driver and explained my predicament, he then said he was headed for Frankfurt and was happy to take me along.

Man, I was so happy to finally get a long ride all the way to Frankfurt. We entered the German border with no problems, they didn't even ask me for my passport because I guess they assumed I was the second driver. Later on, that almost had me deported from Germany as I was trying to hitchhike to Berlin a few months later. The police asked to see my passport and when they saw my initial entry visa stamp they couldn't see a second one from my arrival after Morocco, so they thought I had overstayed my 90 day visa. They then drove me to the Immigration offices and there after careful scrutiny the officials found my other stamps from Spain and Morocco which proved that I had left the country before my 90 day limit. Phew, I almost had an early return to California. Sometimes I wonder how my life would have turned out if they had returned me, I wouldn've met my future wife and kid.

It was so good to be back in Mainz again and I eventually moved in with Karl and his friends in a little old Weissenau house by the Rhein River. It was a very old house with a big coal burning stove and a bathtub in the kitchen. Karl's friends were the owners of the house and were just about to travel thru Africa for one year. Ferdinand and his wife, they were a very nice couple and I liked them very much. So it was Karl, myself and Vince (Ferdinand's brother) and then another girl named Petra moved in, she was very free spirited and used to walk around the kitchen only in panties, I'm serious, she was cute too. That ancient house on the Rein on Langasse 12 had a very pleasant and homey atmosphere. We often had parties and loud live music (since we were all musicians) and no neighbor ever complained.

DESTINY OR FATE, FATHERHOOD.

Then I met her, Fastnacht at the Terminus Club. My friend Karl had almost dragged me out that night, I was bummed out about a girl called Annick. Annick was a half Magadashi and half French girl, exotic and a cute little hottie with more curves on her than Highway 101. I guess her ex-boyfriend was still prowling after her and we got into a push and shove situation on the street. Another time she asked me to come to her apartment in a nearby town near Wiesbaden, she assured me her ex wouldn't be coming by anymore.

But just as we were about to jump in the bathtub she ran to get the ringing phone only in her white thong. Man, she had such a nice round sexy figure and I had never seen a thong before (20 years ago the French invented cool things like these). Her bloody boyfriend was right around the corner and just wanted to talk to her, so she said.

I suspected she might not have been telling the truth to both of us and didn't want to spill any teeth or blood over a two timer chick so I left right away, like a fox in the chicken yard taking the back exit. So I decided to give my love life a break for a little while. Karl talked me into going out that Fastnacht night and we did.

There I was standing having a beer, with a dark tan, long curly dark hair to my shoulders and skinny as a rail from my recent traveling in Morocco. Across from me was Micha, what a cosmopolitan smile she had, and those big green grayish eyes, with a very nice sporty figure. I'm sure we had met somewhere before, another life perhaps. Karl and I approached her and her friend Grazielle but after a few minutes Karl left without a phone number. He just did it to be a good wing man and to back me up. We communicated in pieces of German, English and French because her English was almost nil, my German was also nil, so we mixed everything up to communicate. She had a motherly aura about her.

We got involved a couple of weeks later and she dumped her current boyfriend for me. He didn't take it very well and started being a pain in the behind. He followed us around but didn't want to engage in a fight so I confronted him but he backed off and insulted me in German before walking away. Another time he started insulting my brother who was visiting at the time, he was at a pub in Mainz old town with a girl and this guy starts insulting him in German, thinking it was me, fortunately for him my brother didn't punch him out because he didn't understand a word and just laughed it off. We later got into a wrestling match at the bar at the Terminus club but only because he was with his buddies, I ended up pinning him down in a Judo hold and he pussed out when he noticed his buddies weren't going to help him out.

So that was that, I was saving money to go on a globetrotting tour that year but Micha was deeply in love with me and didn't want to let me go. I knew I would leave in a year or so and my plan was to go by land across the middle East, then India, Thailand or maybe first across to Africa, and who knows where from there. I was going to get a year "round the world" ticket which in those days only cost around $3,000 dollars.

In the meantime in September I had around three weeks off and decided to go traveling a bit. I wanted to go backpacking again to the South but Micha insisted on going with me. I told her I would be hitchhiking and wouldn't stay in Hotels, only camping or Youth Hostels. She had only traveled as a spoiled brat with her Mom and only stayed at nice hotels so I didn't think she was up to roughing it but she insisted she would do her best. She had never packed a backpack and when she showed me her backpack I had to laugh. It was so full of things to the top, like an astronauts air pack. I had a few more laughs when I asked her to try to put it on but of course she couldn't even lift it up over her shoulders.

That was my point I told her, so I asked her to take out all the unnecessary stuff. You wouldn't believe what she had in it, a teddy bear, hair curler, iron, all kinds of elegant gowns and high heel shoes, hair blower, etc. Once she took all that stuff out it was still full but not to the brim like before. Now she could almost put it on herself with a little help from me.

It wasn't really a good idea because on our first night in France we got into our first big fight.

We had taken Mitfahr zentrale (drive-with central), which was sort of a share a ride with strangers going your way. Two German dudes took us along all the way to Biscarroza in France and when we arrived at night we all decided to go to a pizzeria to eat. Micha however said she would first inquire about the Hotel prices next to the Pizzeria. She came out with a gleam in her eye and said, "Shatsi (treasure, but that changed to 'asshole' much later) Let's stay at this hotel tonight and I'll pay for it". Although we had decided to go and stay at the campgrounds after dinner she suddenly wanted to change plans on me.

I said to her, "No Micha, we cannot, we agreed I couldn't afford to stay in Hotels," Well she stood up, grabbed her backpack and said, " it's okay I'm paying so we're staying here yah" to which I responded, "nein, I'm not". She turned around with an air of arrogance and headed into the Hotel with her backpack, I then said to the German guys to ignore her drama, and that we should all go eat pizza, I was sure she'd come out and join us later. And she did a few minutes later, but with fire coming out of her eyes.

I guess she was used to getting away with anything she wanted with her Mom or her ex-boyfriend. She was furious and she contained it but only for a little while. She hardly ate but guzzled down the wine we were drinking, then she started taking our glasses and tried to drink them too. I told her to stop and behave herself. Then she stood up and proceeded to make a fool out of herself by chasing a big shaggy dog that was napping by the entrance. The dog's name was Bubu and she continued to try to grab him but the dog was afraid of her and kept avoiding her behind the tables. "Bubu, come here, kommen sie hier jah, Bubu?" She kept saying. The restaurant was full of French sailors and they were starting to look at her like she was part of the meat menu, so I thought I should take her out of there and have a talk with her.

I sort of gently dragged her out and when we stood outside the Restaurant alone I said to her, "Look Micha, I want you to stop drinking and making a fool out of yourself, please calm down and relax." She looked at me with her big fierce green eyes and said to me, " Du schwein, you pig, you are mean", as she suddenly pulled hard on my long hair. I mean, she was trying to tear my curls off my head and I had to grab her arm tight until she let go. Then she started crying and walking away.

The two German guys came out and we all suggested to drive to the Campgrounds so I grabbed her and put her inside the car. She was calm now but still drunk. The campgrounds had already closed their doors so we all set up our little camp, tents and sleeping bags in the forest nearby. Micha crawled out of her sleeping bag, undressed and forced herself into my sleeping bag. She then proceeded to kiss me wildly, then had sex with me with so much passion and anger that it was a little scary but exciting. Fortunately the other two dudes were a few feet away from us so I don't think they noticed anything.

In the middle of the night I noticed she was gone, I looked for her in her sleeping bag with the reflection of the moon but I didn't see her there either, I thought the worse and wondered if just 'accidentally' she might have jumped in with one of the other guys. I looked over where they were sleeping but she wasn't there either. I then started to look for her around the trees while calling her name softly. I didn't want to walk too far to avoid getting lost in the forest so I stayed close to our campground. Then I heard a noise a few feet away and there she was standing, stark naked like a lost child, just looking around her surroundings wondering where she was. Fortunately she didn't start wandering otherwise she would have been very lost and naked.

I brought her back to the tent and she went back to sleep, I think she went to pee and got lost.

In the morning I had a serious talk with her. After we parted with the German guys I told her I was taking her to the train station to send her back. I told her I didn't' need the stress and that it wasn't a good idea to travel together. I saw the Tasmanian Devil monstrous side of her the night before and I was sure I was going to break up with her as soon as I got back. She cried and said she wouldn't do that anymore and pleaded to please let her stay by my side.

I can't stand a woman crying and I fell for her drama. Things improved, we hitchhiked the rest of the way to Spain, then took a train to Portugal. While at the train station Restaurant after we had some delicious seafood and red wine she followed me to the Men's bathroom. She wanted to make love there but I wasn't too sure about it being a good idea. Especially after having felt the scorn and accusations of a couple of Portuguese religious puritans just because they saw her kissing me in public.

So we waited until we got to the train, we walked into an empty First class cabin and shut the door and curtains, then we made passionate love, sort of dressed just in case. Suddenly, a few minutes later someone started to knock on the door and we panicked, she jumped off me just in time to pull her skirt down and me pull my shorts up. Just then the train ticket guy slid open the door and asked what we were doing there without proper tickets. I think he suspected something because he looked at us suspiciously when he asked us to leave the cabin.

The rest of the vacation went well and we stayed in a small pretty beach town near Porto. The Portuguese people were very hospitable and we got to know some of the local beach crowd who showed us the town and clubs. There was also a great surfing spot by a jetty. The local Portuguese surfers were pretty cool and usually let me use their wetsuits and surfboards. That never happened in France. On our way back we stayed in Biarritz on the Atlantic side of France, (it resembles La Jolla coves in San Diego California) it's a beautiful city on the beach and one of my favorite places in France. There was good surf there but nowhere to rent a board and after asking a couple of guys where I could borrow a surfboard, I stopped trying to ask because every one of them had an excuse not to let me borrow their board.

Then she got pregnant, while we were in Portugal for three weeks I guess it happened, all that excellent seafood, red wine and romantic lovemaking under the stars and in the train must have had something to do with it.

Also, she swore that I agreed to have a baby with her, I understood her question to be "do you like babies" and I said, "JA," but she claims she asked me if I wanted to have a baby with her (She said "machts Du eine baby mit Mir haben?" I understood, "Machts Du Babies"?). While I'm at it, I would like to clarify something. During Micha's pregnancy I never screwed around with any other woman, not even when our marriage was on the rocks. Not even with Santina, Karl's Italian girlfriend who was very good friends with me. I guess Karl always thought I had

had something with her, and so did my ex, but I didn't and I swear it. I hope Karl reads this.

I didn't have the courage to leave her because we were in love, it was a beautiful time in my life because I had never received so much love and attention, not even as a kid.

She was so loving and spoiled me so much, her motherly love was probably what I needed most at the time so I really loved being with her as long as her monstrous side was kept locked up, okay, we were both in love and lust. I was still partly broke and she didn't seem to care, she had a car and always had money because she had a good job and lived at home with her Mom. She was a fancy classy girl, always neatly dressed with shiny clean healthy white teeth and her Colgate smile (unlike other German Frauleins).

So I knew I was at a crossroad and didn't want to screw it up and regret my actions later, so with the regret of putting off my traveling plans, I made a decision. She later claimed that she probably saved me from getting Aids in Africa if I would have continued my travels. Speaking of AIDS, I had the biggest scare in my life.

When we got back from Portugal I started getting some boils, dark spots on my body, also my glands were swollen so I started to get worried. Especially when I read in a German Magazine, Die Stern, The Star, about the later developments of the so called gay disease. They had some new information about what the symptoms of the disease or HIV were. They claimed that boils in the body along with swollen glands were some of the symptoms and that terrified me. Up until that point I knew that it was mostly a gay disease but then I remembered that one of my ex girlfriends from Berlin had had a bisexual boyfriend. Now I was really worried especially since Micha was recently pregnant.

I decided not to say anything to her and secretly went to a German Doctor. The Herr Doctor was very nice but very serene and serious looking. He asked me all kinds of questions like, have you shot drugs with a needle, had gay sex, had blood infusions, etc. I assured him I had a clean and normal record regarding my lifestyle and told him my only worry was because of that ex girl's past with a bisexual guy.

He did the necessary check ups and took my blood, then he looked at me with his serene look and said, " here's my home phone number, if you suddenly develop a high fever you must contact me inmediately". That terrified me even more and I walked out of there thinking he knew something and didn't want to tell me yet. That was the worst weekend of my life because I had to wait until Monday to get the results. I couldn't sleep and I couldn't get myself to tell Micha yet. All kinds of scenarios went thru my head as to what I should do if I had the disease. Should I tell Micha to abort the baby hoping she would forgive me and then go on and wait for a slow death, or just jump off a building without saying a thing. The first one sounded like the right thing to do but I had to wait to get the results on Monday.

On Monday morning I went to the Doctor and held my breath until he gave me the news. He said something like, "you're negative", by which I understood he meant, you are a negative, a zero, gone, finito, history, the past, bought the farm, ate shit, croaked, a goner, etc. Then he looked at my terrified look and explained to me what he really meant. He said the test was negative and that I didn't have any disease. That it was just some infection I caught from dirty water or something while on vacation. He gave me some antibiotics and told me not to worry about a thing. I was so elated I could have kissed his hand, bowed and done the Japanese pigeon dance or wagged my tail off my butt if I was a dog. I thanked him greatly and literally floated along in ecstasy the rest of the day. I couldn't believe how much more you can appreciate life when you find out you're about to loose it. I decided not to tell Micha anything until years later about the terrible experience.

We settled in an apartment in Wiesbaden Biebrich. I had my Honda motorcycle CV 750 for transportation and had a descent job in Mainz Kastel now. As an accounting inventory clerk. Riding a motorbike in Germany on the Autobahn at 200 Km/hr was a rush almost compared to riding a large fast wave.

I knew our stay in Germany was temporary because I still had my dreams of becoming an Airline Pilot. My son was born on July 4th and what a beautiful baby he was, it was the happiest day of my life. We named him Enriko, he had big eyes and always smiled. We were soul brothers since that moment he was born. I remember clearly when I held him in my arms as they pulled him out while he screamed, he heard my voice and remained silent while trying to look at me thru his sleepy sticky eyes. That was the most beautiful experience I had ever had in my young life. He cried a little bit at first but when he heard my voice he calmed down, content to finally meet me. We remained in Biebrich another few months, it was summer so it was our last nice months in Germany, we did a lot of walking thru the Biebrich park and along the River with our new baby in his stroller. Then we moved to San Diego when the baby was five months old.

BACK TO CALIFORNIA, WINTER OF 1986.

We flew to San Diego in November and the weather was still like summer there, it was so nice to get away from another cold winter in Germany when in San Diego it was beautiful with blue skies and mild cool temperatures. I borrowed a VW van from my old friend Carol for the first two weeks and we drove to visit my old friend Inky Binky. Unfortunately, as we were driving into a gas station the next day we arrived, we got hit sideways by a muscle Camaro as it tried to shoot it's yellow red light. The impact was strong and fortunately didn't directly hit the gas tank on the VW bus, however it sent little Enriko's basket with him in it flying all the way to the front of the bus. He didn't even wake up, he just grunted and kept sleeping.

The driver got away and we surveyed the damage, it didn't look good. My friend Carol had asked me to take good care of it and now I felt really bad. She was out of the country at the moment but I was supposed to let her Dad use it for a couple of days and then get it back. They couldn't fix the dent right away so I had to take it to her Dad as it was and explain that I would fix it as soon as he was thru using it, and I did. But her step Mom thought I was trying to avoid fixing it and gave Carol that incorrect message. I later explained to Carol after I fixed it what had really happened.

Inky was now married to Don and had a baby girl in Ocean Beach. We spent a couple of days with them and then we went for a week cruising along Baja California Mexico, I had to catch up to all that delicious food, lobster, fish tacos, huevos rancheros, etc.

Within a week we had our next fight. This time it was another one of her tantrums because I wouldn't spend money crazily. We were on a budget because I didn't have a job yet and she was upset because I didn't want to spend money freely. Anyway, we were parked by the Coast Guard Light house at the end of Sunset Cliffs when she suddenly grabbed my wallet and threw it up in the air with all the fifty dollar bills flying with the wind. There must have been around three hundred dollars inside my wallet and they all went flying outside the van. I told her to pick every one of them up or else I was leaving her there. I started the van and my bluff worked because she started to pick them up in a hurry. I pretended I was going to drive away and she ran after the van screaming at me and assuring me she had found all of the lost bills. I felt sorry for her, she seemed like a confused little girl at times and she just couldn't stop herself from having her tantrums. She had suffered as a little girl obviously when her Father passed away when she was only nine or ten years old.

Eventually we settled down in Ocean Beach on Santa Cruz street in a cozy little one bedroom cottage only half a block from the cliffs. I hooked up with my old buddies George and Charlie who where still there and now working as carpenters in Construction. They oriented me to get a job working as a carpenter sheeter in the construction of homes. Then I continued University and Flight School at National University, my counselor Kimberly was a real help, she was the attractive blonde pilot who helped me thru the loops of the University. Thanks to her help and my persistence, I pursued and completed my dream.

I really cherish those moments when I remember them in detail. Enriko my little boy was just starting to walk, Micha was trying to adapt to the beach atmosphere and to our tight financial situation. I was making enough to survive and we had the essential necessities at home. Sometimes, she would have one of her outbreaks and start screaming and yelling over anything. Fortunately it was all in German so the neighbors didn't know what it was all about. One evening I swear I don't' remember why, she found a Johny Walker bottle that I had hidden from her and started drinking it by herself. When I got home that evening she had already turned into the Tasmanian Devil.

I just don't understand how such a cute normally lovely quiet girl could transform into a monster sometimes. She started her usual drama of blaming me for her rotten meager life in California, telling me how I ruined her life, and what an asshole I was. So this is how I went from being Shatsi, Liebling to being a Schwein, Ashloch, etc. I decided to walk out the door hoping she would calm down but she grabbed a knife and pointed it towards me, so I challenged her to aim it for my heart (of course I was ready to block it just in case). It threw her off and she appeared confused so she said she would cut her veins and I would be blamed for her death.

I thought she was bluffing so I said to her, " okay, but clean up your bloody mess before you pass out", and I slammed the door shut. I did look thru the window before I left to make sure she wouldn't do anything stupid and I left quietly once she put the knife away and calmed down eventually.

Other than a few dramas life was good, although stressful at times due to Micha's jealousy streaks and dramas, I enjoyed most of those years in Ocean Beach. We often hung out with my old friends and had a few of our old friends from Germany visit us as well. Heike and Herbert, her Mom, Karl Hiller and Santina, Alexandra and Happy (Andreas Puttner), and my brother Joe and his new girlfriend from Berlin. I remember one of his girlfriends was so naïve that when she brought her hand held radio from Germany she was trying to tune it to her favorite station. When we explained to her that it wouldn't work she asked very disappointed, " why not, it's a German radio". Another time they came by to pick up their mail at our apartment and she was disappointed because she wasn't getting any mail. I explained to her that it would take a week or two to get a response and then she replied, "But how is my hometown mail man going to know where to find me here?". And you thought Americans were naïve?

Micha sometimes worked baby sitting a friend's child (baby Daniel) so she could pay for her yearly ticket to Germany where she would stay with her Mom for four to six weeks. Her Mom also visited us every year. When her Fiancé Visa was about to expire we decided to tie the knot. I was a little scared of marriage but I knew that was the only way we could stay together so we had a nice little wedding in our neighbors backyard on Santa Cruz avenue. All of our friends from Ocean beach were there and also my old College friends, Bud, Theresa and Jim. Even her Mom and her best friend Heike flew over for a few days. It was a great Beach Wedding. Our neighbors Jamie and her husband organized it for us in their backyard. That was really nice of them.

Her Mom was the nicest Mother in law anyone could have, she truly believed in me and in my flying dreams. On one of the visits she made us she handed me a check for $5,000 Dollars and said to me in German, "here you have so you can continue your Flight training, you can pay me when you have enough". I couldn't believe she had more credibility in me than her daughter and my own parents. I was so grateful to her and all these years I have gotten along very well with her. About seven years later I paid her every penny back including interest for those seven years. Micha's best friend Heike and Herbert also loaned me out a couple of Thousand without me even asking for it. I also paid them back with interest. They are the nicest people and that's one of the many reasons why I always felt like Germany was my second home.

By the end of 1988 we had moved to a larger Duplex on Niagara avenue which was only two blocks from the pier where I usually surfed. I was getting burnt out from working, running a family, attending National University and Flight School on weekends. My days consisted of early wake up at 6am, cup of coffee, cereal, load up my Honda 750 with tools on packs, electric saw in the back, bundled up in sweaters and leather jacket, gloves for the early winter 35-40 Fahrenheit chill and the fast drive on HI-15 North to the Construction areas around Escondido. At 6:30 am I hardly encountered much traffic or cops so I was able to make the drive at 80 to 90 mph, hugging the fuel tank and leaning low over the engine to stay warm. I wouldn't do that now , I'll tell you that.

CRUISING BAJA CALIFORNIA, NIGHT BANDIDOS.

By now I was in need of a long vacation. I took my semester student loan of around $3,500 dollars and bought a better VW Westphalia van than the one I almost burned down. The older one actually caught on fire on the freeway, I noticed people passing me and saying something like "Fire" and I thought they wanted a smoke. And then I saw it when I stopped and looked at the back, the smoke was coming from behind the van where the engine was. I ran back to the front of the van and pulled my kid out and climbed up a little hill away from it. Then a good Samaritan stopped to help out and handed me a can of cherry Soda, he said to shake it and extinguish the fire with it. It worked perfectly because it wasn't that huge of a fire yet, it was mostly the rubber around the engine that started burning.

So that's why I bought a newer van for my dreamed up Surfari vacation down to Baja and beyond (Enriko called the VW bus the Bye Bye Bus because we told him we would go on it on a long Big Bye Bye).

I took two months off from school in the winter and we packed and rolled. Micha, Enriko who was two years old by now, and myself. It was a great adventure but Micha wasn't used to roughing it and she complained a lot, phew, that wasn't easy. We were so different and sometimes I wondered how long we would last. But we had a great time camping, fishing, surfing and exploring Baja south followed by the Ferry ride to the mainland Mexico, then coasting southbound to Puerto Escondido, the Mexican Pipeline.

It' a hollow wave similar to the Pipeline on Waimea except it's a sandy shallow brake, one of the best surf spots on the Pacific coast where I almost broke my neck when I hit bottom on my head and shoulders during a wipe out.

I was scared I would end up crippled but I only received a sore body and back for many weeks thereafter. Even now I still get a stiff back and shoulders I think as a result of that injury.

During the time we stayed in Puerto Escondido we befriended most of the other travelers camping at the Campgrounds. However, my ex-wife Micha was a little jealous of two cute English girls in cute skimpy bikinis. Every time they walked by and said 'Hi' or 'Good morning' she would ignore them. Then one night as we were all having a fire on the beach and playing guitar, Micha promptly got up and said she was going to bed. Later on that night more people joined us, including the two cute English girls.

Then sometime around midnight when we were out of drinks we all agreed to go dancing next door to the open air beach Disco. We had a great time dancing and drinking and we didn't get back to the camping grounds until about 5 am. I thought it would be smart to sleep on the hammock tied to the VW bus and a palm tree to avoid waking Micha up.

When she woke up in the morning and saw me there she didn't suspect anything. But then one of the neighbors asked me if I had a good time at the Disco. Of course Micha heard him and asked me if I went with the English girls too. I said I didn't remember clearly because we were all pretty drunk

Man, she was pretty furious and proceeded to throw stuff at me while I was trying to sleep in my hammock. I just kept her at a distance with a little bamboo stick at her ankles, as if she were a wild lioness. Then she tried to cut the hammock with the machete.

So later that afternoon she said, " Now you're going to take me out dancing too, ja", shit, I wasn't ready for this, still hung over and tired from the night before. So I agreed and off we went for dinner first. She was dressed up all sexy in a mini skirt and all made up, she had a great figure and a pair of sexy legs with an attractive cosmopolitan face on her neck so she looked dressed to kill. (as a matter of fact she was dressed to 'kill' me).

First, she started poking at my ribs and pinching my butt while we had dinner and sangrias. Then she downed a couple of drinks and started getting aggressive, I really dreaded seeing her drink because I knew that any moment now she would transform into the Tasmanian Devil. I asked her to please stop doing that and it pissed her off. She suddenly stood up and said "Shaisse, you don't have any energy for me?, let's go now Ja". So as we walked out into the wide beach walk she said to me in a soft calm voice as she handed me baby Enriko who was sleep, "can you hold the baby for me, ja bitte?".

I was surprised at how calm she suddenly became so I didn't suspect any surprises. However, while I was holding him, all of a sudden she slapped me so hard on my left cheek that my face started to vibrate. Also, the slap resounded like an echo due to the wide street. I didn't know what to do because she inmediately ran away back to the Camp ground. My cheek was still vibrating and I decided to calm down and breath deep. I knew that if I chased her down I might not hold myself back and it would most likely trigger a street fight with someone jumping in to defend her. So I was smart and remained calm and kept breathing deep and slow.

When I got back to the van shortly thereafter I was pretty calm, I put the baby to sleep, then I sat in front of her and said to her in a mild voice, " look Micha, you should not have done that", I expected her to apologize and promise never to do that again. Instead, she had a smirk on her face and she said with a bitchy witchy voice, " I'll do it again if I want to". I couldn't believe it and while my thoughts went thru my head on what to say next, I swear my hands moved on their own. It was like a mysterious entity had grabbed them and swung them at their leisure.

Like the fastest gun slinger in the west, both my hands lightly slapped her almost simultaneously. I really wasn't planning on doing that, it just happened, they were pretty light slaps thou compared to the one she landed on my face a few moments earlier. It caught her by surprise and she started crying. Now I felt like shit and told her I was so sorry but that if she did that again I might not be able to hold my self back.

I hugged her tight while she cried and she almost fell sleep in my arms, in the middle of the night she made love to me and in the morning she pretended nothing ever happened. "Liebling, vat do you vant foa breakfast" she just said.

After that serious talk and to make the story short I think she got the message never to do that again, so she didn't try to slap me anymore but she did try to claw my face a couple of days later. I knew she had crossed the line and there was no way back, we were on the verge of separation and we both knew it.

Unfortunately, because of her Dad's drinking and girl chasing actions she had gotten a bad impression about men and thought I was going to do the same things, so she was over reacting to everything with jealousy. It happened often where we would be sitting having coffee and breakfast in California (when we first arrived from Germany) and a young waitress would approach us in a friendly way, she would assume I knew her and would ask me why I was flirting with her and if I had slept with her. I mean, it was funny at first and I would laugh because I thought she was joking. But she wasn't, and suddenly she would get up and say, "Let's go, I don't like it here". She just wasn't used to having overly friendly Waitresses attend us in this way.

So back in Mexico, we returned via the mountains and deserts over the Mainland and across the vast desert towards Calexico. It is said that you shouldn't drive at night because of night Bandidos. However, I took my chances because we were running out of time and Micha had to catch a flight from LA in a few days.

So one night as we were driving in the pitch black night on the empty Highway, it was an endless straight desert road for hours on end and I started getting worried with "what if" scenarios.

Then I noticed a pair of headlights catching up with us from behind, at first I felt relieved thinking I wouldn't be that alone but then they approached very quickly and didn't pass me. They stayed at my speed right behind me, hmm. I started wondering why when another set of lights approached at pretty high speeds from behind again, this other vehicle was a muscle car such as a Firebird and when it passed us it stayed in front of us and stopped accelerating. Now I was sandwiched in between both cars and I started feeling my nuts up in my neck area.

I was really sweating now and started imagining what I would do to defend my family. I noticed they both were switching from low to high beams on their cars and they still surrounded me for about ten minutes now.

Then the car in the front accelerated and almost disappeared from view over a slight hill, stopped and started switching to high beams again facing towards our direction. Now I started making a plan because I really thought that now they were prepared to block the road and force us out. I told Micha to hide in the back with the baby, cover up with blankets and if found, to scream that she was pregnant even thou she wasn't. Then I started loading myself up like Rambo, without the muscles and the automatic weapons but with a working brain. With just a dagger in my boot, a machete on my lap, a hack ax behind my belt and a cutting knife in the other hand. I was really going to fight if I had to.

But just then, the car behind us, also a Camaro type passed me and sped up pretty fast until both vehicles disappeared from view in the darkness of the night.

We all felt so relieved and then I realized what had just taken place. Drug runners, that's what they were, hiding behind me at first. Then the guy without the drugs speeds up and checks for Military checkpoint areas and if none, signals the guy behind my car and then he speeds by, that's how they used to do it in the past.

Now they use high Tech equipment and even modern aircraft to scuttle drugs into the Country.

GRADUATION DAY. ONCE AGAIN, ALL BY MY LONESOME.

By the summer of 1989 I was able to work less as a carpenter and more as a Flight Instructor. Micha had been working as a baby sitter and an Aerobic Instructor part time and now she was working as a cashier at the Food store across the street from us. This is how the beginning of most Pilots' careers begin, first making flight hour experience thru instructing until a small Air Taxi or Commuter Airline can hire you as Co-pilot on small or medium passenger aircraft. That could take two or three years to accumulate one thousand flight hours depending on how much you flight instruct.

Now, this is why I tell everyone that if you get into aviation for the money, you shouldn't be in it in the first place. Because on your first commuter Pilot job you only started making around 900 Dollars a month. Yes, well that was a few years back and I don't think it's changed that much now, actually it has, now some companies make you pay for the aircraft training. That is the beginning of a starving pilot career and only if you have the passion and love for airplanes you will succeed past those hard cashless moments of eating ramen noodles, rice or bean burritos for breakfast lunch and dinner.

I did have fun Flight instructing and was lucky to get a few nice students from Europe. One of them was Urko from Spain, Enrique also from Madrid and Alessandro from Italy who I later visited in Florence. Urko was just a kid with a dream to fly, the kid was a genius and he flew like an ace. What didn't help him was his accent which was so strong that sometimes the Air traffic controllers couldn't understand him. On one practice Instrument flight he was giving the time in hour and minutes to the Female controller as we over flew a navigation station. The twelve o clock didn't make sense to her and she asked, "what about twelve o clock"? To which I responded without touching the microphone, "twelve o clock, your place or mine baby," I froze when she answered, "watch it, your mike is stuck", meaning my microphone had remained open and she heard what I said. Oops, I lucked out she didn't sue me.

Flying with Enrique from Madrid had it's frustrations because he had a bit of an ego, he thought he always knew everything and wanted to do things his way. Well, I wasn't' going to let him kill me so on a Flight training day, on one missed approach over the airport with a twin engine aircraft, he did something that I considered dangerous. He refused to use more rudder control instead of aileron control after I simulated to fail an engine, so I took control and said to him I wasn't going to continue training with him anymore. I suggested we take a single engine aircraft and practice spins so he could see what would happen to him if he kept using aileron instead of rudder during an engine failure after takeoff.

This was my favorite kind of training, spinning the airplane out of the sky on it's back and then letting it plunge down nose first towards the earth while spinning around. I told him to shut his eyes and then when I had it on it's back falling backwards and then dropping and spinning on it's nose I yelled at him to take control and recover. He tried but he couldn't and literally begged me to take control and recover. I recovered after the third turn after he started getting really nervous, he then said he'd had enough for the day. I figured that little experience shook that ego of his out of his system. After that we went and had a few beers and we talked about it. He understood the message and controlled his ego after that, other than that he was a funny guy and I continued his instruction until he finished his Commercial License. Urko and Alex also finished successfully. Alex was always the perfect gentleman, he'd stop anywhere to let a lady go by and sometimes I pictured him stopping the airplane above to let ladies go by on the road below him.

I also had a few other free lance students thru the Gibbs flying club. One of them was Santiago the Argentinean. He had a private Pilot license but wanted to finish his Instrument License. We became friends and eventually I ended up giving him free instruction in exchange for a place to live in his nice house in La Jolla, just a couple of blocks from a great surf spot. We stayed friends for a long time and still get together sometimes in San Diego. His brother and him started that company years ago, advertising with a hot chick's rear end in a thong, a good wave and the Reef sandal in the second page of Surfer Magazine. Nice going Santi.

I was lucky I was able to get Multi-engine hours quickly since I had a wealthy student who chose to do all his ratings on a two engine Duchess Aircraft. Most companies will require at least 300 hours multi-engine before they hire you so it is important to get those soon. Therefore getting a Multi-engine Instructor rating right away is the key. In 1989 I graduated from National University and had all my ratings by then.

At first I was a starving Flight Instructor for about one year and a half. But before I ended my Instructor days, Micha and I separated in 1990 in peaceful terms. It was inevitable, she really had changed since she arrived to California. Thanks to our fake blonde lawyer neighbor that coached her into changing into a liberal big mouthed emancipated woman. This is the same woman who later tried to screw me and hid my car and cottage keys when I refused her advances. I think she was always jealous of Micha and wanted to make us split.

So we decided for her to take a longer vacation in Germany as she usually did every year, except this time she threatened she wouldn't return. So I believed her and then when she did come back she thought I was screwing pretty Lorna whom I met at Winston's reggae nights in Ocean Beach (guess who told her, yes, that fake blonde lawyer). But I wasn't screwing her, we were close but I wasn't having sex with her because we were still married. She used that as an excuse and took the next flight out and went back to Germany with our son. We parted in peace and remained good friends for long.

We could not have forced ourselves to remain together anymore. Micha had gotten pretty aggressive and had lost all respect for me. I couldn't sleep in peace anymore after she threatened to be a magician and disappear my bratwurst for good. A few days before she split, after we'd had a big fight that caused her to jettison her diamond wedding ring straight out to space, (I later climbed the roof to look for it and found it) she had her master drama of all dramas.

After I went surfing to calm down and let her diffuse, she grabbed the big knife in the kitchen and proceeded to slash our futon mattress about three times. Then she lifted it up and dragged it out to the front lawn, together with a lot of my belongings, books, clothes, surfboards, etc. Not my acoustic guitar because she knew that was taboo, it was sacred to me. When I returned I had to drag everything back in and asked her why she did that. She said she slashed the mattress because she wanted to make sure no other Bitch slept in it after she left. I had to sow it up and turn it on the other side because I couldn't afford to buy another one.

The night before she left she came over to the coach where I was sleep, she said she wanted to cancel her flight and that we should try again. I knew it was all beyond repair and said we should see it as another vacation, a time test to see how we would feel after some time. We then made love for the last time. I drove them to the Airport as I usually did every time they went to visit Grandma every year and tried not to think that it was probably the end.

It was nevertheless the saddest day in my life when they left. I remember very clearly when I came back to our cozy little apartment, it was suddenly so empty and quiet. There were no footsteps or screaming or laughter of little Enriko anymore, just silence bouncing off the wooden floors. I heard a jet aircraft fly overhead and pictured them in it, looking down towards Ocean Beach where they used to live and my heart broke. It was the first time in a long time since I had really felt my heart ache, I sobbed like a kid for a long while but I knew it was the best for everyone. I knew that if I had prolonged this forced relationship because of my little son, in the long run it would have been more traumatic for him, more dramas and fights between his Mother and I, bad example after bad example. Besides I didn't want him to see what I saw as a child with my parents, it wasn't the best example of parenthood.

It's amazing and sad how you realize sometimes too late how much you loved someone after you've lost them. After you've become attached to each other for many years even when you didn't get along much of the time. You're still paired up as a couple making good and bad experiences together and living life while sharing the good times and bad times. So when separation sets in, it is a difficult moment to remove yourself from that personal attachment you had with your partner. Especially with your kids, that's the hardest part, it's like someone is tearing part of your heart out.

Micha and I became better friends after we separated, she's a very spiritual person and is also a yoga Instructor now. We have become more like soul brother and sister and I respect and cherish her friendship very much. I guess our experiences together led us to improve ourselves from within and made us better persons. So I never regretted the times we shared together, they were actually great times and I never got bored with her. We still sometimes get together in Hawaii when she comes to visit with her partner Ralf.

THE SERIOUS NINETIES

I had to sell almost everything to raise money and I couldn't afford the rent in the Duplex anymore. So I moved into a garage studio by the cliffs in Ocean Beach, it was a cozy little place with a fire place on Santa Cruz street. It was rented to me by Jen, our ex- neighbor lady, the lawyer fake blonde with the BMW. She's the one that eventually got pissed off at me because I rejected her sexual advances. I was at my desk in my cottage studying with my door opened and there she was naked, wrapped around in a towel after her shower, high heel shoes and red lipstick.

She looked like a beefed up beef burrito wrapped in a very small flour tortilla, with the beef hanging out. She stood by my side while she put her hand on my neck and suggested I take a break to relax. Gulp, I knew what she wanted and I just acted aloof telling her I really had a lot to study. Another time while she was in the shower I asked her if I could get my toothbrush since the bathroom door was left open.

She responded that I could and then she added, "you can look behind the curtain if you want, I know you want to". Hell no,, I didn't want to, she was flabby and I had no intention of looking at her, far less touch her.

I guess I hurt her deeper ego so she decided to hide all my keys one day. I knew she had them because I heard her get them while I was in the shower, but I couldn't prove it. She used to stalk me and spy on me every time I would have girls over at my cottage. She used her position and status to try to get even at me for shattering her female ego. So I moved out and told her she would get her house keys back when I got mine back, to which she responded by calling her friend cops and they threatened to arrest me if I didn't return her keys inmediately. So much for another lying lawyer. She was usually trying to impress people. One day she drove around the block with her old surfboard (someone else's board) sticking out of her sunroof, without a fin, calling me out to go surfing.

I was so pissed off but I had to humiliate myself and return her keys in front of the cops. They didn't want to hear my story because they were her friends. It had taken me three days to remove the steering wheel lock off my Mustang with a Diamond tip drill so I wasn't very happy. I'm sure karma or her alcohol abuse dealt with her eventually.

I started dating again but mainly European girls. I had a good circle of single friends that were mostly Europeans from an English school where my friend Boris the Menace attended, the crazy German from Frankfurt. Thru Boris I met the Sicilian Swiss chick called Dina, man she was hot blooded, in every respect, attractive with the nicest pair of breasts. We dated for about two months and had a couple of honeymoon trips to Baja Mexico where she insisted on paying for almost everything because I was still partly broke.

One day she exploded in anger when I bought a gift (with my own money) to send to my ex wife for her Birthday, she then accused me of using her and that what I really wanted was to go surfing to Baja, which was partly true because I did bring a surfboard with us, hey, there was good surf that weekend down in Baja. After all the romantic times we had in Ensenada, the great sex on the beach and in the Hotel and she spoiled it all, no sense of humor there. Well we did have a great time together and I did dig her but she was looking to catch a husband with US status and I wasn't in that mood so she split a couple of months later.

I discovered the Latin girls and their warm qualities, actually I discovered a half Latin girl before that called Lorna. She was beautifully gorgeous, we had a great time together and helped each other emotionally. She was a love and we built a close friendship pretty quick.

And for the record, NO, I didn't have sex with her while Micha was in Germany. Well, we came close one night when we returned from dancing at a club, she was a little tipsy so I suggested she crash on the couch. She didn't find the couch comfortable so I told her to stay on the other half of my bed. She took her skirt off in the dark but I could see that she only had a little dental floss thong. I tried to ignore that and stay on my side but my lower little head kept trying to lead me into trouble.

In the middle of the night she somehow moved her nice derriere into my groin and I couldn't resist touching and feeling, oh, the pleasure of such a nice butt and it was strictly forbidden according to these stupid marriage laws. She started responding but I had to take a piss. While I was taking a leak I remembered that I was still married and shouldn't go thru with it so I returned to sleep on the couch with my disappointed soldier saluting all night. Well, what also played an important role in helping me stay loyal was the fact that my now ex, threatened to bite my bratwurst off if she ever would know of me cheating. Also the fear of Aids and that I didn't have a condom at the moment. Talk about having mind over body control.

I did love Micha in my own selfish way but maybe I should have shown it more. I was just so busy with pursuing my dream career that I probably didn't try hard to show it to her so she reacted in an insecure and jealous way. I will always appreciate and cherish the moments I spent with her since we met. She was the woman that showed me the most motherly love and boosted up my self esteem with her praises and compliments when we were still much in love while in Germany. Thanks to her, it helped me find my own internal love and it also made me a more secure and self assured person.

BIG SURF AT SUNSET CLIFFS, WINTER OF 1990.

I must admit, the separation was a little tough at first and often I would miss them terribly. So I started surfing even more to cope with it. The ocean has always been my Temple of Meditation so that's how I kept my sanity and mental balance. I'm not even close to a pro surfer level but I have surfed many great known spots around the world. Tamarin Bay and One Eye in Mauritius, Reunion Island, Uluwatu in Bali, Tarrazhut in Morocco, Northern Spain and Portugal, Western France, Piha and Raglans in New Zealand, Eastern Australia, Fiji and Hawaii, Puerto Escondido and Pascuales in Mexico and many of the great surf breaks in Baja California. Not to mention many of the great breaks on Oahu and Maui.

In San Diego county I surfed my biggest winter surf in the winter of 1990. There was a monster swell and Sunset Cliffs was pumping. One day me and my buddies George and Chris decided to try our luck at a spot called Garbage at the Cliffs since the Pier was pretty blown and closed out. It looked big and clean with some beautiful steep peaks held up by favorable offshore winds. There was nobody else out there that day so it turned into an epic day with just me and my friends.

We walked down the concrete stairs and paddled out in between sets.

I was the first one out there at the take off zone and had my favorite surfboard with me, a Murphy classic semi gun, about nine foot long, thick with a double stringer and a long single fin. I waited until the cleanest sets started to show across the horizon and by then I had gathered up my courage to go for the biggest one. George and Chris the Belge were still paddling out when they saw me drop in on this wave. I remember clearly as I was on my feet on a pretty vertical drop that felt like it would never end, I heard a very loud roar coming from behind me and wondered where it was coming from.

It was unusually loud and sounded like a growling lion trying to catch up with me. As I made my backside bottom left turn into the face of the wave and saw my buddies eyes bulged out trying to scratch for the shoulder of the wave, I realized what a monster wave it was. I looked over my left shoulder and up and amazed myself at the size of it, the face of it was at least three times overhead according to George and Chris, which made it around eighteen to twenty feet on the face.

I S-turned up and down into it's face in slow motion, soul surfing it for what it was worth. Time seemed to come to a standstill and I was in such ecstasy even after I pulled out over it's left shoulder. My buddies were hooting at me when I got back to the line up and they noticed I had this stoked look on my face like I was in heaven. So far, that had been my biggest wave and I knew I was gonna remain stoked for the rest of that day and week. The ecstasy you get from riding a powerful wave is similar or better than the best orgasm you can think of with the hottest chick. A couple of waves after that one, I lost my board during a wipe out and my leash popped so I started to swim and body surf the big sets coming in, until Chris rescued me on his long board. I was so stoked by that first big wave experience and it remained fresh in my mind as the best surf session of those times.

Sabine and my 72 Mustang posing in Baja Mexico

MEXICO, ROOT RETURN.

The year 1990 was coming to an end and I was ready for a serious change. I wasn't getting a lot of offers for good Pilot positions so I decided to try my luck in Mexico, there was a pilot boom there, my friend Pepe had told me. Pepe was a Corporate Pilot that I met while walking thru General Aviation at the Guadalajara Airport, he was a super nice guy and we made a close friendship pretty quick. He wanted to take Instrument Flight training to improve his English in San Diego so I arranged for him to stay in my old crash pad in Pacific Beach and he offered me his apartment in a nice neighborhood of Guadalajara whenever I would return.

Sabine, my new very cute French friend from Paris and I drove across Baja California on my 72 Mustang convertible. I had decided to leave California for now and try my luck in Mexico based on what Pepe had told me. He said that because of the Pilot shortage there and with my US based Flight experience I would have no problem finding a jet job. So I packed all my belongings, surfboard, guitar, bicycle, books, clothes, etc. into my loyal Mustang and said goodbye to San Diego and my friends there once again.

We took our time driving across the desert-like Peninsula, camping out, surfing, exploring, etc. Twice I fell sleep on the wheel as we drove (after having lunch and a beer) in the heat of the sun with the top down (not hers). We skidded off the road but fortunately didn't slip off into the cliffs below, that was a close call.

The other time, as we were driving along at about 80 miles an hour, one rear tire literally exploded and burst from the intense desert heat, the car skidded and fished tailed but I kept it on the road, Sabine was sleep and it scared the hell out of her. Fortunately, a good Samaritan in a green truck (they call this voluntary group of road mechanics the Green Angels) stopped an hour later and helped us cut the wrapped tire off with a saw. He also left us a bottle of water. I didn't have cash at the moment but I offered him my beloved Norwegian French corduroy hat as a gift, It had been my favorite hat (I bought it in Oslo while with Marit) but I was glad to give it to him. Thank God there are good people in this world.

Then, one night as we were looking for a safe place to camp out and sleep, we noticed three guys in a truck had been following us, in wild Mexico that can be dangerous because there have been rape attacks on surfers' girlfriends camping at the beach. One of the three guys walked behind us into a store as we asked for directions to a beach, he intervened and said, "I know of a nice beech neer heerrr my frrrend, I can shou you". I said thanks but no thanks because I knew he was obviously planning to join the party later with his buddies. My radar (sixth sense) was ON and we kept driving until we found a safe Motel.

Sabine loved it in Mexico but she had to return in a couple of weeks to San Diego. From Baja south we took the ferry to the mainland and arrived to Guadalajara to my pilot friend Pepe's apartment. We went to my parents hometown and attended a few traditional feasts and rodeos, bull riding and fighting. Sabine was entranced by those experiences and she didn't want to leave. My Mother liked her very much because she was also a Catholic and agreed with her in religious discussions (unlike me) and even hinted to me that she'd like to have her as a daughter in law.

But by now Sabine had to return, I really got to like her and wanted her to stay with me but I didn't have much to offer her at the moment, so we parted with tears (I'm not sure if she cried for Mexico or me) in her eyes and again, I was alone all by my lonesome. It really sucked being alone again but I was used to it by now. I stayed in Guadalajara for almost two months while I went thru the red tape of converting my Commercial pilot License to a Mexican ICAO one. Fortunately I got a job flying a Sabreliner private jet out of Puerto Vallarta a couple of months later, just when I was out of money and starting to get worried.

Pepe had been a very good loyal friend and even loan me out five hundred Dollars towards the end so I could finish my License Conversion. I valued his friendship very much and even when I was tempted by one of his ex girlfriends I declined having sex with her in order to respect Pepe's friendship. It wasn't easy, one night she needed to stay in the city at his place but I was occupying the guest room with two beds. She didn't want to sleep with him on his bed so she asked if I didn't mind if she slept in the bed next to mine. Of course it wasn't up to me and I said it was okay with me. I think she was trying to tease Pepe because when we turned off the lights she got completely naked and jumped under her sheets. I could see her beautiful figure and I wished she wouldn't have been his ex girlfriend. I had a hard time falling sleep but I held out and was proud of myself the next morning. I told Pepe that I had not had sex with her and he said he wouldn't have cared, but deep inside I think it made all the difference because that proved he could trust me as his friend. (if I can trust a friend with a girlfriend, I can trust him with anything else).

I drove from Guadalajara to Puerto Vallarta with about 50 pesos in my pocket and a full tank of gas. I was so elated to finally have been hired to fly a jet for the first time.

I guess I was in a hurry so I started passing cars along the narrow highway in order to get ahead of all the slow traffic. Then just as I started passing a bus, the whole traffic came to a stop and I was left out of the lane, as a huge 18 wheeler truck was coming down a hill headed straight into me, shit, I couldn't get out of his lane and he couldn't stop because it was down hill for him. I was choking, just then the bus pulled over into the grass halfway and left me in between both lanes as the truck approached. I was sandwiched in between them but the truck cleared and went on it's way. The bus passengers were pissed off because they thought I had pushed them off the road and they started cursing at me. I waved and went on my way with my heart ticking at the speed of sound.

At that moment two cops on motorcycles (yes, they also sport thick mustaches too) appeared a few hundred feet behind the truck. They saw the commotion but didn't see that I had caused it. I sped away from the scene unseen by them and kept speeding away. Obviously, the passengers in the bus told them it was my fault and they thought I was driving drunk or drugged. It really hadn't been my fault, I was passing properly but when everybody stopped there wasn't anywhere were I could squeeze in anymore.

After 20 minutes of pretty fast driving I figured I had escaped the motorcycle cops and besides, I was getting hungry and could smell the grilled chickens being sold by the side of the road. I hadn't eaten recently and all the driving action had awakened my appetite, so I stopped to have a grilled chicken at the side of the road. My biggest mistake here was that I didn't think of hiding my car behind the chicken stand hut because I didn't think they would pursue me for so long. Then I saw the cops and my heart stopped just as I was about to sink my teeth into the chicken.

They walked up to the chicken stand and asked, "Who is the driver of this car?" I wished I could have pointed at the chicken but someone pointed at me and they immediately grabbed me by the arms and dragged me towards their car.

They were furious because they said they had been trying to catch up with me for the last twenty minutes. They pinned me against the car and searched me. Then they wanted to arrest me because they thought I was drunk or drugged. I managed to calm them down and explained to them what had happened but by now they wanted to be rewarded for their troubles. They insisted I follow them back to the city to pay a hefty fine and wouldn't give me back my Driver's License.

The situation got worse when the bus full of pissed off passengers pulled up next to us and they started to point at me and cuss at me again, they were yelling at me, " hijo de puta, cabro'n pendejo, chingenselo," etc. They really wanted the cops to arrest me.

After the bus left, I asked the cops to accept my gift of my last 40 pesos if they let me go. I didn't have more to offer them because I needed 10 for the chicken. I even offered to give them any of my belongings in my car, the surfboard, guitar or how about a bicycle. (I didn't want to push my luck by offering the grilled chicken as well). They acted offended but I managed to establish a good rapport with one of them because he liked Mustangs, in the end they took the 40 pesos (the chicken wasn't included) and let me go with a warning not to drive away for the next half hour so the bus passengers wouldn't see me catching up to them again. And I was free, that cold chicken tasted so good but now I was penniless or should I say, pesoless.

LIVING IN PUERTO VALLARTA.

It was great to have a flying job, specially getting to finally fly a Sabreliner jet while living near the beach at Nuevo Vallarta. It was an FBO (Fixed base operator) at the Puerto Vallarta Airport, sort of a private Hangar with jet air service for the rich and powerful. We used to fly the owner, celebrities and some politicians, also some Drug Enforcement (DEA) agents who looked more like drug lords, sometimes I think they were actually one and the same. Sometimes we would fly eight of them loaded with weapons to another city where they were to do a sting operation. The next day we would pick them up minus one or two. They actually sometimes tipped us a couple of hundred dollars each. Word was that only the drug lords did that.

Life was great again. My new boss, Captain Tron was a super nice guy, he trained me on the Sabreliner and I got my Type rating from an Instructor in another city at their cost. The other Captain wasn't always that nice to me. Jet-Set celebrities would fly there in their private jets and we would provide further transportation to their villas south of Vallarta. I met and conversed once with Sir Richard Branson and another time we received and attended Rod Stewart and Robert De Niro. There was also a Hollywood movie being filmed in the jungles of Mismaloya South of Vallarta and the film crew were flying out in their Helicopter out of our FBO, I think the Hero actor was Mario Van Peebles.

When they were finished filming they had a major beach party on a beach Hotel and we were invited. Man, it was crawling with babes, models, wanna be actresses and all the booze and loud music you could imagine. It's amazing how pretty girls are so gullible in this business, willing to do anything for a chance at making it into a movie. After dancing most of the night, I ended up taking a cute local girl home while my brother Joe waited for me at the same table chatting with two chicks, I couldn't believe he was still there when I arrived about two hours later to pick him up. It must have been 8 am and he was sleep at the table.

There was an interesting story that I was told by a very nice Gentleman as I drove him and his family to the Main Terminal for his flight back to London. He was returning earlier than planned due to a misunderstanding with his host Mr. Goldsmith. Apparently the host, didn't take it very lightly when he was pushed into the pool in a friendly and funny way by this Gentleman, who was just playing along as the other guests started pushing everybody else in the pool.

So he was asked to leave early. No sense of humor I must say. I enjoyed talking to him because he seemed like a very easy going and down to earth individual. I knew I had seen him somewhere before but I couldn't pin point where and when. Unfortunately, I didn't know at the moment who he was until I returned to the FBO, it was no less than Mr. Sir Richard Branson. Had I known before, I might have asked him for a job as a Pilot. (Heck, it might not be too late to ask if I suddenly loose my flying gig).

Shortly before I left Aero Tron, there had been mysterious disappearances of expensive alcohol from the passenger lounge and around $2,000 Dollars in cash. One of the trusted Employees was a suspect but because they liked him so much due to his charismatic personality they didn't want to proceed and press charges even thou the suspicions pointed towards him. I had the impression thou, that the other Captain that wasn't that nice to me was acting suspicious towards me even thou the real culprit was probably right in front of him pretending to be his friend. I didn't want to tell them what I knew because I never like to play snitch, but every night after work, this Employee would have large doses of the best cognacs, rums, etc. He had a drinking problem.

I liked the guy too, he was a nice guy but he had problems. It was never proven to be him and I think the situation solved itself eventually.

They rented me an old weekend home surrounded by bush and jungle, it was very quiet and dark at night but I enjoyed the solitude sometimes. I wasn't always alone since I had plenty of animal company. Huge flying cockroaches the size of sparrows, lots of scorpions, some rats, mice, coral snakes, iguanas and the occasional stray cat. Coral snakes were to be taken seriously because they are highly poisonous. I almost stepped on one in the middle of the night while barefoot one night.

Fortunately it was a full moon and I saw it's silhouette before I stepped on it. That would have been it for me, I probably would have ended my career right there and then. I can't imagine all the fun I would have missed and all the ladies that would have missed out on me, LOL.

Every evening the crickets and their choir would serenade me to sleep on my hammock outside in the patio. It wasn't that bad actually, I had no furniture so I started sleeping on orange crates with a sleeping bag over it. I had no electricity the first two weeks but it was quite romantic with candles at night. Then the situation improved when I met Mika from the San Francisco area. Her and her sister were vacationing with their parents when my friend Pepe and I met them at the promenade in Vallarta. Man, they looked great in bikinis.

Mika stayed an extra week after her parents left, she stayed at my empty new place and adorned my surroundings with her lovely self and cheerful personality. Her Dad sort of gave me a friendly warning before they left, he said to me, "Enrique, if anything happens to my Daughter, I'll make sure you'll never fly again". She did get pretty sick in her stomach, Moctezuma's revenge or something like that, she didn't eat anything but crackers for four days and I was afraid she was going to dehydrate.

Eventually she recovered after having lost a few pounds, she still looked attractive although thin.

I had a great time in Puerto Vallarta Mexico, on my days off I would explore the surrounding area for good surf and found lots of it. In Sayulita town half an hour away, and Punta Mita. Unfortunately that whole area of Punta Mita is now closed off to public traffic since the previous corrupt government bought the fishermen out.

I loved living there but I wasn't flying much and I wanted to fly for the Airlines. I met and dated a few local girls, Leyla, Pati, etc. I also had been dating a cute girl from a neighbor fishing town near La Cruz, The fisherman's Daughter I'll call her, her name was actually Adriana. With beautiful long black hair, a petite figure and pretty full lips on a very cute face, also big sized mamantary devices. I vividly remember one lovely night with her, having tacos and beers at a little café' on the beach at La Cruz, she had her arm around me and her head on my shoulder, she sensed I was leaving soon and had a sad aura around her. I had to go on with my career so I left shortly there after.

I did see her once again a few months later when I came to pick up my Mustang but it wasn't the same anymore. We did make love a few times that one last night and I always had the doubt if she could have possibly gotten pregnant. Years later when I went back I tried to look her up but she had moved away to the city. Goodbye Vallarta, I loved that place. I will always remember Adriana, she filled some of my empty nights with her warm love and cheerful smile.

VERY CLOSE CALL DUE TO FIRE IN FLIGHT.

I almost ended my career and life before I left Vallarta. I had been hired by Aviacsa and was supposed to leave for Amsterdam for two months of training the following week. But I still had one more flight to do as a favor for Enrique, a ferry empty flight to Houston Texas to pick up the owner. We took off out of Vallarta with just Capt. Tron and I flying. With enough fuel to reach Houston and enough holding fuel just in case. Fortunately the center fuel tanks had not been filled, which are in front of the firewall separating the tail cone section of the empennage. Right before Takeoff, Capt. Tron had switched hydraulic pumps because the pressure showed a bit low. Normal procedure, then after rotation as we were climbing thru about 1,000 feet and turning along the coastline the fire alarm sounded.

RRRiiing, the Fire alarm and Red Warning lights caught our attention, I handed the flight controls to Capt. Tron and proceeded to discharge one fire bottle extinguisher after the other but the Fire alarm continued, which meant that the fire was still active. By then, we had already declared an Emergency and started to return for an emergency landing. A request for the emergency fire personnel to be on standby was made as well. We knew all hydraulics had been lost which meant we only had accumulator pumping, maybe only three applications to stop the jet. We couldn't sense or smell a fire but obviously it was still going in the tail cone section, fortunately separated by the firewall.

We landed and rolled off the high speed taxiway stopping just at the end of it. We each grabbed a fire extinguisher and ran outside, that's when we noticed how the whole tail section was still smoking and flaming like a torch. We ran away from the airplane fearful it might explode and just then the fire personnel got there and started trying to put it out. They did put it out but the private jet was a total loss.

We talked about it that afternoon and then it sunk in how close we got to dying. Our mechanic Miguel, who checked the wreckage said that the intense heat and fire had almost melted the cables leading to the elevator, which is the flight control that operates the pitch control, up or down. It was hanging by one little thread, one more second or two in the air and it would have had catastrophic results that would have sent us for a final dive into planet earth, like an arrow into the ground. Also, if we would have had fuel in the center tank which was right next to the firewall, maybe it would have blown up in the air. For the second or third time I cheated death once again. Let's see, how many lives do I have left? I think I lost count by now.

In reality Flying isn't really that dangerous, the most dangerous thing in an Airline Career is the trip to the Hotel and back by taxi or airport shuttle. Also, the other most dangerous things about flying are: A Lawyer in a Bonanza, two ego driven Captains flying together, and last, a (hostie) Flight Attendant with a chipped tooth in strong turbulence. The thing that I am most afraid of is when a pissed off Fright Attendant accidentally or revengefully tries to spill your hot coffee on your precious goods like on your lap.

Other than that, I haven't had any other mishaps or close calls except two car accidents caused by serious accumulated fatigue and jetlag. I had been flying an entire month to Europe and back up to eight times in one month and my biological clock was obviously confused. I finally came home and that night as I was driving home from having dinner with my girlfriend, I fell in a deep sleep while driving my VW Van on H-5 North. I woke up when my van kept going straight right into the concrete divider and I smacked my head on the side window. That hurt, I woke up screaming like in a horror movie, my head spinned and I tasted blood in my mouth. I realized it wasn't a nightmare and then I stepped out to survey the damage. Both wheels on the left side were shredded off by the constant scrapping against the concrete divider, all the way to the rims. I lucked out that the curve went to the right instead of left, otherwise I would have ended up in someone's living room, decorating their wall like an egg smeared on it. I called my girlfriend to pick me up and left the van locked. The next morning when I went to fetch it with spare tires it had been broken into, glass broken, stereo and cassettes gone but that was it. It happened to be in the middle of a bad neighborhood near Barrio Logan.

AIRLINE SAFETY AFTER 911.

You might be thinking that flying has gotten safer because of all the restrictions and Security screening that still goes on at every Airport. Maybe to a certain extent, but in reality a lot of it if not most of it is just Theater or Kabuki. To make the Public feel like they're really getting their money's worth in increased Airport taxes, decreased freedom and more humiliating experiences induced by our no commonsense TSA agents at the security areas. Because of the fear of stereotyping only certain individuals that would fit a terrorist description, they feel compelled to treat everyone the same way even if they don't fit the description at all, such as a baby in a stroller or an old woman. It's ridiculous to a certain point.

I was traveling last year with my family and our two young babies, one year and two year olds, it was early and the babies were tired and cranky, comfortable in their very small strollers. Well, the TSA agents insisted for us to remove the babies from their strollers and to remove their shoes. The babies reacted to all the harassment and started screaming. Plus, the agents weren't even polite or considerate, when we went thru with the two year old the alarm went off and they insisted on searching the baby from head to toe. Even his diaper was opened and searched, (I kind of wished there would have been a big ugly doodoo inside it), the babies were scared and kept screaming. I mean, is all this really necessary? Why can't they train these people to be more polite and courteous, and it wouldn't hurt to use a little common sense.

QUESTIONS REGARDING 911.

Have you noticed there is more public abuse lately or is it my imagination? Either by security agents or policemen. Beatings, abuse with taser guns, accidental shootings, etc.

What have we allowed or given up in exchange for a safer life from terrorists?

There have been many questions being raised ever since the 9/11 events took place and no one has proceeded to demand for answers yet. Sure, they'll call it a conspiracy theory but the questions are there, and there are plenty of witnesses, documents, recordings, sightings, enhanced video shootings to back them up.

For example:

Why was our entire Air Defense System ordered from a very high Command Body to stand down, not to engage, to expect a Drill simulating an attack on US soil on that particular day of September 11th. While senior Bush was having lunch with a senior Bin Laden.

Why was there an Air Force One Boeing 747 circling over New York City at very high altitudes the morning of the attacks? There is enhanced video footage of this.

Why were the Bin Laden family members and other Saudis allowed to leave the country in their private jets that night until the next morning, when every other aircraft in the entire Nation was grounded for a few days.

Why were there a few witness reports the day of the attacks, from credible citizens on the street that the aircraft that hit one of the twin towers looked actually grayish-greenish in color instead of the colors of United or American Airlines colors.

Why did some of the Firemen who were interviewed initially agreed that the Towers had exploded as if they had been rigged for demolition, and the third building? It wasn't even that close to getting damaged and it came down perfectly in one mound of dirt too. Word is, the Jewish owners collected a large sum of money in the millions from the insurance pay-off for all three buildings. Not only that, all the workers of Jewish descent didn't show up to work on that particular morning to the Twin Towers. (That's why there were only around three thousand victims and not many more thousands.) The firemen who made the initial comment about the Towers being rigged later refused to back up their initial comment, it was as if they had been scared not to talk.

Why had many of those flying terrorist been allowed into the country for flying lessons, even thou they checked out as possible Al Quaeda operatives.

Why does Bin Laden have such a history of working in the past with the CIA, and trained as an operative.

Too many Why's should raise a flag, but why do most people refuse to pursue the truth?

It's up to each and everyone of us to seek the truth, remember, where there is a murmur there is usually a river.

Now, let's be clear about something, I'm not making this stuff up or trying to instigate something. I am merely the messenger and am just sharing some information that I think is worth looking into. There is lots of material on the Internet on certain websites, enhanced video shootings, photos, recordings, documents, etc.

Above, Dad flies with me on the Fokker 100. Below, Me in Merida Yucatan.

MY FIRST AIRLINE FLYING JOB, SUMMER OF 1992.

So now I had to leave this Vallarta paradise. Fortunately, I ended up living in another nice place, in Merida Yucatan. Flying for Aviacsa Airlines on a Fokker 100, it was a 108 passenger jet plane with state of the art avionics made in Holland. The company sent a Simulator partner and I to Amsterdam for eight weeks of training. My Simulator partner Mejenes and I had a stressful but fun time in Amsterdam that summer (Mejenes was a young Mexican Pilot who couldn't get his priorities straight, he eventually failed the in Flight training in Mexico because he concentrated more on chasing the flight Attendants than flying the airplane).

We used to call the Simulator 'The Torture Chamber' because of the hard times our Instructor Capt. Special used to give us in it. But we released the stress by going out, having a few beers and chasing the Dutch girls around. Then I settled in Merida, a three hour ride form Cancun on the Caribbean Ocean side.

Two months later my Dad helped me drive my Mustang from Puerto Vallarta to Merida Yucatan. It was a nice adventurous three day drive with only my Father and I. I really enjoyed those moments alone with him. He then flew back with me a week later on one of my flights and The Captain of the flight let him take his seat while on the ground. It had been my Dad's unaccomplished dream to be a pilot, but it now seemed to have come to reality at least for a few minutes. I took video and pictures of him sitting there with the Captains hat on. Yeah, you could do that in the old days. It made my Dad very happy and gave me an unforgettable memory.

I had been dating Marci from Coyoacan in Mexico City during the initial training with Aviacsa. She had rescued me from my boring hotel and brought me to her nice apartment in Coyoacan. It's a 500 year old traditional town in the middle of Mexico City, where Cortez the conquistador that defeated the Aztecs, (no, not the Aztec football team) initially started building the new Spanish Mexico city. She lived in the Beautiful old town square of the City and only two blocks from Frieda Kahlo's Blue House.

She was a wild flight Attendant that liked partying, surprised? I really dug her but her wild life and her smoking of strange tobacco didn't suit me very much, neither did her 'wilder' girlfriends who were worse than her. Anyway, when I moved to Merida she said she wanted to move on her own over there too and was going to stop flying to start a new life in Merida. So she sent her furniture to my future house in Merida city. She then resigned with her Airline for reasons of pregnancy and even flew with her airline there with a pillow in her stomach, she had guts.

I discovered the real fun of Airline Flying and went crazy chasing Flight Attendants or letting them chase me. I was seeing a few at the same time and wasn't committed to any particular one. Marci found out and moved her furniture out, I guess she had assumed we were going to settle down together and was disappointed when she realized

I wasn't the settling kind. So it was back to sleeping in a hammock again until I bought some of my own furniture. We managed to remain friends and occasionally lovers. We did have a lot of fun together and even had sort of a little lovely Honeymoon weekend together at Playa del Carmen once.

MERIDA YUCATAN. FRIGHT ATTENDANT TROUBLE.

I couldn't commit to one girl and besides I was having a grand time. I got caught red handed once when Vera walked in on me with Itali in my room, that wasn't a situation I would want to repeat. Unfortunately, I was sexually involved with all three girls that were the flight attendants on my flight that night. MG was cool about it, she knew what was going on, Itali was acting Bitchy cause she wanted the whole rights for her only and Vera was furious because she had thought she was the only one. During the flight, the latter two were at war, running over each other's toes with the galley carts, spilling coffee or drinks "accidentally" over the other, etc.

Then Vera tried to spill my coffee on my lap in the cockpit during flight, I caught it just in time before it burnt my goods. I felt very sorry for Vera because I had been her first love and lover. I didn't realize she had deeply fallen in love with me and was the old fashioned one man for life kind of girl, very pretty and intelligent too. But I couldn't seem to want to settle down with her, I was enjoying my single life and had further plans to fly for the next largest International Airline in Mexico. I wish Vera would forgive me for hurting her, I deeply regret that. I did enjoy and loved every moment I spent with her, I also loved the experience of being her first man.

Merida is a beautiful City, with Colonial architecture and a very lively Maya culture. Very warm and humid with lots of archeological Pyramid Sites around the whole state of Yucatan. Uxmal and Chitchen Itza to name a few. Also the local beach Progresso was picturesque and had it's fair share of great beaches. I spent a lot of time at almost deserted beaches sometimes by myself, other times with flight attendants. I would put up my huge hammock under two palm trees and spend hours on that hammock. Sometimes I would be the only one on that beach or whoever I was with and it wasn't' rare to make love on the beach or on the hammock, under the palm trees or in the water.

I also went often to the South of Cancun where a two hour drive would take me to some of the most beautiful beaches, near the Tulum Maya ruins, overlooking the beautiful turquoise sea, with white sandy beaches and thousands of palm trees. At night everyone would converge at the restaurant bar with Reggae music filling in the night sounds and candles all around. It was fairly easy to meet nice girls mainly from Germany or Scandinavia but sometimes I would just spent time in complete solitude, meditating or reading.

On my days off I would go there and stay at bamboo huts on the beautiful beaches, I won't reveal the spot because I hope it never becomes commercialized. Many Europeans go there and it is often a nudist beach. One of them anyway. I also visited all the Pyramid sites and explored the Maya region and culture.

The flights we did with Aviacsa were mainly within Mexico and Guatemala, it was a great atmosphere at the Airline and the overnights we had were long enough to explore the cities and have fun with the crew.

THE TRUTH ABOUT AIRLINE SAFETY IN PRESENT TIMES.

Airline flying is usually the safest method of traveling these days. However, if the public would know what really goes on sometimes they probably would not fly as much. Generally it's human nature that we must be wary about. Pilots for example are a rare bunch. Generally ego driven but very confident and secure of themselves. You have to be, but sometimes egos get in the way of safety and that's when safety gets compromised.

Also, when most men are in their twenties and thirties we are still experimenting and adventuring. Not quite mature yet but mature enough to fly a commercial jet with many passengers in it. Drinking has been a problem for some Air crew and some Pilots have actually gotten caught drinking and flying. But to my knowledge, there has never been an accident caused by drinking and flying. The biggest threat to flying are the Airline Management themselves, bean counters that is, Accountants, etc. Here's why.

While trying to make the Airline more profitable they keep reducing the Crew's night rests to save on Per Diems, Hotel accommodations, etc. Also, to maximize the Crew's work load, the Crew Scheduling (screw scheds) departments schedules Crew members on pretty tight return flights with longer hours in the cockpit.

With minimum night rests for days, lousy in flight meals, night flights and jet lag, voila', you have a bad cocktail. And that my friends, is the biggest cause of Airline accidents, fatigue. ACCUMULATED FATIGUE caused by the System itself. How the FAA and the NTSB ignores these causes I don't understand.

In the end after an accident, when it is determined as Pilot error, they overlook the fatigue factor, and it's almost always due to fatigue which leads to poor decision making and slow reactions by a tired Crew.

Now add to that, drinking, parties, or girl chasing and it would add up to the fatigue factor while at the same time it could relax the crew from Airline Management related stress. But we all know what our responsibilities are and I think almost all Pilots will be responsible and avoid drinking too much when flying the next early morning. Besides, we are subjected to a twelve hour no drinking rule. Some countries have a 24 hour no drinking rule (most don't really adhere to it).

I must admit thou, sometimes those nights get out of hand, drinking and having sex all night was not rare. Speaking for myself, I never compromised safety when it was my turn to fly.

Here's one example. In 1993 I was flying for my first Latin American carrier as First Officer. I was nearly thirty, single and loving my job and lifestyle. I had a late evening flight from Merida city to Cancun and then to Villa Hermosa. The Captain was a super cool guy but he loved chasing girls and drinking (perfectly understandable in our job). So this night he had plans with one of the Ticket agents at our second destination which was our overnight stay. He hinted to me that I should stay sober and sleep well that night because he had plans. Sure enough, he had a bottle of wine with him and was having his girlfriend over. I heard most of the passionate commotion almost all night since his room was next to mine. Fortunately I did get some minimum rest because our departure was pretty early, 6:00 am from the Hotel pick up.

That morning we had five legs to fly, all about 45 minutes to one hour long. When Captain Lover Boy showed up, he had his dark shades on and he appeared okay.

We did the necessary checklists, started engines, pushed back and then he told me I should fly. After takeoff and gear up, he leaned back his seat, put his hat over his face and said, "you have control, I need to sleep". When I saw his eyes I noticed they were bloodshot.

I ended up flying all legs and did pretty much everything on my own, including speaking on the radios while he slept thru every flight. He did wake up to operate the gear handle and flaps for me for every takeoff and landing. I was enjoying all the flying I was getting and I felt he was okay except a little tired.

185

I don't think it compromised safety because I was doing all the flying and had had a decent night sleep.

Another case. I was flying for a second Latin American Airline on a Boeing 757 as First Officer, we had many red eye, or night flights with up to five legs or destinations. Since we did an average of three all nighters per week, most of us were pretty tired during the flights. Occasionally I knew of one Pilot falling sleep while the other one was landing. Good thing it wasn't the other way around. Well, on one of these night flights during the last leg we were headed back to base, to a city near the US border. It was to be a three hour flight in the middle of the night. We were both pretty tired and the Captain said I should take the first nap, so I did.

Thirty minutes later a certain growling noise woke me up, it was the Captain snoring. I looked around at our Instrument panel to determine where exactly we were and what time it was. We had crossed into another ATC, Air Traffic Control sector and where close to approaching our Point of Descent. I started trying to contact ATC on every possible frequency for the area until they answered, they asked if everything was okay because they had been trying to reach us.

I said I had been given the wrong frequency and things were back to normal. I suspect we both fell sleep for at least twenty minutes. It sounds scary but flying on Autopilot at heights up to 39,000 feet above sea level is much safer than approaching or departing an Airport. Yes, disaster could have struck but it didn't. We were also getting pretty close to the ADIZ zone. As a worse case scenario, we could have run out of fuel and have to glide down for a very silent landing to a long enough airport. Or, if we would have overshot the ADIZ zone (Air Defense Identification Zone) into the US, we probably would have been shot down by US fighter jets if it were in present times.

Another time over the Pacific, we were all tired during a night flight. The FO was reading and I asked him to stay awake while I closed my eyes for 10 or 15 minutes, he assured he was wide awake so I leaned back and shut my eyes. I can normally stay in sort of a meditative trance-like nap, where I am aware of any changes or unusual noises and can sense what's going on around me. I opened my eyes when I sensed a certain purring or better said 'snoring' sound. I looked at the FO and he was sleep with his head hanging down and the back seat guy was also napping. It had only been 15 minutes but I've heard of these events happening for longer periods of time.

After that, I changed my rules to "no reading" for the guy that stays awake.

I don't want to scare the public but these events happen more often than they should. Chronical Fatigue is a serious problem with Aircrew. It's not natural for humans to be up all night, specially in high workload situations such as approaching an Airport that has very poor weather, low visibility or adverse conditions.

It is true that we sometimes take turns power napping in the cockpit in our seats. Some longer flights carry an extra Pilot to take over so the Crew gets some rest. That is the key to maintaining a safe flight, keeping ourselves as Pilots safe and alert by being rested and relaxed.

On larger airliners like the Boeing 747 we carry bunks in the cockpit but we only use them when we carry supplementary crew.

It is not normal for a human body to take on the loads of crossing different time zones while staying up all night. We eventually adapt as best as we can but it still takes a toll on us. Sometimes we wish we could just be cuddled in our warm beds with our wife or girlfriend (even with our dog or inflatable doll) instead of being up all night, trying to stay awake and alert in order to make sound actions and decisions concerning the safety of the flight and our 400 plus passengers who are comfortably snoozing in their seats trusting us with their lives.

Power napping has actually been sort of approved by the FAA, besides, NASA has made extensive tests with Astronauts and Military pilots. There was a study they did with three sets of Pilots in a simulator on an all night flight simulation. One set was to stay awake all night on coffee, with no rest, then their alertness level was measured and the data recorded during a simulated high workload approach and landing in adverse conditions.

The second set of Pilots were told to take a Power nap for twenty minutes each and then they were tested like the first set of pilots. Then there was the third set of Pilots who were given some alcohol to drink before the test flight, napped twenty minutes each and were then given the same scenario and tests.

The results were amazing. The first set of Pilots who stayed up all night, sober but without Power napping had the lowest level of alertness. The second set of Pilots who each Power napped had the highest level of Alertness. And the third set who had a drink before flight actually had a better level of alertness than the First set of guys who stayed up all night sober. Hmmmmm! it makes you wonder doesn't' it.

Human nature is to blame for most Pilot error related accidents, but Fatigue has always been a factor during these accidents. The public never hears about it because it's not beneficial for Airline Managements to increase the Crews rest periods and to reduce our long hours of night flights.

UFO SIGHTINGS.

(to be read with twilight zone music in the background.)

In the summer of 1993 I was still flying for my first Airline. There was one particular flight from Merida to Monterrey City, followed by Juarez the next day. It's a city that is next to the border town to El Paso at the US Borderline. The flight between Monterrey and Juarez took about 2 hours and 15 minutes over a vast dessert. On this particular afternoon on a clear blue sky day, fifteen minutes into the flight, Captain Aguilar said to me, "Look left, very bright chicken aluminum farms".

There were six very bright lights on top of a mountain ridge. After a few minutes the Captain said again, "freaking chicken farms don't fly, do they?" I looked again and this time those bright lights were above the ridge, like floating in mid air while still in formation. We kept observing them as they got closer and closer to us while they also seemed to be climbing with us. We were climbing thru 24,000 at that moment.

Now they were at a distance of 5 to 7 miles off our left. They didn't look like bright lights anymore but were clearly elongated disc shaped objects. A Military or commercial aircraft is easily identified from the vapor trails, windows, winglets, etc. These objects had none of those, just plain milk white flying discs, six in formation. We called the flight attendants to the cockpit one at a time of course, and they all agreed they looked like UFO's. We kept them in sight for about 10 minutes and they just cruised along sort of floating but not in direct formation like fighter jets do.

Then I asked Air Traffic Control on the Radio if they had some military exercises in the area and they said NO. They asked us what we saw so we answered, "six bright white disc looking objects in formation next to us". Absolute silence, and then someone on the radio, obviously crew from another aircraft said something like, " what have you guys been smoking, we want some too" followed by sneers and giggles.

Right away after that radio transmission the six white disc look-ing objects veered left and took off at the highest speed I've ever seen. I wasn't sure if they disappeared momentarily after they veered off at such speeds and then reappeared, or we just lost sight of them due to the high speed they achieved. Within seconds they turned into bright lights over the distant ridge where we had originally seen them at first. And they remained there, hovering over the same hills. A few minutes later, an Aero Mexico airliner reported them also at the same position as we had. I saw them again on two more occasions that week but only hovering over the same mountain ridges in the distance, as bright lights, five or six in formations. That desert area is called the Area of Silence and is a mysterious region with various phenomena sightings.

I have a very open mind and can't say for sure they were Extrater-restrial craft or advanced Disc Shaped looking Secret Military Aircraft. As far as I know, the US military doesn't have such developed craft yet. But there are rumors and some evidence that they have been trying to develop prototypes ever since Hitler's German scientists were "invited" after the war to help with the US Aerospace programs.

In fact, it is a fact that the Germans had been working on hover-ing craft since before the end of the war and after they lost. Then the US and the Russians captured many of their secret craft and scientists working on them. That is how the race for Space began.

Many Airline Pilots have seen strange craft in the sky but they usu-ally keep it to themselves for fear of being scrutinized or investigated. I know of at least five Pilots that I have flown with that claim they saw what was very clearly UFO looking craft in the sky. I can't really relate what they saw because only they know what they saw. One thing is for sure, it cannot be denied that we have been visited by intelligent life.

I don't understand why governments keep denying their presence after so many years.

UFO presence has been on this planet for thousands of years. Just read the detailed description of the prophet Isaiah or Ezequiel (as well as the prophet Enoch) of his flight in the angel's chariots of fire. He actually describes it almost in scientific detail, the engines, the landing gear, glass windows, the fire emanating from the rockets, the roaring of the craft, etc. The old Testament is full of encounters of this type.

The Elohim, according to the Old Testament, were their Gods and Angels in Chariots of Fire that flew. In many other more ancient texts, such as the Hindi and also native Americas from the Olmecs,Toltecs, Mayas, Incas, Aztecs, they all talk about their Gods that arrived from the East and brought them knowledge ranging from science, agriculture, mathematics, astronomy, astrology and Pyramid building.

In the more ancient writings from the Sumerians from ancient Mesopotamia that date back to 4,000 years BC up until the deluge 11,000 BC, they actually describe these Gods in detail, such as their arrival, reasons to be here, creations, wars, and their names and positions. They also talk about Nibiru, the 12th planet where they came from. These translations are very credible because in addition to the clay tablets where they are recorded, there are sufficient artifacts, monoliths, drawings, statues and much more evidence of their history on Earth. There is too much left behind as evidence around the world to just discard as a coincidence. Every other ancient advanced civilization credits their flesh and bone Gods for the knowledge and guidance they gave them. In ancient Sumeria they were called the Anunnaki, which meant "Those who from heaven came to Earth".

According to various ancient texts and the Bible, after the great flood 13,000 years ago, the survivor descendants of Noah started the new human population all over again. But this time they eventually were taught many sciences, art, astronomy, astrology and architecture from the Gods. They even were given Kingships. This is how Intelligent Mankind eventually emerged suddenly around 4,000 years B.C. All this started in Ancient Sumeria, the Central and South American Continent, ancient Egypt, Greece, etc.

It makes you wonder were all these ancient ruins left behind around the world really came from, around the same time period ranging from Egypt, in Peru: Machu Pichu, Lake Titinaka and the Nazca lines, in Mexico: Teotihuacan and all the Mayan Pyramids. Not to mention the ruins of Balbeek in southern Lebanon. Modern scientists still can't figure out how these immense rocks and monoliths were carried and lifted to such heights.

They actually sometimes come up with the stupidest theories on Discovery Channel where they actually think they know what they're commenting about. I had to laugh when I heard one respectable Scientist claiming that the ruins of Machu Pichu were built to accommodate Inca Royalty in their Summer Homes at those high altitudes where they could get away from the hustles of the city.

Such shortsighted ideas only keep people more ignorant. Most people prefer to believe in fairy tales or child stories (such as the snake and the apple story) than in concrete history with concrete recordings of events backed up by physical evidence (pyramids and other ancient artifacts). They are very quick to discredit and deny facts even when it's right in front of their face, some even argue that all those ancient writings were probably a product of their imagination, oh yeah? What about the unexplainable huge 1,200 ton monolith granite slab block laying around in the high plateau of Lebanon? Even today's modern equipment wouldn't be able to lift it up with any crane or equipment. The statues depicting men and a woman goddess in astronaut suits and helmets, the Nazca Lines, the clay tablets from ancient Sumeria depicting the story of their arrival and creation.

Even the Bible gives us hints in some sections of the Old Testament, such as, "Let us create man in our image, let us let man toil the earth for us". Or how about the story of the fallen angels, "They found the daughters of man to be fair and took them as concubines and wives". Oh, so all of a sudden they get anxious and want to have some fun with the girls, hummmm? That doesn't sound like spiritual beings to me, isn't that what the Spanish did when they came to the Americas? They liked the cute little naked Indian chicks and started proliferating with them, while at the same time using to their advantage the fact that the Aztecs thought that they were the Gods that had promised to return. And they also angered their commander and were punished initially, until eventually it all got out of control and there you have it, voila', many new independent Latin American Countries. Sounds to me like the same thing happened with the Anunnaki but at a much greater scale on planet Earth.

For those of you who would like to know more on this subject I recommend a great book by Mr. Z. Sitchin, one of his books is called, The 12th Planet.

You probably have heard of the Bermuda Triangle and the Triangle of the Dragon I suppose.

The Bermuda triangle is around the area near the southern Eastern tip of Florida, Bimini island, Eastern Bahamas. Where as the Triangle of the Dragon runs South to South West of Japan in the Pacific Ocean and it covers a large area all the way to the Mariana Islands. These two areas have plenty of stories and many mysteries from the past.

The Dragon triangle probably has more history since a millennia ago. All the reports from Chinese and Japanese ships that encountered mysterious beasts they called Dragons, coming out of the ocean and destroying their ships. Curiously enough there are more detailed reports and drawings of Japanese texts dating back only two centuries of UFO looking craft that would surface near the coast of South Western Japan. In addition to that, during the second world war some cargo and US ships encountered mysterious sudden gigantic waves that sometimes sank some ships. Fishing vessels from Japan have a few of those reports as well, including personal reports and documentaries of ship Captains who claimed to have seen UFOs or better said USOs coming out of the ocean near their ship and thereby creating rogue waves that sometimes reached 100 feet in height. Many ships and aircraft have been sunk mysteriously without a trace in that area.

One theory is that due to the large volcanic activity in the bottom of the ocean there are gases released that destroy the buoyancy of some ships, therefore sinking them. The Bermuda triangle also has that theory. But there is also some electro magnetic disturbance going on that affects navigation instruments on low flying aircraft. Amelia Earhart, the great female aviator and adventurer is know to have disappeared in that area of the Mariana Islands. Her case also still remains a mystery.

Most Commercial Aircraft over-fly those areas, including myself pretty often on the way from Japan to the Philippines, Guam and Australia, but apparently it doesn't affect high flying aircraft.

The vast ocean retains many mysteries we probably will never know about.

Think about it just for a moment, if you had the technological means to defy gravity and adverse liquid atmospheric surroundings such as the deep ocean, wouldn't you hover in space or hide under the depth of the oceans from predators who probably would want to possess your technology and destroy you in the process with their diseases, greed, ignorance and arrogance?

The way I see it, our planet and our creation has been restored, enhanced, and genetically improved to sustain intelligent life, by higher intelligent beings who visited earth many thousands of years ago. They helped mankind take that quick leap of evolution from being un-intelligent ape looking beings called Hominids to being Homo erectus, Homosapiens, (homosexuals?), etc. etc. They came and went as they pleased and when things got out of control due to overpopulation and destruction caused by the new earthlings, they decided to leave the arena and the humans to their own destinies and hide from them. Either down below the oceans or in the vast Universe, while waiting for the right time to intervene before the Earthlings blow up the planet. In ancient manuscripts they hint that planet Mars was also one of their bases (hence, the sphinx looking pyramid and other square monuments from pictures from Mars). There are plenty of hints, archeological remains, writings, carvings, drawings, ancient texts, etc, all over our world that support the theory of their presence on earth.

Me and my Taesa friends. From top clockwise, Enriko, Me, Fabian, Antonio and kid, Nose', and Mau the jungle man.

TIME FOR A CHANGE IN SCENERY. MY SECOND AIRLINE JOB IN 1994.

Anyway, back on Planet Earth I was living my dream of being an Airline Pilot, traveling some and having fun with Flight Attendants. But I needed more, I needed to see my little son in Germany so I focused my attention on getting a job with an International carrier. I did get on with Taesa Airlines out of Mexico City towards the end of 1993. It was also excellent timing because one of the Flight Attendants, Itali was claiming to be pregnant by me, I knew it couldn't be true because I had been careful. Besides, she couldn't have been pregnant because she always made sure that after she played with that flute and finished her song she ingested the notes. She was the type of girl that lusted and loved sex so much that she wanted to posses whoever she had it with.

I asked her to produce some Doctor results of her so called pregnancy but she never did and eventually she admitted she had made the whole thing up.

Once again I was packing all my belongings into my good old Mustang and cashing out my bank account. Just in case the company would go bankrupt and freeze the assets, I withdrew all my savings which were about Ten Thousand Dollars in Mexican Pesos. I knew that was not a good idea to be caught driving thru the jungle with all that cash stashed in socks but I took the chance. It was a long drive all the way to Mexico City, about a two day drive without cop problems or modern Bandido holdups this time. I really enjoyed the panoramic views and the primitive roads I sometimes had to drive thru in the south. Sometimes the road was so bad I had to S-turn a lot on the road to avoid huge potholes.

Finally I was driving up into the beautiful Volcanic Mountains South of Mexico City, what an awesome sight, the Popocatepetl Volcano smoking on one side, and the thick forest on the other. Then my transmission started failing on me from the heavy weight, constant up-hill and fast high altitude driving. I was now driving on two gears only but I made it to my Pilot friend Arturo's house deep in the City. Arturo and I had flown together at Aviacsa Airlines and he was the son of retired DC-10 Captain Vargas from Aero Mexico. I stayed with them in the center of the city whenever I was in town as thou I were part of their family. Capt. Vargas was the nicest gentleman I had encountered in aviation so far, and Arturo was a replica of him.

I lucked out and was sent for training on the Boeing 767/757 a few months after flying the 737. All of our Simulator Training was done at the America West facilities in Phoenix Arizona. I had to adjust to life in Mexico city and that wasn't what I really wanted to do but that was my new base. I really missed Merida and the beaches very much, and my friends and girlfriends too. At first I felt amazingly lonely in a city of 24 million people. I hated it at first, but then Marci my old flame stepped into my life again and invited me to move into her nice apartment. Marci was really like my soul sister, I did love her but I couldn't settle down with her because she and her friends were just too wild.

She was of Italian origins, with beautiful green eyes, light brown long hair and a cheerful happy pretty face and personality. She was a very passionate woman, making love with her was a like a constant eternal orgasm. But her lifestyle was too wild for me, her friends were sometimes musicians with bad drug habits and I didn't think that was appropriate for me at the time.

One four day weekend, Marci, her girlfriend and I went to a deserted beach two hours south of Acapulco. We wanted to camp away from civilization so we had everything we needed. Tent, sleeping bags, guitar, Tequila, food, etc. There was a little village nearby where we could buy cold beer and hot food too so we weren't completely alone. It was Christmas night and we had a nice big fire going. I played guitar while Marci and her friend started rolling what I thought was tobacco but it wasn't. I wasn't' very comfortable with that but I just sort of ignored it.

Suddenly in the middle of the night I heard footsteps and saw a few figures walking towards us. At first I thought they were night Bandidos about to harass us or force the girls into sex and when I saw that they had guns I instinctively got up and grabbed a burning thick stick from the fire to stop them with. I only saw two of them at first but it turned out to be the local Sheriff and three assistants and they were just patrolling the beach for safety of the tourists. I inmediately thought about Marci and the joint she was rolling and wondered if they noticed that, but she was a clever girl and pushed the stash under her skirt as soon as she saw them. They then told us to have a good night and left.

The next day we all decided to explore the North side of the beach towards some prehistoric caves and rocks we had been told about so we started walking in that direction, it was so desolated and beautiful so the girls decided to walk topless. We all challenged each other to swim naked and as we all were in the water we noticed some human heads looking at us from behind the bushes. The girls got nervous and got dressed quickly. We hadn't noticed but we had been followed by some Indian locals who probably were the ones who had been spying on us at the camp a couple of nights ago. The local Witch doctor lady had warned us about not going too far from the village for that reason.

We continued our walk towards the prehistoric rock formations with ancient drawings on them. Suddenly as we approached the rocks, two Indian locals came out from behind them. They had fake and treacherous smiles on them and asked if we wanted to buy some fresh crabs. My intuition warned me not to trust them and I asked them if they were alone.

They said they were but I knew they were lying because I'd seen three heads back in the bushes.

I asked them about their other friend and they said he was in the water catching crabs. I knew what they were planning and I grabbed the thickest stick club that I could find just in case. I had no problem taking on the first two but I wasn't sure exactly how many more there might be hiding behind the rocks.

Then one of the guys leaned over to me and said with a smirk on his face, "hey cousin, why don't you share one of the girls with us," I inmediately replied, "No I cannot because one of them is my wife and the other one is my sister". I knew they were trying to round us up in between the rocks so I instructed the girls to grab sticks and rocks and we all climbed on one of the big rocks. From up there we saw the third guy hiding waiting for us to walk in his direction. He had some fishing gear and a machete and I knew how close we'd come to being trapped.

From our safety rock they couldn't reach us and we could throw rocks on them so they eventually gave up and left.

We were now pretty nervous at night, well I was mostly. Because here I was in the middle of nature with two attractive chicks in my tent at night and only my machete and guitar to defend ourselves. At night I would wake up many times with any sound coming from the bushes. Marci wanted to make love by the fire after her friend went to sleep but I was worried they were watching us, so we went inside the tent to do that while her friend continued sleeping or so it seemed.

Then in the middle of the night I felt her friends butt rubbing on my groin, she was snuggling into position into me either knowingly or dreaming I don't know.

At first I wanted to believe that they were both gearing me up for a threesome, great, I was game. So I thought I'd test the waters and follow her lead so I started caressing her tummy and thighs. Suddenly, as if she realized what was going on she moved away and I thought, "Oh shit, she's going to tell Marci about it". So in the morning as we were having coffee I said, "hey girls, stop changing sleeping positions on me because last night I didn't know which one was which and I accidentally grabbed the wrong one". It kind of worked because they just laughed and said something like, "sure, you pervert".

On our last night there we finished a bottle of tequila and stayed up late, singing, dancing and drinking.

The next morning I got up with a groggy head and decided to go for a little swim. I had left my shorts hanging over the tent so I grabbed them and just as I was putting them on I remembered that I forgot about my rule number one, shake everything before you put it on. It was too late now because I had my shorts up to my nuts and that's when I felt it. A hot powerful burning sting just one inch from my co-jones, my nuts. Oh that hurt so bad, it was like someone drilling a hot nail into my skin. I shook my shorts off and then I saw the little bastard S-turning down the sand, it was a red little scorpion. He obviously felt the effects of the tequila in my blood because he was S-turning a lot so I stomped on him to straighten him out.

We walked and limped up to the Witch doctor 's (llerbera) hut a few hundred feet away and she told me to lie down on the hammock and have lots of cold beer. She said I was lucky I had lots of Tequila in my blood because that would reduce the effect of the poison.

Then she put some gun powder in the wound and told me not to walk much. She said I could stay in her hammock as long as I wanted. Sure enough we had a few beers, laughed it off and I ignored the pain until it eventually subsided. Those four days were nevertheless the best time I'd had in a long time.

Later on in Mexico city, Marci and her girlfriend had just opened up a Little Cafe' in a nice part of town and were having a lot of clientele. Sometimes I would stay and help her shut down and prepare for the next day. Then afterwards we'd make love in the kitchen, on the counters, tables, chairs, etc. man, it was wild and beautiful. Shortly thereafter I moved out of her apartment in good terms. Her and her friend told me I could eat there the rest of my life for free and they never paid me back the loan I made them to expand their Cafe', it was only about $1,200 US Dollars. I figured she paid it back with many laughs, good times, Love and Sex.

My flights with Taesa Airlines were mainly to Germany, lucky for me, because on my long layovers of a week I would stay at my son's and his Mom's apartment and give him all my undivided attention and time. Those were probably my happiest times in Wiesbaden with my son. I always looked forward to spending my days off with him, it was much better and satisfying than having a weekend with a good looking flight attendant. We were very good friends with his Mom and we always respected each other.

A few times I took my son with me on my flights back to Mexico or Dominican Republic, as well as New Zealand, Mauritius, Australia, Fiji, Hawaii, Hong Kong, etc. (but that was further down the road). I also took Micha on a flight with me to Vallarta, in the cockpit because the flight was full. Yes, it was legal in those days. Then I set her and Enriko in a nice Hotel with enough spending cash for ten days. I came by and joined them when I had days off. She always loved Mexico so that was my way of making it up to her for her patience and cooperation in allowing me to see my son anytime.

Often my son would fly in the Flight deck with me too, which was then allowed. On one or two occasions I let him sit on my lap and let him think he was flying, of course with the Autopilot engaged and me in my seat it was not a safety hazard. (Not like the Russian Airliner that left the Captain's teenage son in his seat when the Co-Pilot left his, you know the rest of the story I suppose, the kid disconnects the Auto Pilot and they plunge down to earth for some aerobatics followed by a very rough and uncontrolled crash.)

Those where the great days of Aviation. You could bring your family or friends to the Aircraft Cockpit or just bring them along with you on your trips.

Often we would invite girls to the Cockpit Enroute, and often we would seal a deal for a date for later after we landed. Unfortunately, this present paranoiac airline security has done away with the fun and pleasantness of airline flying. Some of it is needed, but not so much as to not be able to show your kid the aircraft cockpit.

I spent a lot of time in Puerto Plata and Santo Domingo since we were based there for a month at a time. Flying charter flights to Germany and back on weekends and resting on the weekdays. There I sort of dated Joasta and other girls, one of them was a very pretty mulata by the name of Francia Lanti, she looked like out of a fashion magazine when she was dressed up, she was sweet and had a good heart too.

I also hooked up with a very elegant lady from Vienna, she was married to a wealthy Doctor and had come to the Island by herself to play. I saw her on the beach topless and it was a beautiful sight to behold. She was around 34 yeas old, very firm medium breasts and a great sporty figure. Her face was also very aristocratic with beautiful big green eyes. The next morning I saw her sitting by herself having breakfast at our Hotel so I walked up to her and said to her in German if she'd like to join me, the Captain and the other First Officer.

She accepted and we got acquainted and talked for a long while. Then we made plans to go out dancing that night all together. That evening when she showed up at the Lobby she was dressed to kill. A sexy tight low cut dress with barely enough to cover her panties above her beautiful sporty legs. She was a sports instructor at her home town and therefore had a very athletic figure. We danced and had a few rum and cokes and I then parted with her alone. We started kissing on the dance floor passionately and I could hardly wait to see the rest of my evening present. Voila', when we got to my room I feasted my eyes on that beautiful face and body, she was like a Goddess. Very experienced in the art of sex and willing to please me. I think I must have pleased her too because we got together again before I left on my next flight.

That's a great place to be if you're single, dangerous if you're married. But some of the married guys used to say. "I might be married, but not castrated". There are all kinds of exotic girls on that Island, the culture is so rich and life was so full of passion. You really had to exert a lot of self control to avoid getting out of control. I was single at the time so I had many girlfriends in various places, In Frankfurt, Zurich, Vienna, Puerto Plata, Mexico. HIV was a big risk everywhere so a man's best friend had been traded from a dog to a condom.

BACK TO SAN DIEGO. LOVE, PAIN AND KARMA.

It was around mid 1994 and within a year of that kind of flying I was getting burnt out by the jetlag and lifestyle. I requested more of the local flights and moved back to my hometown in San Diego. The airline had opened up a base in Tijuana so that was practical for me. It was good to be back in my old turf again. I moved into a friend's of my old friend Inky Binky, Sue's friend's boat at the Point Loma Harbor, it was a 65 foot classic motor yacht called Ebb Tide. Sue and I became good friends and roommates. Ron, the owner was a very cool Canadian dude who sometimes stayed on his boat on weekends. We also shared the boat with a cat called Kika. I loved the lifestyle living on a boat because it just had a sense of freedom that appealed much to me. That's when I discovered my love for living on boats and sailing. Ron taught me to sail and sold me his old 20 foot sailboat called Termite, all for $800.00 Dollars. That's how I discovered my hidden passion for boats and sailing.

That fall one night I stopped at a Spanish Tapas Bar called Cafe Sevilla in downtown San Diego. I was actually on my way to the airport for a midnight flight but some friends were supposed to be there that night so I thought I'd have a coffee and chat for a little while. I didn't see my friends, but I did see those bright eyes, enchanting dark expressive eyes on that very pretty face with long black hair. She had a beautiful smile when our eyes crossed, I instinctively smiled at her and she did too. I'll call her Nena, it was like Deja Vu, that was no coincidence, I wasn't supposed to be there that night so somehow I believe it was my destiny or fate, whatever.

I approached her on the way to the bathroom, I asked her if the public phone worked because she had just used it. Then I pretended to make a call and came back towards the bar. When her friend got up to go to the bathroom, I approached her again and we talked and I introduced myself. After a few minutes I said I had to go and we exchanged phone numbers.

That night during my flight I stared at the stars and saw her face in them. I felt strange, as if I had found something I had been looking for. We went out for a few weeks as friends and then we started a very passionate sexual relationship, it was unlike other sexual relationships. It was more profound, intensely passionate and beautiful.

One late evening I took her on a cruise of the Harbor on my little sailboat 'Termite'. We had champagne and snacks, even candles that stayed lit while we anchored. It was a windless night and when I dropped the anchor next to Shelter Island, it didn't set well and started dragging without me noticing it. It was so romantic with a full moon and I thought I had prepared everything accordingly.

We started kissing to the full moon and before we could unglue our mouths suddenly we were lit up by a bright light right on our faces. I looked up shocked thinking we were about to be run over by a larger boat. It was the Coast Guard who very politely told me, "excuse me sir, but you're right in the middle of the channel and your Navigation lights are set backwards". I apologized and felt embarrassed by my lack of Seamanship and knowledge. I was still knew at this and had put the red and green Nav lights on the wrong sides. Then the anchor hadn't set properly because I failed to let out more scope, so the boat drifted to the middle of the channel. Fortunately there weren't any large ships passing by that late into the night.

I didn't want to be with any other woman and I wanted to be loyal, I really did. But I guess we hadn't talked about anything serious, it was just sort of happening. I didn't know if I was falling in love, I'm not sure if I was. Maybe it was just the passion that was blinding me, well it was falling in love with lust too. Then suddenly four months later, she told me she was pregnant. I was shocked because she said she couldn't get pregnant. I started having my doubts about the whole thing and I noticed how she was changing, as if she knew she had me by the cojones and didn't have to try to be nice anymore.

One day I confronted her about it and she got furious, she said something like "if it doesn't work out we'll just get divorced". Wait a second, we're not even married and she's already talking about divorce. I lost trust in her and didn't believe her anything anymore.

Suddenly my freedom felt threatened. I felt she had planned the whole thing, acted the whole thing to get a husband. Some Latino girls do that when they start getting desperate for a husband. I felt trapped and fooled, I felt as if she had acted to be in love just to trap me in her love commitment marriage trap. I was hurt and disappointed.

I did try and gave her the benefit of the doubt by moving in together in Imperial beach (most guys would have split on the argument that the baby could be from someone else, but I stuck around based on my sixth sense or intuitive feeling). I figured it wasn't the baby's fault so I would still give him a nice welcome into this world and then see how it goes. Baby Sebi was born shortly thereafter, I welcomed him to the world and wondered what I had gotten myself into this time. He was a cute big fat baby with lots of hair everywhere. (I kept all my doubts to myself and suffered internally with all kinds of negative thoughts that went thru my head). Fortunately, my doubts and mistrust were a false alarm and I later knew she had been telling me the truth.

I stayed with Taesa Airlines until Air New Zealand offered my aviation broker a contract for rated B-767 Pilots. I was the only one from the America's since they only wanted ICAO (International Civil Aviation Organization) ATPL's (Airline Transport Pilot License) and preferably from Britain or Kiwi and Ozzie (New Zealand, Australia). I lucked out since they decided to accept my ICAO ATPL from Mexico but not my US ATP (US ATP's are not ICAO based and not accepted in Europe or other Countries).

The secretary from the Aviation Broker office was sweet and very helpful after I charmed her on the phone, I got the contract and was happy to be flying out of Auckland.

There are various Aviation brokers such as Parc Aviation or IAC who recruit experienced Pilots to fly short or longer term contracts around the world. These contracts are usually pretty well paid and if you're single and Type rated with the required hours of flight (usually above 3,000 hours and above 6,000 for Captains) on the particular type of Aircraft, then it might be something for you.

At the time, First Officer salary was $5,000 Dollars per month, tax free, plus 2,000 New Zealand Dollars for rent allowance and approximately another 2,000 from per diems. That was pretty good especially since I was only making one fourth of that with Taesa after the huge Peso devaluation.

So I sent my letter of resignation to Taesa and accepted employment with IAC for that contract. Taesa by now had been reduced to one third of it's original size (thanks to the crooked President Salinas who had just left office, took the money and ran, and left the country in economic turmoil) which caused my Left Seat training on the B-737 to suddenly come to a stop, so there was nothing holding me there.

Air New Zealand initially said the contract could last anywhere from six months to two years.

I knew I would have to be looking for another job soon after this contract but that was a chance I was willing to take. There were quite a few job offers around Asia so it didn't seem that difficult to stay employed. Besides, Air New Zealand gave me an additional ATPL from their country with a B-767 rating and that eventually opened the doors for the next contract.

I had been chocking for air living with Nena because she wasn't ready to live together in a relationship since she had never done that before. She had always lived at home and had her spoiled ways and temper bursts that I didn't want to encounter. Of course her family and her had some resentment towards me because I still didn't want to get married after the baby was born. I knew I had to get out of that situation because neither her or I were ready to settle down with each other. I did give the baby my name thou.

I told Nena I'd be back in a few months and once again packed and left, (I sent her Tickets to come visit me a couple of months later) it was supposed to be only a short 6 to 8 month contract but I needed an excuse to escape. Don't' forget how I had felt trapped, plus we didn't get along anymore.

I must admit that I didn't understand her, I couldn't comprehend that due to her hearing disability handicap, she misunderstood or wrongly explained many things, her situational awareness hadn't been developed normally due to her condition. She had been deaf mute until seven years old and after an operation she was able to regain half of her hearing on one side and only 30% on the other side (it didn't help that she didn't like to wear her hearing aid). So that's why sometimes I misunderstood her or thought she was lying about little things, I think she probably didn't remember or didn't hear me clearly whenever we were in conversation. Unfortunately, I didn't realize all this until years later when we finally were able to build a good friendship.

Celebrating my Birthday with friendly natives.

NEW ZEALAND LOVE. MY THIRD AIRLINE JOB.

I felt relieved to leave but when I got there I was lonely and missed her and the baby. Can't live with them or without them, that is so true. She remained in our little house in Imperial Beach and we saw each other a couple of times when she visited me there and when I flew to San Diego. Coincidently, as I was in Auckland feeling lonesome I met a cute Kiwi 22 year old named Mindy, we struck a friendship that pretty soon turned into a sexual relationship. She had a very pretty face with big eyes, a very nice fit body and milk white soft baby skin. I loved having sex with her, it was like discovering sex in my early 20s all over again.

At first we saw each other only when she had free time, not on weekends. So I felt like I was just her part time toy boy and didn't mean anything to her. So one weekend, Patty, a Flight Attendant friend invited me on a double date dinner where she introduced me to Kara-lee. She was originally from my side of the woods and I loved speaking Spanish with her. I really felt warm all over again being with her. That warm human touch that I hadn't felt in a while since I left. It was a nice friendship that soon developed into a relationship.

Now I had to try to stop what I had with Mindy, I figured she wouldn't even care. So when I told her that I had met someone that weekend and that I wanted to continue seeing her, I saw her eyes turn red. She said she had been cold to me because of fear of falling in love, but that it was too late because she was now in love with me and didn't want to stop what we had. She said she wouldn't stand being dumped for another woman. I couldn't bear it seeing her cry so I kissed her pretty face, lips and eyes and told her I would try to manage to stay only friends with Karalee.

Man, that wasn't easy being me. That night after dinner and some red wine, she seduced me once again and we ended up in her bed having sex. I thought it would be the last time. I really didn't want to get into this situation but somehow I was in the middle of it and couldn't get out that easy.

When I was with Karalee I was happy and enjoyed everything with her, including sex. When I was with Mindy I was in lust and passion mostly, she was hot looking and eager to learn more about the joys of sex. But I was going to try to stop it. The next time I saw her I told her I had decided to stop seeing both of them, that we would have to remain only friends. She was okay with it as long as I didn't take the other girl instead of her.

Now, I had told Karalee about her in the beginning and that we had already remained only friends because I did plan to do that. Then I had to try to be as diplomatic as possible with Mindy because I didn't want her to be hurt, she had had a bad experience where she almost got chocked and raped and was still a little frail from it. I did feel compassion for her but I also had to be extra careful not to piss her off because she said she felt like burning my house down, and it wasn't even my house.

Then one day she called me and invited me to watch a movie so I thought it was okay to go as friends. She was dressed very sexy with a super mini skirt, high heel shoes and a sexy blouse with her beautiful breasts showing partly. After the movie we had some dinner and a bottle of red wine. Then when I dropped her off she said. "Oh please come in just for a little bit so I can show you my new clothes". I tried to say no but I couldn't. I came in and she started displaying her new clothes around, dressing and undressing. (A couple of years back in San Diego, the Sicilian chick did that to me too, while her geeky male roommate who was in love with her, waited for her to come out while she displayed her sexy underwear for me in the bathroom, followed by having sex in front of the mirror. I had to put my hand on her mouth so the other dude wouldn't hear her moan in pleasure.)

She looked so good I couldn't stop myself, she came close to me and rested her face next to mine, we hugged, kissed and ripped our clothes off, well mine because she was already partly naked. We were once again devouring each other in a passionate frenzy. I didn't care about the world at that moment, it was like floating in heaven. But I did feel guilty thereafter. I kept fooling myself thinking it would be the last time.

I know, I can't feel that proud of myself but somehow I felt like a victim of love. I loved being with both of them and I couldn't give either one of them up. I knew something had to happen soon before I got caught. Auckland is a relatively small city and I was afraid I would be seen sooner or later. Then I found out the contract was about to end in October and I knew that would be my way out anyway. I had really enjoyed living in Auckland, I had bought a New surfboard and surfed all the good spots on the Island, Raglans, Piha Beach and others I don't remember anymore. I also went on a week long camping trip with Karalee all over the North Island. It was all so beautifully clean, natural and green. I went surfing one morning at Raglans, and that same afternoon we were skiing down Mt. Ruapehu, not many places where you can do that eh. So a few weeks before the contract ended, I sold my car and started packing.

I came to see Mindy one more time before I left. I took her to a nice restaurant for a nice romantic dinner just in case it would be the last time. I didn't tell her that thou, I just said I was on a Standby ticket for my return and I still didn't know exactly when I would leave.

We had dinner and wine followed by a quick short passionate sex and love session. She was crying and just as I was getting ready to leave, as she laid there naked under the sheets with her beautiful milk white baby skin body reflecting against the candlelight, she grabbed my hand and tried to pull me towards her. I could see the passionate desire in her eyes, she wanted more loving and I had to leave because I had to pick up you know who at the airport by midnight. I felt bad and wished I could have stayed all night with her, to hold her one more time and make love to her all night until she would fall sleep in my arms, but I couldn't.

I deeply regretted leaving but I was standing in between two guns pointed at my head and I didn't know which one to dodge. I will never forget her pretty face staring at me with her big green watery eyes holding on tight to my hand, naked like an angel and burning with desire. I will always regret and cherish those last moments I had with her. I really wish she has forgiven me. She asked me to promise I would tell her when I would fly out so she could bring me to the airport and see me goodbye. I told her I would but I couldn't, because by then I was staying at Karalee's house and she was driving me to the airport on my return flight. She had actually requested that flight so she could work on it and be with me in Los Angeles.

I did call Mindy from the airport on my departure night and apologized, I explained to her that because I was on a Standby Flight they had suddenly called me that day to assign me a flight. She cried on the phone and was upset but we agreed we would meet in Honolulu during her vacation with her grandfather in a couple of months. I really wanted to see her again but we never got around to it, or better said, I never got around to it. I didn't receive her letter with the dates she would be in Honolulu because Nena had hidden the letter. I didn't see her letter until one year later.

So my stay in New Zealand was coming to an end, it had been a great experience, also a great experience as a Pilot, flying that part of the world and discovering new places and cities. We had some excellent overnights, two days in Fiji on the way to Honolulu, then three days in Honolulu, oh boy, that was risky. We stayed at the Ilikai Hotel facing the Ala Wai Marina and often we'd go partying in town with the flight attendants. On one of these layovers, my old mate Ross was the Captain and a flight attendant friend of Karalee was on board. We all went out dancing and stayed out until late, we danced a lot with her friend but nothing happened that night.

Karalee always thought I had slept with her but I swear I didn't, even thou she was pretty hot looking.

On another layover (before I met Karalee) when we all went out with the Flight Attendants, we almost got into a fight with a couple of drunk Sailors, they were desperately trying to drag our girls away to shag them, I overheard them talking in the men's room and planning how they would force them into a taxi "so we can fuck them" they said. I told them they were so full of shit because I wasn't going to allow it (you should have seen their faces). There were three guys (my flight crew) including myself and we were guarding them like good shepherds.

Besides, I had my eyes on one of them that had been flirting with me, so if anyone was going to get them it was going to be us. The girls were pretty drunk by now and one that I didn't like so much started kissing me at the bar. Later on she just disappeared (went back to the hotel) because she found out I was interested in her friend.

The Navy dudes followed them outside when they went for a smoke and when I approached them to tell them that we were planning to leave, one Swab sailor inquired 'who the fuck' I was, one of the girls responded that I was their Pilot and they laughed. I said to him that because he was young and ignorant he couldn't grasp reality from fiction and that there was no fucking way outside of his fictitious imagination he was getting laid by these girls tonight (you should've seen their faces this time). The girls laughed and left with me and the other crew members.

When I got to my room I got a call from the cute one I liked, with an invitation to her room. I did visit her and we had some pretty exciting sex, (she was a cute and exotic half-breed Kiwi girl with a nice little body with great titties), she appeared hungry for love and reacted very passionately and wild like a cat in heat. We made love until we both fell sleep and then I went back to my room in the morning. I never flew with her or saw her again, (I think her name was that of a fruit that rhymes with berry) she had told me earlier that she had a boyfriend in a distant country in the Indian Ocean area. Little did I know that I would end up living in that area shortly thereafter.

From my balcony at the hotel I would stare to the marina and dream that one day I would live here and have a sailboat there at that Marina. Dreams do come true remember?

So still in New Zealand and getting ready to leave, but as they say, "it's not over until the fat lady sings", and I was starting to get nervous on how I was going to handle this. The situation got more complicated because Nena had insisted on picking me up at the LAX Airport. Although we had sort of separated she obviously wanted to try and get back together again. I had mixed feelings about it because I was really into Karalee at the time. It was now too late to make her change her flight plans.

Now I had to figure out how to deal with Karalee and Nena and to avoid them from running into each other with me at the Airport. I explained to Karalee that my brother was picking me up and that I should go to San Diego with him, and then I would be catching up with her three days later on her return from her Flight pattern LAX-FRA-LAX. She agreed, also I told her that in case we got lost at the exit, not to wait for me, to just go ahead with the crew to her Hotel and I'd be calling her there. So when we landed at LAX, I knew I had to scram and pick up all my luggage quick and try to make it out to the exit before she did, spot Nena and go to the parking from there, all without being seen by Karalee or her crew.

I was making it to the exit when I spotted Nena, then I looked back and I saw Karalee with all the rest of the crew not far behind me, I started sweating. I didn't think she saw me so I veered left behind a pillar and called over to Nena to come to that side. She looked so beautiful, nicely dressed and made up with her long black hair and bright eyes and she had our baby boy with her. She was nervous and excited to see me. I was also nervous and sweating but mostly from the fear of being seen by both at the same time. Karalee knew about my predicament with Nena and understood, but she didn't know she was picking me up. As far as she was concerned we were separated and I wasn't going back to her. I didn't think I was either.

So far it looked like I was clear, but know we had to walk in front of Karalee and her crew to get to the van. We crossed the street to the other side towards the parking area, I then took my surfboard in it's bag that I had bought in New Zealand and laid it on top off my luggage on the cart, I pushed it from the left side and hid behind the surfboard, that way Karalee or her crew could only see my luggage and Nena with baby with somebody's legs pushing it.

Phew, I made it unseen to the parked VW van and we drove back to San Diego. It was a sad moment, being back with Nena and not having feelings for her, or better said, have my feelings for her blanketed by my feelings for Karalee. I wanted to try to be at least loyal to Karalee, she had believed me that nothing would happen between Nena and I. Nothing happened that weekend, I slept on the couch, and although she did come over to the couch to try to kiss me and seduce me I remained cold and motionless.

That Sunday I drove to Los Angeles to meet up with Karalee. We had a great two days together but she was sad because she knew it was going to be difficult to continue seeing each other. We made love over and over again in her hotel room and we parted. We weren't sure when and where we were going to see each other again because I still didn't have a future flying job and didn't know where I was going to end up. She said she'd call me again on her next flight into LAX.

So I went back to San Diego with Nena and the baby, by then I had fallen again for her and we started having a relationship again. I didn't think I would see Karalee again so it didn't feel like cheating. A month later I got hired by Air Mauritius as First Officer/Cruise Captain on the Being 767.

I told Nena I still didn't think I was ready to settle down and that I couldn't promise anything but that we could still meet whenever I got a chance to visit, and that I would also fly her over there too. She was sad because she felt me flying away again, but she still had hopes. It was sad to see her dark eyes engulfed in sadness every time I left, watching her pretty face watching me intensely as I walked away into the airplane. She didn't want to let go and she told me she'd be waiting for me even after I told her to go on with her life and not wait. She said I would eventually mature and when I would be ready to settle down she would be there for me. I couldn't believe her at the time but it turned out to be true eventually.

Hanging out with very friendly Mauritian natives at my bungalow.

L'ILE MAURICE, BEAUTIFUL MAURITIUS ISLAND. MY FOURTH AIRLINE JOB.

So off I went towards Africa in November of 1996. Mauritius is fairly close to Madagascar (actually East of it, and next to Reunion Island) which is next to the South Eastern Coast of Africa. I had spent a warm stay at home in San Diego and was starting to get attached to my little son, but the thought of Nena's plans to entrap me was fresh in my mind and I couldn't just erase it. I felt relieved to leave but at the same time I felt lonely and sad to be without them.

The Air Mauritius interview was the easiest Airline interview I've ever had. It consisted of an interview with the then Chief Pilot Capt. Bhanymundub (he was a very nice and respectful gentleman) and two other Management gentlemen. They asked me a few technical questions and that was that. One question they asked me was to define the meaning of ETOPS, which means Extended Route Two Engine Operations. I was so jetlagged and acting like a zombie so I thought I would try my chance at being funny. So I answered that it meant, "Engines Turning Or Passengers Swimming". They rolled in laughter and then asked me for the real meaning which I told them. Apparently they liked me so they asked me to wait outside. Ten minutes later I was given a letter by Miss Pierrot the secretary, it said I was found acceptable for enjoyment or better said, employment.

This was by far the funnest Airline I have ever worked for. On my very first flight operating out of Zurich, I was welcomed to the Airline by the whole crew at the bar, then we all had a snow fight outside the Hotel and then headed to the Disco downstairs. I was trying to give a good impression so I was being careful not to over do it. I was ready to go back to my room at around 3 am and as I said goodnight, one of the cute Flight Attendants stood up with me and said she was leaving too. She was a pretty attractive fair skinned French Creole with a nice set of big breasts, squeezed in their bra and trying to get out. She had been flirting with me the whole night and I thought she was up to something. We got in the elevator and she said to me to call her to her room if I got bored, but I was afraid to just in case I was being set up.

Interestingly enough, her name when translated meant Horny in German and it fit her well. Miss Horny called me about twenty minutes later and asked me what I was doing, and when I told her that I couldn't sleep she asked if I wanted to come over to her room. I said I didn't think it was a good idea so she said she could come to my room instead, so I accepted. She gave me the warmest 'welcome to the Island mon' reception. She was voluptuous, had a pretty face with big green eyes and you know what else, and was a great lover. We had a steaming session of Island sex and then she left two hours later. I asked her to be discreet about it just in case, and she agreed to it.

Then on another flight a week later, just as I was getting ready to do my Route check out of Paris, I had another nice warm welcome from a lovely Chinese Mauritian girl. We all went out to the Montparnasse area to a Tex Mex Restaurant where we all had tequila's and a good time. There was Nick my training Captain and Didier the other First Officer. They were trying to get me drunk on Tequila but in the end I was the soberest of all. As we were walking back to the rooms in the Hotel, Nick said to me not to worry about the Route check the next day. That I was okay and was pretty much passed. Then he said, "There's one more thing you need to do, call Niky and go shag her, she wants you". I couldn't believe it and at first thought he was messing with me. I jokingly asked him if that was an order and he replied, "yes it is, now call her and go have sex with her", that's the way he put it as he handed me a condom (he actually said "go f…. her"). They both stared at me, laughed and said, "Welcome to Air Mauritius".

So I called her and sure enough, she was already waiting. The "my room or your room" sentence came up and she came to my room within minutes. Mon Frere, Qui Posicio'n, c'ette' Mari Bon. That was pretty hot Island sex, that girl had the hottest lips and the most flexible tight little body, no kidding. We both went at each other like a couple of Tequila fed Piranhas on a feeding frenzy. That petite girl was so good at pleasing a man that it seemed she was reading my mind. The next morning everyone knew about it and they sort of made light jokes about it during the flight.

Later that weekend in Mauritius she came by one evening to my Bungalow, she brought weekend luggage with her because she thought she was spending the whole weekend, unfortunately I had plans and couldn't entertain her anymore than one evening, but that was enough. I didn't want to get too serious to quick because I wanted to taste more of the different fruits of the Island.

It's funny that the same thing happened with another girl that went with me to Reunion Island for a few days, when we got back she said she didn't want to go home to her parents yet. So she stayed three more days at my Beach Bungalow until her Mom started making calls looking for her. It was easy to get overwhelmed with so much attention, sex and love' lust, so I was enjoying it but I could only have so much of it. I also needed my space and free time to do other stuff like surf, explore the Island, explore the clubs and bars, meet other people, etc.

Mauritius is a beautiful Island about the size of Oahu in Hawaii. It is neighbors with Reunion and Rodrigue Island, they used to be called the Mascarene Islands. There are about five different cultures that apparently get along with each other, that is until there is some kind of cultural turmoil that ignites racial conflicts amongst the Hindus and the true African Mauritians. Then all hell breaks loose as they start burning cars, throwing rocks off bridges and clashing with each other. This happened twice while I was there and it caused me to be confined to my apartment complex for a few days at a time.

One of the times it happened, it was instigated by the Indian police because they massacred the Rasta leader of the Reggae Rastafarian community in prison. He was at a street concert singing for the legalizing of marihuana, so they thought they would use him as an example. Then they threw his naked body in front of city hall after they pumped it with drugs to make it look like an overdose. This caused the African Mauritians to go crazy and they started attacking government buildings, burning police cars and throwing rocks off bridges. The Hindus joined forces with Muslims and then the government threatened to implement Martial Law in addition to bringing in mercenary racist soldiers from South Africa to shoot with pleasure at the African descendants. Eventually everyone calmed down and peace came to the Island once again.

This Island was at first inhabited by pirates, although the Spanish and Portuguese discovered it first over 400 years ago, they weren't interested in it's volcanic surroundings. (That was when the Spanish and Portuguese Navigators had pretty much charted most of the oceans of the world, way before Captain Cook or any others.) Then the Dutch claimed possession of it giving it it's name in honor of their King Maurice. The French later came and took it from the Dutch and later lost it to the English, which eventually left them to their Independence around 1958. The Dutch sailors were responsible for the extinction of the famous Dodo bird, a big bird chicken duck looking thing with little wings that couldn't fly. The French brought Africans mostly from the East of the African coast to work as slaves. Then in the early 1900s the English decided to import Indians to work the sugar canes that the Africans no longer wanted to work. There also came many Chinese. The Hindus multiplied quickly due to the lack of Television (sort of kidding) and pretty soon they outnumbered every one else. Now they are over 65% of the population and pretty much run the government and major textile corporations. The minority are the Franco Mauritians, which are the remaining French or Dutch descendants. They pretty much have all the wealth and own most of the beach properties. The ones with the bad end of the stick unfortunately are the true Mauritians, the African descendants of the original slaves they imported. They are also a minority and are affected by poverty and mistreatment by the wealthier Francos and Indians.

So all this mixture really created some interesting and attractive people, not to mention the exotic beauties running around. Also a very rich culture and great cuisine. The Mauritian people are some of the friendliest and relaxed people I have encountered.

Once I got settled at a nice beach Hotel near Maeburg in Mauritius for the first couple of weeks, I started concentrating on my new life. That first week I experienced a full on cyclone hitting very close to the Island. My room was up to half a foot of water and my ceiling was about to fly away from the winds outside which were blowing at hurricane force. This went on for two days and was quite a different type of Welcome to the Island Mon. Like the other 'welcomes' this one also included a lot of blowing and shaking but of a different cyclonic type, and without a 'Happy Ending'.

Eventually I moved into a gorgeous beach house on the Grand Bay side with my Simulator partner Clement from Canada and Patrick the French Moroccan. I was still a little bummed out and really missed San Diego, Nena and the baby. I still couldn't bring myself to accept her yet and somehow felt that I'd eventually get over it.

The first Mauritian friends I made were Bilal and his sidekick Chips. They helped us get settled and were always there to help us out thru the red tape. They were Muslim Hindus with very honest and ethical backgrounds and you could literally trust them with anything.

That weekend we went out to the Club Med close by and hooked up with two local sisters that one of the guys knew. One of them was promised to be married to a Muslim guy, she was nineteen years old and was out to have fun that night. She was okay, very nice little body and a cute smile. That night they ended up at our place at the beach because it was too late to go home. I had an extra bed in my room so I offered it to her, she just started undressing down to her panties and then I noticed she did have a hot little body. Our hands met in between the twin beds and she jumped right over as soon as I gave her a little tug. She loved playing the flute like it was going to be her last song, with a lot of feeling and passion, if you know what I mean, and that was fine with me. Then she mounted me and gave me another 'welcome to the Island mon' and very wildly made love to me. She had a big smile of satisfaction on her face before she went to sleep. In the morning she wanted another go before she left, and then she said, " we should do it again before I get married", to which I responded, "I don't think it would be a good idea, it was nice meeting you thou". The last thing I needed was trouble with a pissed off fiancée'.

There was an occasion were Clemont, Patrick and myself almost got into trouble without even knowing it. There were a couple of guys who wanted to rent the bungalow next to ours and they were introduced to us by a couple of neighbors. These guys were supposedly from Jordan and were in the business of shopping for race horses for the King himself, or so they said.

They were coming from Madagascar and said they had been looking for horses there too. When they came to our house after we invited them in for drinks, they brought a couple of very attractive Madagashi girls with them. The first doubts I had about these people were their appearance, the King's jockey was overweight and not small enough to be a jockey. The other two guys looked like they were Olympic athletes and the girls were very silent and weren't allowed to talk much.

I just sensed something was wrong with this picture.

They came by a couple of more times to see the bungalow and to talk to us and then they disappeared for a few weeks. Then one day our friend Bilal showed us the daily newspaper with their pictures on it. It turns out they were heroin dealers and were looking for a house to rent were they could stash drugs coming from Africa or India, and then send them out to Europe or Australia from there. They got busted when the local Police investigating one of them found a mysterious key on him and obliged him to show them the house it belonged to. It happened to be the house they had rented to stash their drugs. We looked at each other in disbelief and wondered what would have happened had the police thought we were in business with them. Mauritius is know for being used as a midpoint for transporting drugs to other parts of the world, drugs that get delivered from India or Africa. Sometimes on our own flights from India we would witness a passenger getting arrested at Customs, for transporting heroin on them inside their bodies in rubbers they swallowed tied to a tooth with a thin line. Usually they were poor family men that were willing to take the risk to feed their families back in India.

The way they would send the drugs from Mauritius to a container ship bound for Europe was via a smaller boat from a harbor. Sometimes they would steal a boat and then sink it. That happened to my friend Patrick the French Moroccan. He had just bought a $40,000 Dollar, 36 foot sailboat that he kept anchored off in front of his beach house. One morning it was missing and he never found it again. It either was taken to Madagascar where they sell them or use them for further drug trafficking.

A week after I got settled near Grand Bay, I went out to the Banana Café at the beach by the Bay. From there I went to Secrets, a little Club near Pereybere where I met Preescy with her friend. They were both very pretty Mauritian girls of Indian descent. Preescy and I hit it right off and later that night we kissed goodnight and decided to meet during the week. Eventually we got passionately involved, she was a very sensual woman, very clean and perfumed with natural oils, passionate and very sexual. I really hadn't experienced girls like her before. After two weeks of dating, she hinted she wanted a serious relationship and when I said I wasn't in for that, she decided to go back to her ex boy-friend who was managing a night club near Cure Pipe. We remained very good friends with Preescy and she became my closest friend on the Island throughout my whole three year stay. She was my "confi-dent" and my buddy and I really missed her when I left. I still clearly remember her at The Cotton Club, a little clothes shop across the Grand Bay beach where she worked. I would spend hours in conversation with her inside her little shop sometimes.

Preescy and me boating in Grand Bay.

That week I went and bought myself a pickup truck, a Nissan 4 wheel drive for easy access to all the secret surf spots of the Island.

There was a lot of uncharted surf there. That week I was driving towards Tamarin Bay, South of the Island with my new Kiwi board (the one I used to hide myself from being seen at LAX) strapped to the back of the truck. I was excited because there was a big swell hitting that part of the coast and I was going to get to surf famous Tamarin Bay. It's a great powerful left wave when it breaks overhead. On this wave, you really have to quickly make a left bottom turn and maybe get barreled, otherwise you end up on the coral beds just ahead, which I did once on my butt.

So anyway, there I was underway crossing this wide plateau headed south, the winds were pretty strong but I didn't think about my board flying off. Well it did, I noticed in the rear view mirror something like a kite flying behind my truck, I screamed in horror when I saw my beautiful surfboard just barely clinging to one of the bungees and flying like a kite (it was a seven foot tri-fin, wood imitation color with a thick stringer, round pin tail and shaped like a mini gun, just beautiful).

I stopped just as it became loose and flew right into an incoming small truck. The truck rolled over it and stopped suddenly. I ran over to the truck and pulled the board in it's bag out from under the truck. It looked still in one whole piece but when I pulled it out of it's gray bag it had one large crack across it and all fins were missing. It was actually a glass epoxy board, made strong and light for traveling, which is why it had survived in one whole piece. Still, my precious board was ruined. It was like watching my dog getting run over.

I decided to pick up the pieces and head south anyway, maybe I'd be able to borrow someone's board. To make matters worse, on the way to Tamarin Bay I got stopped by three Mauritian cops who were hiding at the bottom of a hill, they claimed I was going 90 kilometers an hour in a 50 km zone. The last zone marker had been at least half a Km behind at the last village. And they were waiting at the downhill side of the road because they knew that cars would automatically accelerate due to gravity, besides, there was no speed zone in that sector where they were.

I was already pissed off about my board and these cops really started to get on my nerves. I knew I could push my luck when they found out I was an Air Mauritius Pilot because they respected that. But they kept insisting politely. Finally I told them in my broken French to go harass someone else and that their little cheating trap wasn't going to stick with me. I started to get back in my truck but they wouldn't give me back my California Driver's License, they said it didn't say it was an International License, so I told them it didn't say it wasn't and therefore it was an International license. They then asked me to sign and fill out their ticket. I filled out the name El Zorro and made up a very fake address. I put down "Ocean st, #69 planet Mars". The Morons couldn't read or what? Finally I was on my way to Tamarin Bay. Fortunately an Aussie surfer I met there let me use his board, and now I could forget about the lousy day I had earlier. I had an excellent surf session and felt great again.

Flying the Boeing 767 with Air Mauritius was a great job. The crew atmosphere was warm, friendly and wild at times. We had flights from Mauritius to Africa (Cape town, Johannesburg, Durban, Zimbabwe, Kenya, Mozambique) and Europe, Paris, Frankfurt, London, Rome, Zurich, Manchester, Geneva. The best flight pattern was the one to Perth and Melbourne Australia.

On a Rome three day overnight, visiting Santa Margarita near Rapallo.

We had seven day layovers there and the per diems we got were pretty well above 140.00 AD per night, multiply that times seven and that's enough to pay for your monthly groceries. We could usually save half of the per diems and spend the other half dining and drinking. Other destinations also had three to five day layovers which is mostly unheard of nowadays. Tja, the good old days of aviation when Airlines used to be run by Pilots instead of bloody accountants, lawyers and crooks.

We also had flights to India, Delhi and Bombay. One night in Bombay I hooked up with three girls from Alitalia that were staying at my Hotel as well. The cutest one Marzia, seemed a bit snobbish and not interested in me at first. But as the day went by and we hung out together they all seemed fair game for hunting season. That night as we all danced with tequila in our bloods at the Disco downstairs at the Taj Mahah, Marzia started giving me what I thought were mating signals (kisses on the neck). I suggested to her we go alone to my room but she was worried that the rest of her crew would criticize her for that. I think we were both getting sexually attracted but I couldn't break her apart from her herd and I knew I was running out of time because I had to be out of the hotel at 5 am for a deadhead flight back to Mauritius.

So I tried my last card and told her she wouldn't know the true meaning of the term Latin Lover unless she would spend the last hour with me in privacy (I couldn't believe myself for using such a corny line). I told her what room number I was in and left to get ready for my flight, about 15 minutes later she was at my door in her jammies. She had taken the bait and accepted my invitation for a good healthy bout of passionate hot Italian sex. She was a beauty and I was sorry to have to leave so soon, that hour was the fastest running of time I have ever felt. I knew I had one last condom somewhere and I was frantically looking for it after smooching and kissing for a few minutes but I couldn't remember where it was. As a last resort I turned my Flight bag upside down and there it was, stashed away for an emergency. Now I knew the meaning "time flies when you're having fun". I was dressed up and ready to go while she laid in bed asking me not to leave, she said something like, "love me more, don't go, please stay". I knew I could have called in sick since I was only returning back as passenger (deadhead crewmember) but my sense of responsibility didn't allow me, also the fact that I was traveling back with a training Captain by the name of Alapoudakis (I'm almost sure he would have understood). I was also getting close to upgrading as Captain so I didn't want to risk being seen as an irresponsible Pilot. So I deeply regretted leaving but I did. I never saw her again and that was a pity.

Oh, those great times in Mumbai (Bombay). "Mumbai Radio, Mumbai Radio, this is Air Mauritius 74 on HF". It was a long quiet night over the Indian Ocean on the way to Bombay. High Frequency radio was almost impossible to make contact with. Strangely we could hear other aircraft calling Shannon Radio on the Atlantic but not Bombay Radio which was much closer to us. High Frequency waves bounce off the Ionosphere to the other side of the world and back down to Earth at very long distances.

We were looking forward to three nights in Bombay at the beautiful ancient Taj Mahah Hotel on the waterfront by the English Gate Monument (the same one where tourists were taken hostage by Pakistani terrorists and the Hotel was badly damaged by fire that they started).

I was starting to date a new girl there called Miroslava who was a waitress for the fancy Mexican Restaurant at one of the nice Hotels in town. She could bend like a pretzel because she had practiced ballet for many years. It showed because when she walked around she puckered out her sweet ass and stuck her chest out. But on this night La Petite Fille was with me and her and her girlfriends wanted to celebrate my Birthday with me.

So we all went to the Mexican Restaurant to start the celebration. My Mexican friends from the Mariachi band were there playing as usual. They were there on a renewable contract with the Hotel every six months, Javier, Juan and Jose' from Guadalajara so I felt right at home.

Except this time I brought a sandwich to the buffet because I had no choice but to bring Petite Fille (Desiree') with me and she was ready to party. Miroslava didn't seem very happy to see that but after they finished their shift, they all came to my room at the Taj Mahah to join the party. We had Tequila and beers and my whole crew were there.

Miroslava was dressed up pretty sexy and so was Petite Fille who was wearing a mini skirt with a thong, versus a tight thin dark pants. I really wished I could have been alone with Miroslava but I felt somehow committed to Petite Fille because we were just in the process of breaking up. We had been trying for a few months but she was so perseverant and her lovemaking and other lovely qualities about her made it difficult to stop all of a sudden. Miroslava on the other hand was a young sexy waitress who probably just wanted a way out of her waitress job and she was willing to try anything new.

So I made the decision to give Petite Fille the first choice that night. After the party, we wet kissed with Miroslava in the elevator good night and I sent her home with her Mariachi band.

She looked disappointed but it had to be done. Decisions, decisions, that's what it's all about in my line of work, making the right decisions.

What a night I had with Petite Fille, she made sure I had a superb Birthday night. Her tongue caressed all of my body and mine hers. Our passion was at the end of it's rope so we made the best of it. I didn't get to make it up to Miroslava because the next time I came back to Mumbai she already had another boyfriend.

Something I really enjoyed about Bombay was the people and the magic of the city. Despite the misery, smog, noise and stench during the monsoon season, there was something about it that made it interesting. Sometimes as we were descending towards the Airport we could already smell the stench of the city, sort of like a dirty public toilet. Fortunately, our hotel The Taj Mahah was our little world of safety and hygiene.

The part I didn't look forward to was going thru all the red tape of the left behind British Beaurocracy mixed with Indian Red Tape incompetence and voila', you had a terrible mixture. It took us almost one hour to clear in thru Customs and Immigration. It seemed that every Official that had to stamp our Documents had a larger stamp every time and the guy with the largest of them all, was the head honcho. But they were nice and polite and never lost their patience.

Then it was another hour to the city thru the most chaotic and noisy traffic I have ever seen. The funniest part of driving was dodging the Holy cows just kicking back in the middle of the roads, it seemed like they had more respect for these animals than for humans crossing the road. The most important part of a vehicle in Bombay is the horn because without it, it probably wouldn't pass a safety check. On one occasion as we got into a Taxi we asked the taxi driver not to touch the horn and we would pay him double the fare. He agreed and was eager to make some extra money. Unfortunately for him he couldn't help it and as soon as he made the first block he forgot and used it, beep beep.

It's like they can't drive without touching the damned thing many times, that's all you hear all day, beep beep, beep beep, all day long.

Just one block away from our nice Historic Hotel the misery lurked. The beggar children, the lepers, deformed children and adults begging for money. All this while the (owners) pimps of the small begging children sat in their nice Mercedes Benz watching their operation. We had been told to ignore the children but I couldn't help it trying to help them. The minute I handed one child some money, dozens appeared out of nowhere and swarmed all over me like bees, "mister mister, give me money, buy me milk", etc. I started getting worried when they tried to touch me so I started running away until I made sure they stayed behind. Phew, it was hard to try to ignore them but I knew it was for their good.

It doesn't help to help them because it just feeds the system of corruption and abuse by the Handlers of the children. These children are sometimes bought from orphanages and trained to beg in different languages. No kidding.

One morning as I was headed back from some shopping, a little girl approached me and asked me in good Oxford English if I would like to shop at a special discount. At first I tried to ignore her but then she said it in French and then in German, finally in Italian and then I tested her in Spanish but that one she did not know.

I was surprised at how clean and tidy she was dressed and combed. She wasn't like other beggars because when I tried to give her a bill she refused it and said she didn't want my money. She got my attention so I asked her what she wanted. She said she wanted to take me to a Bazaar where I could get special prices. When I told her I didn't have any more money she insisted and said if I didn't come with her, her Handler was going to beat her up. That again got my attention and I felt like kicking her handlers ass. I could see him at the corner in his Benz, a fat ugly fellow monitoring the scene from the safety of his Benz. As we were approaching my Hotel she started trying a different approach and this time she started crying and begging me to come with her. When the Hotel guard saw her he directed himself towards her and she knew she was about to get a kick in her behind, literally, I didn't want to see her get abused in that way so I offered her the bill which she took and ran away really fast.

Despite the miserable conditions the lower casts live in, they always have broad very white teethed smiles and are very genuine. I liked conversing with them whenever I could.

We also had layovers in Singapore and Hong Kong. Not to mention the best, one week layovers in Perth and Melbourne Australia which I used to fly to other cities such as Brisbane to go surfing for five days. The other favorite one was the six day layover in Singapore where I would then catch a flight to Bali for more surfing.

That was the life I had been dreaming of as a kid, traveling thru Europe as a Pilot, surrounded by pretty women and flying big jet planes. The money wasn't bad either. It wasn't the best but the savings capability were great. You could literally live off your per diems and save all your salary. I had saved all my Air New Zealand salary and was saving most of my Mauritian salary to buy an ocean crossing sailboat. That was another of my crazy dreams, to sail the world by sailboat.

I was now living in my own beach bungalow near Pereybere north of Grand Bay in Mauritius. It was a lovely place with a few other bungalows around and a community pool. It was also facing the beach and snake Island. It was a beautiful place really. I lived there most of my stay in Mauritius. My friends and I called it Hotel California because we had many wild parties were people came and never left until the next morning, specially chicks. Often we'd also have live music with loud bongos echoing thru the night, also flight attendants, local girls and the occasional tourist girls we'd meet on the beach. A couple of times we all ended up in the pool with the girls only in their panties and with bottles of Tequila or Rum floating in the water. Life seemed great at times, other times it was still a solitary life.

But everything eventually comes to an end. Sadly but truly. I was getting fed up with being so far from home and getting bored from the same old every day on the Island. My good Aussie friend and surfing buddy, Damian, was leaving the Island and my musician friends had left. Also, some of my pilot acquaintances were getting married and I was remaining as the only single guy in the group, so I wasn't hanging out with them much anymore.

My best friend Juan the Artist was my only remaining bro but he was mostly involved with his business, painting and his family and I didn't want to invade his privacy too much. Still, I frequented his home and hung out with them often.

During my first year in Mauritius I started dating Desiree, La Petite Fille I called her, she was a very pretty girl from Cure pipe and a Flight attendant. We dated for about one year. She was very adventurous, spontaneous and energetic. She was also a great lover and I never got bored with her. She had some amazing qualities for her 23 years of age. She was a great cook, a great friend and good humored girl and as I said, an excellent hot sexy lover. She had a very petite sexy figure with very nice medium sized breasts, fair lightly tanned skin, blondish curlish hair and nice full moist lips (she was basically a white Creole, French, English, and some African which you could tell by her round sexy petite figure and sexual full lips) . We traveled together often on flights with the Airline. We also traveled to Reunion Island for a little sort of honeymoon, Rodrigue Island, India, Australia and on Air Mauritius flights to Europe. I really felt something for her, but I think most of it was sexual. 'Oui, Je la aimee'. She really was a fun and intelligent girl.

She looked hot in a bikini, specially topless, and even better in a mini skirt. I almost got into a couple of fist fights with the horny locals because of their disrespect for other guys' girlfriends. One day at the beach as she was laying topless and another time as we were crossing the street in Grand Bay, we had just had dinner at the Pagoda Chinese Restaurant. She was wearing a short skirt with a white top and as we were trying to cross the street to the parking, I noticed an old car with four local Indian guys in it.

They were drunk and stopped in front of us to point at her breasts and say things to her. I couldn't believe their cynism so I cussed them out and kicked their car, I know, a little primitive male reaction. They momentarily kept going but then suddenly they made a 180 degree turn while screeching their tires, just like in their corny Indian movies. Then they followed us to the empty parking lot facing the beach.

I saw them coming and jumped into survival mode, I gave Desiree' my keys and told her to get in the truck, I knew I had to act fast and knock them out one at a time as they came out of their car, first come fist served. Fortunately only two of them stepped out at first, the older one with an empty bottle of beer in one hand staggered out saying, "Que est que tu a dit"? (What did you say to us?) As he raised his hand and tried to walk towards me I was already headed towards him with my foot aiming for his mouth, he looked behind him thinking that his friends where backing him up but they weren't, two of them stayed in the car and the other one was still holding on to his door, looking insecure. When he saw that I was headed towards him with a very pissed off look, he backed off, lowered the beer bottle and said, "Pas probleme" No Problem.

They got back into their car and drove away. I thought that they had never seen a pissed off Mexican before and when I looked behind my shoulder, two big Chinese guys from the restaurant where we had eaten were walking towards me ready to back me up. I was loaded with adrenalin and really wanted to kick some ass but Desiree was holding on to my arm and holding me back, that was pretty smart of her.

But as I said, everything eventually comes to an end. I think her Father was expecting something serious out of it and started pressing her, specially her Mother who was a hysteric controlling woman. And as they say, mothers like daughters, I could sense some of that in La Petite Fille. It had to come to an end. It was nevertheless sad for her and me too. That week after we returned from our last little Honeymoon from Rodrigue Island we parted in good terms.

One afternoon as we met at Le Cauda'n by the waterfront in Port Luis, she was reading me a good-bye romantic letter she had written for me, as she read it she cried and almost made tears come to my eyes too. I put my arm around her and we hugged each other for a little while. Actually we were interrupted by the Moral Police who tried to break it up, the idiot came up behind us and suggested that indecent behavior was not permitted in that area. We were just hugging not having sex on the bench, I snapped at him and said, "it is immoral for you to interrupt a romantic moment" after which he apologized and walked away. Those are the kind of things that I was fed up with in Mauritius.

We did meet occasionally thereafter for a quick bout of exciting sex. By the way, that was a beautiful getaway with Desiree'. We had a great time in Rodrigue Island, it's a beautiful, natural and virgin island, almost untouched without cars and big hotels. It's almost like going back in time one hundred years with only small villages and little bungalows by the beach. We could explore around and find our own little empty beach cove, with friendly colorful fish swimming around us. Sometimes we'd spent long hours of the days naked on the beach and in the water.

So that's how Adam and Eve must have felt at one time, when things were still good with their Creators, before they found out the truth about their Godly origins and existence.

A few days after returning from Rodrigue Island, when I was at the Banana Café' I met Kesi, she was a voluptuous blonde, half Italian and half Eastern European. She was '24 and a whole lot more', and there to have a good time while she worked at one of the hotels. We met the first time at Banana Café and I saw her again a few days later at JP's party. I arrived to the party with a bottle of Tequila and two British chicks I had met at the beach, they were cute but when I saw Kesi again I quickly signed off my two young and attractive companions to my pilot friends and gave Kesi my full attention.

She looked super Hot, she was wearing a tight white pants with her thong visible thru, a sexy top that looked like her breasts were about to escape out of their prison and her blonde hair down to her shoulders. She was happy to see me and so was I (so was my friend downstairs). We all had lots of drinks and ended up in the pool, in our underwear with the girls topless. Then later on Kesi and I ended up on someone's bed (I think it was JP's bed and I suspect that later on when he got married he didn't invite me to his wedding because of this or because he felt insecure that I might be a threat with his new wife) and we got sexually acquainted. She was sex all over, she emitted sex, her face was sexual, her lips, her voluptuous body, her ass, everything about her. She was a hot, passionate and wild girl, not shy at all.

That night I asked my good friend Ian to give the British girls a ride home (I introduced Ian to Leti my neighbor and they ended up having a happy life together, much later they visited me in Honolulu). Wrapped in towels and wet underwear they left, one of them not very happy because I didn't drive them home that night. It was fair game because we were all just having a good time. That night Kesi and I spent the rest of it in her apartment. After that night we dated for a couple of months and when Desiree' found out she was furious and delirious. I didn't understand why because we had already broken up. I guess she wanted a grace period after our brake up, it wasn't like she had died you know.

Skinning and fishing mermaids with sexy Kexy.

Kesi was a lot of fun and a very nice and helpful person but I couldn't take her seriously. It was too good to be true. I mean, she really was Hot looking, she would stop the traffic in Grand Bay whenever she walked around in her mini skirt, high heel shoes and loose blonde hair. Even when we where out dancing, there were local guys trying to hit on her when I would get up and go to the bathroom, it was like walking around with golden jewelry around your neck in a bad neighborhood. She was also a good friend and was there for me when I dislocated my knee and ended up in a cast for three weeks, she was like my private nurse, driver and lover.

By the way, the way I almost broke my knee was kind of embarrassing. I was showing up for an early flight to Durban, and when I was entering the Boeing 767 I didn't see that the Electronic Engine compartment on the floor by the entrance was open, it was six feet deep. I walked in and as I said "Bon Jour" to the Flight attendants I disappeared into the hole, I sounded like this, "Bon Jooooouuuuuuuuurrr". I didn't even know what hit me, it was like being eaten up and swallowed up into the belly of the beast.

I instinctively spread my arms and was able to hold on to the sides after scratching my back and banging my head on the rim, but my left knee stayed outside and tweaked sideways. I went to the infirmary at the Airport and had the scratch on my back cleaned and disinfected, my knee wasn't broken so I decided I was okay to make the round trip flight to Durban. It was a bad idea because on the flight back, my knee was so swollen and I couldn't walk on it. I didn't want to be rolled out on a wheelchair so I waited until all passengers exited the aircraft and away I limped out of the airplane.

My left knee really hurt like hell so I had a taxi take me to the Clinic. There a doctor examined it and suggested to drill a little hole inside my knee so he could see what damage there was inside. I came close to telling him to drill the hole up his dark side and asked if he could just put a cast on it. He agreed and disappeared to prepare the cast while his nurse stayed behind with a huge needle ready to stab me with Morphine. I politely declined and said I didn't need it. I asked her for a Tequila instead but of course she didn't have any.

Then the Doctor came in with a water proof cast and they rolled it up all around my leg, from top to ankle. He suggested I stay overnight but I said that only on one condition, if his cutest nurse would stay with me as well, he smiled and said I was free to go. I was limited to what I could do with this cast on but I still went swimming and snorkeling with it. It also didn't stop me from letting Kesi jump all over me.

Fortunately, she was still around and really took care of me, she would drive me around, get me groceries, take me to the beach and make love to me. Thanks Kesi for looking after me, we remained friends thereafter and years later we met again in Las Vegas and San Diego.

Then I started having a secret sexual relationship with a local Mauritian girl who was supposed to be married to some rich Muslim guy, I didn't know it at the time, let's call her RM. She had the nicest petite figure, like a ballerina, cute little face and a nice tanned complexion. I suspected she was hiding something because she wanted to have absolute discretion, which was fine with me because I also wanted discretion.

Sex was excellent with her because she was exotically sensual and sexual. She knew exactly what she was doing and wasn't shy about anything. One night we had sex on the ceiling of my apartment, I felt like we were two cats in heat, she was and she meowed like one in pleasure. With the stars and the moon above us, the ocean below and the reflection of the waves, it was so romantic and exciting, you all should try it sometime. Let's just say she had no boundaries and was willing to try anything. Then I started worrying when I found out who her "boyfriend" was.

By then I was getting ready to leave the Island anyway so I just hoped I would make it out of there alive. Muslims don't take it lightly when they find out about these kind of news.

I knew of an Air Mauritius Pilot from South Africa who was murdered on orders of an influential local guy. One version was that during a flight, the Captain kicked this drunk guy out of First Class because he wasn't supposed to be there and he was harassing someone's wife. The Indian local guy told him he would regret his actions and took revenge. The other version is that the Pilot was involved with a Muslim Flight Attendant who was promised to be married to this evil guy, he found out and had the guy killed. Except, the two thugs he sent to the Pilots apartment got the wrong pilot, it was another South African guy who was visiting and had a pilot uniform on as well. When the Pilot got home he realized what had happened and left the Island for good.

I had already been threatened by an ex-boyfriend of Desiree's when I made her cry during the breakup. He put it this way "you might end up like a dead Mexican in Grand Bay". I thought he was bluffing, but I don't think he was, and I jokingly responded that it wasn't that easy to kill a Mexican. Those people are unpredictable and they don't come from the front at you. They send someone to take care of you or gang up on you with a few of their friends, very cowardly I must say.

Needless to say, I was getting desperate to get back to America.

I had met a very nice young girl in Guadalajara Mexico during my last vacation there and she made me realize that I needed to be closer to my own kind. Before I left, her and her two other sisters organized a surprise goodbye party for me. With balloons, music and even presents. She was tall, with big dark pretty eyes, very attractive and her name was Lizet. She was quite a few years younger than me and her Mom seemed to mind, so eventually nothing came of it, just a few sort of love letters while I remained in Mauritius. She was a very warm and lovely person and we remained friends for a long time, she was like a forbidden love or maybe a soul sister.

National crew in cockpit.

National crew at Miami pool.

This was my Alcatraz paradise view from Pereybere, in front of my bungalow.

ESCAPE FROM ALCATRAZ, OR MAURITIUS. NATIONAL AIRLINES, FIFTH JOB.

So it was time to leave Mauritius, I was also glad I was leaving due to a few other reasons. I had also gotten involved with a French cutie who was vacationing with her Mom, brother and friend. They were staying at the bungalow a few feet from mine. I saw her and her friend topless at the pool and got introduced by Leti my neighbor (who evened the score because as she said she owed me one for introducing Ian to her). She was only 21 but mature and a woman in every sense. A redhead with some freckles and a real hot redhead nude all over, beautiful breasts and a pretty baby face. Her name was Rebi. She started sneaking out of her bungalow at midnight and staying with me until 5 am or so because she said she didn't want her Mom to find out. Her Mom was pretty attractive and still fairly young, in her early forties. Very well kept for her age. I think Rebi was just having a good fun time with me but her Mom fell in love with me in a kind of possessive way.

She didn't know what was going on between her daughter and I but she probably suspected. She eventually started hitting on me big time. She'd come to my apartment in her bikini and try to fondle and tongue kiss me, I really didn't want to get involved with her because I was already involved with her daughter and plus, I sensed she was maybe a little nuts. She was just to pushy, I literally had to go around the table in my patio to prevent her from trying to shove her tongue down my throat, while the rejection made her madder and more pushy.

She started stalking me and waiting for me outside my terrace. I had to literally close all windows and pretend I was sleep because she wouldn't take no for an answer, eventually I left the island but didn't tell her when. Phew, was I relieved. I did see her daughter in Paris one more time. Rebi gave me love and warmth during my last lonely days in Mauritius and I appreciated her for that. Then I made the big mistake of giving Rebi my details in San Diego and when her Mom wanted to travel to California she called me and asked me if they could visit. At first I thought her Mom must be over me by now and I thought it would be okay, but it wasn't. That night I picked them up in San Diego at the Holiday Inn, they had their luggage with them because they had checked out.

Hmmmmm! I wondered what they were up to. The Mom was happy to see me and she said she wanted to look for a hotel by the Beach, so I drove them around all day showing them the beach towns and hoping they'd like one of the beach hotels that I showed them. To my surprise, the Mom kept saying, 'Non Non, I zon't like iiit'.

So when night came and they still had no hotel they asked me if they could crash on my sailboat that I was living in. Of course I couldn't say no.

I got to admit it, I did look forward to getting it on with Rebi one more time but later I found out she had a boyfriend in Australia. I gave both of them my aft berth to sleep in and took the small berth in the front of the boat hoping they would be more comfortable. We had some wine and said goodnight because I had to get up really early for a morning flight. But not before she tried her old tricks of slipping her fingers down the back of my pants or grabbing my upper legs under the table, in front of her daughter who couldn't see anything while we had dinner and wine.

Shortly after the lights went off, I heard footsteps coming towards my bed and I thought maybe it was Rebi, but when she climbed in my bed and I felt for the hair, to my surprise guess who it was, yes her, the Mom, 'Holy Shit, what do I do now', I thought to myself. I told her to let me sleep and go back to her bed but she kept hugging me and trying to kiss me while saying, "I mizzt yu, I luv yu all zis taim". I really felt awkward and told her in a very stern voice that she had to leave or I would be going to her daughter's bed, bad mistake saying that but it worked. She looked at me with piercing eyes and got off the bed. I really thought she was going to stab me at night but she just quietly went to the settee next to my berth and said she would sleep silently there.

I could hardly sleep that night and when I woke up, there she was, rolled up like a little puppy on the settee, next to me in the salon area. I didn't know what to say and I asked them to lock the boat whenever they left. Then I secretly told Rebi what happened and that I couldn't have that anymore, she understood and said they'd leave that day. I really felt sorry for her Mom and I sort of felt obliged to Rebi, I guess she was trying to make her Mom happy.

That weekend Rebi flew out to Australia but not before calling me and asking me to please join her Mom for dinner one more time because she wanted to apologize, as friends only, and she said she would behave this time, so I accepted. I was very good friends with my long lost girlfriend so I told her the story and she said she would come with me to sort of spoil things for French Mom just in case, I thought it was a good idea so I went along with it.

We went to the Spanish Old Town and had a great dinner with some Margaritas, she was getting a little tipsy and occasionally she would slide her hand under the table and grab my leg. I wanted to laugh because the waitresses were watching this and they were having a kick of the whole show. When my girl friend got up to go to the bathroom she slid next to me and put her hands on my lap and only left when she saw my girl friend come back. It was nevertheless a good evening and I think we all, including the waitresses watching us had fun. However, when we dropped her off at her Hotel, she kissed me goodbye, hugged me with desperation, and said in my ear that she would love me always "Je te aimerai toujour". That was the last time I saw her, she did e mail me quite often and we did continue an Internet friendship for a while, that is until I made a negative comment about the excessive French strikes in France, she was pissed off at my comment and never wrote me again.

The main reason why I wanted to leave Mauritius was because my friend Ross had contacted me about the job at a new Airline in Las Vegas Nevada. They needed Captains to fly their Boeing 757s and I jumped at the opportunity. I was getting fed up with Air Mauritius due to the constant changing of Rules that applied mostly to the Foreign Pilots, changes made by the new chief pilot there. I basically escaped from Alcatraz. Well, I wasn't supposed to leave and break my contract otherwise they would have pressed charges on me.

So I decided to leave on the last midnight flight with Air France (This was after I gave plenty of notice a couple of months before and they still refused to allow me to go). I arranged for Juan the artist to drive me to the airport. I had been transporting my stuff to Frankfurt little by little so I didn't have that much to move. Nevertheless, It was kind of sad to leave because Mauritius had been good to me, I had grown very fond of it but I needed a change. I had eventually become a recluse during the last year there.

While in Mauritius, I did a lot of meditating, yoga, swimming, reading, etc. to keep myself occupied, but my heart wanted to get back to California. There was nothing holding me there anymore and I felt I was living dangerously, specially with my situation with the discreet lover I had and the death threat hint I heard from a source. Damian and Juan were both my closest friends and when Damian left I had no other surfing partner so that sucked, specially because I didn't like being by myself when exploring new distant surf breaks in case of curious sharks around.

Juan the artist was a very special person, down to earth and a very relaxed kind of guy. He was originally from Spain and had lived on the Island with his wife and kids for a few years. I was very happy to have a friend that was like a brother to me, specially when I was running out of friends towards the end. I didn't feel so secluded having Juan and his family there for me.

There was also Bilal and Chips, Ian and Leti, Jane my neighbor, Patrick and Verena, Preescy, Clement and my good Mauritian musician friend, Gislain, and of course my Rasta friend with the huge dread locks down to his waist that looked like a large baguette behind his head, Rodo Camarel who was always at Pereybere Beach ready to talk about the philosophy of life. They were all good to me. I dreaded leaving but at the same time I was excited for a new beginning back to the western civilization. And so I left.

I left my truck for Juan to use and eventually sell, my bicycle to Leti and my guitar to Juan's kid. Also my nice Kiwi surfboard that flew out of my truck I gave to Gislain. Many other house items I gave away to the cleaning lady, guardian, etc.

This must have been about the tenth time I moved in the past eight years or so, again, I was leaving a trail of bicycles, guitars and surfboards around the world, as well as girlfriends and the occasional kid. Well, only the two I knew of. I felt some sense of responsibility towards my little kid in San Diego with Nena, so that was another reason for wanting to come back. Nena and I still had some passion and love for each other whenever we saw each other but I still couldn't take her seriously. It's hard to explain, when she came to see me twice to Mauritius I was excited to see her and then when she left and I was alone at night outside looking at the stars, I felt like the loneliest man on earth, I really missed her and that's when I realized that I did love her. I wished I would have told her that.

Nena and Sebi visiting me in Mauritius, it was a beautiful time.

I was fighting it, little did I know that you cannot fight love away. I didn't want to accept her yet, I thought I would meet my ideal person sooner or later, my imaginary ideal woman was waiting for me somewhere else. What a fool I was, there is no such thing. That's why many people end up alone in the search for the ideal person that never shows up. Love is not perfect, when it's there don't refuse it because it doesn't meet your expectations or monetary aspirations as many women often do.(I fought it for a long time and ended up falling in love with her all over again years later)

I took the midnight flight with Air France to Paris sort of disguised with a Rasta hat on, unshaven and in jeans. I didn't want to be recognized for the fear of someone phoning the Chief Pilot, and simply by his orders, having the Airport Authority deny my boarding and pressing legal charges for abandoning my contract, as he had threatened to do a few months before. All worked well and I made it to Paris the next

morning. Then from there I went to Wiesbaden with my son En-riko and his Mom.

Enriko and I visiting other small towns in Germany.

I had to do the right thing so I called the Chief Pilot long distance from the Airport. I said that I had

left the Island and at first he thought I was doing a flight pattern to Paris. I explained to him that I left for good because he couldn't grant me the time off to care for my parents, kid and girlfriend. He was furious and started to cuss on the phone, I said I was sorry but that he hadn't understood my urgency to return home after I had given my ninety day notice, so I had to take the matter into my own hands. Then he said something offensive and hung up on me. My reasons given for leaving Air Mauritius were partly true, and I had tried following the proper procedure to give enough notice prior to leaving the contract. However, the chief Pilot denied me the 90 day rule and extended it to 6 months, he had also changed my contract to four yeas instead of the three that I had originally signed for. So I ended up loosing around $18,000 Dollars from my end of contract gratuity.

Not only that, every time I came up for a Command position chance, he would change the rules again and raise the required flight hours for the Foreign Pilots. For example, initially 5,000 total flight hours were required to get a chance for Captain upgrade, then he changed that to 6,000 and later when I met those he changed it again to 7,000 hours. But that only applied to the Foreign Pilots and not for the inexperienced Mauritian Pilots who were being upgraded to Captains with the 5,000 hours. Of which one third had been spent in the bunk, another third as boy pilots, (second officers who don't take off or land) and the other third in the right seat of the turbo-prop. If lucky, the remaining few hundred hours were in the right seat of the B-767.

Some guys who didn't meet the PIC (Pilot in Command) requirements to obtain their ATPL s, (Airline Transport Pilot License) actually went to Reunion Island to fly around the Island multiple times in a single engine propeller airplane to build up the required Pilot in Command hours required for the French ATPL.

I had requested time off to go to the Interview in Las Vegas and I even had to make something drastic up in order to get the time off. I told him that my girlfriend in San Diego had had a nervous breakdown and I needed to be there to take custody of our son and to take care of her. When I came back after the interview I stayed another two months before I left for good.

About two weeks after I left Mauritius, my new Chief Pilot John received a letter concerning me.

It had been generated by my ex-chief pilot Tribally who accused me of being irresponsible, unreliable and dishonest for breaking my contract with them. He also had false accusations claiming that my land lady had complained about me thrashing her apartment and not paying three months of rent.

Now, all these accusations were made up to try to get me fired from my present Employer. None of these were credible since I had a good reputation, recommendation letters and had Hong Kong Bank receipts of my rent being paid with direct deposit to my land lady in Mauritius, I even let her keep my last deposit just in case. I also paid to have the place cleaned up thoroughly. I think he had her come in and sign a blank letter when she called to inquire about me, I couldn't tell her I was leaving for fear of her telling someone and that someone telling the lying chief pilot. Anyway, that didn't affect me at all because I showed my present Chief Pilot proof of my rent being paid on time.

So you can see what kind of boss I was dealing with in Mauritius. It was believed that he was partly responsible for the downfall of a female Mauritian First Officer. She was an attractive young pilot who had upgraded from flying the Island Hopper turbo prop to flying as Junior First Officer on the Boeing 767. He had been trying to get into her panties from the time he hired her and now that he had upgraded her he pressured her even more. Even at home she was looked down upon because she had been dating a Western guy. The poor girl had so much pressure that she eventually cracked and had a nervous breakdown. The typical phrase some Captains would tell the female Pilots was " I'll give you my leg if I can have both of yours", meaning their leg, their flight sector. Usually it was meant as a joke and there were no sexual harassment charges filed because in countries like these no such thing exists.

Anyway, the way it happened was during a flight from Brusselles to Manchester. They were Deadheading as passengers with a Captain who was a friend of mine and another male First Officer, also all the Flight Attendants. When she tried to enter via the wrong line thru Customs, the Official told her to go to the non-resident line. She in return reacted by spitting in his face, just like that.

The Official called his superiors and she demanded to be arrested. She then proceeded to press charges on the whole crew, claiming they had all sexually molested her. She remained in Manchester getting various Medical tests and eventually they found out she had some kind of paranoiac nervous breakdown. At first the Company put both Pilots on suspension for a couple of weeks until they were proven innocent. When she returned to the Island, she was trying to sue the Airline because she lost her Airman Medical Certificate and her job.

I must say that I don't think she was cut up for the job because she was perhaps too feminine and vane. When she was flying, she used to put her beauty kit next to her seat in the cockpit, instead of her flight bag. In my opinion, women in a cockpit who have a bit more male hormones than the average woman do a better job as pilots. Where as the very feminine ones probably don't have it in them quite as well. In the US there are many female pilots and some of them are just as good as men, but most of them have been hired due to government pressure to hire more minorities. The same goes for men that are too feminine, you don't see them in cockpits often, maybe in the back of the cabin where most do well as Flight Attendants.

Well, I made it back to San Diego and tried to establish a friendship with Nena, we had one eventually and at first sort of kept a platonic relationship. I tried living in Vegas at first while roomating with my good old mate Ross Brightman and another guy (I had flown with Ross back in New Zealand in 96 and we had remained good mates since, I called him 007 because of his personality, his life style and his mysterious life. He had quite an interesting work history, various Aircraft type ratings for all Commercial jets except the Concorde, and had flown contracts for over 30 Airlines and Countries). That didn't last long because Ross and his buddy ended up in a physical quarrel over shit that built up as roommates. Then I ran into my old flight school buddy Gary (alias Gaza) at the Crown and Anchor, (Gary and I knew each other from National University and Flight School). He never ceased to amaze me at his ability to piss off women with things he said.

Here's an example, he was hanging out in Waikiki once at Duke's bar when the working night girls (prostitutes) started approaching him with the typical hunting lines, "What's your name, what do you do, buy me a drink, and I'm yours for a fixed price, etc". Twice he was approached in the same way and both times he told them he wasn't interested and that they should move on. Well, a third time another girl winks at him, approaches him and starts the same conversation, not to mention that she also fit the same slutty description. When they got to the "what do you do in life" lines, she told him she was an Accountant. At which Gaza responded, "get out of here, you're a fucking prostitute". She couldn't believe that he caught her at her game and made a scene accusing him of being disrespectful with the bartender. He was kicked out of the bar but was there the next day again. It was very obvious that the chick was a working girl but since he caught her at her game she decided to get even at him.

On another occasion, I was having a beer with him at the Mai Tai bar in Honolulu when two very cute girls sat next to us. They were normal professional career girls and when they told us they were studying to be Doctors, Gaza said something that the cutest one next to him took offense to. I don't think it was something offensive, it was just a sarcastic remark about Doctors and their drinking rules compared to Pilot drinking rules. The Doctoress to be got on his face but Gaza held his cool and told her he didn't need a young girl yelling in his ear at his age, and that she should back off because he didn't offend her in anyway. Miss cutie obviously wasn't used to having a guy telling her basically "down girl" but she did back off and things got back to normal. Of course a massage was out of the question by then.

I tried to intervene and make peace and it seemed to please her because in the end when they left she came over to my side and gave me a goodbye kiss. I had to rub it in and told Gaza not to ask for one and we just laughed it off after they left.

Back in Vegas Gaza and the Zimbabwean Ian, alias "General Skaffa" were flying locally there and shared an apartment, I roomated with them for a few months before I decided to move to San Diego and live on my sailboat.

Oh yeah, another dream come true, I did buy my sailboat with my saved cash from contract flying. It was a 1975 West sail 42 with a 4 foot bowsprit or overhang, a cutter with a strong full keel as part of the bullet proof fiber glass hull. It was a strong blue water ocean crossing boat and needed some tender cosmetic care. I got it for $67,000 Dollars. I was ecstatic with it and that weekend my friends Ross and Skaffa joined me to take it out for a sail. We went out the Harbor beyond Point Loma, hoisted all sails and let the breeze carry us at about 6 to 7 knots. It was such a feeling of freedom, slow and quiet melodious freedom with only the waves, wind and swells.

My West Sail 42 anchored in front of Coronado Island.

After a few hours out, as we wanted to turn back the wheel wouldn't turn, it was stuck. We couldn't figure out what the problem was so we lowered sails and just floated a couple of miles of Point Loma while trying to figure out the problem. We looked at the mechanical linkage to the steering chain and other components but nothing came of it. So we called the Coast Guard and they said to contact Vessel Assist. Then they told us to drop the anchor and wait for them for about an hour.

We were in deep water and the Depthsounder read almost 200 feet. Since we didn't want to drift further out to sea we dropped it out. All 300 feet of thick chain with a 65 pound Anchor.

I promise I'll never do that again. After an hour or so of tinkering around to find the problem I instinctively found the Auto Pilot engage switch under the start box panel, apparently thinking it was part of the latch to that door, someone pulled it and coupled the Auto Pilot. So that's what it was. I pushed it back in and voila, the wheel moved.

We celebrated with a few beers and decided to start hoisting up the Anchor and 300 pounds of chain. We also called Vessel Assist to cancel.

But now it took about another hour to finally pull up on all that weight by hand cranking the manual windlass hundreds of times while taking turns and having beers. Eventually we made it back to the dock by nightfall. Nevertheless, it was a great day out to sea. My lovely West Sail is still with me and has been restored and well taken care of. I have probably invested at least $30,000 Dollars in it since I bought it and have done most repairs and changes myself. All electronics including the Auto pilot has been replaced, as well as the standing rigging along with other safety items.

It was exciting living in Vegas but all the superficiality eventually got on my nerve so I moved back to San Diego. After I bought my sailboat I started living on it whenever I was there. Nena and Sebi would stay with me on the weekends. It was cozy inside and we had beautiful warm moments inside my floating home. Life was good, I was flying closer to home and living on the water, I also had Nena and Sebi so I was happy. But I didn't want to take it further. Nena seemed content with the open relationship we had, or at least I thought so.

Before I moved to San Diego, I had my own separate lifestyle. I still considered myself single so I occasionally dated. For about a year I went out with a very cute Kororican petite Asian Latina. BR and I occasionally saw each other a couple of times a month and she came to visit me to the boat a few times. She was a little aggressive with her New York attitude at first but she improved and then her whole attitude changed when I suggested she should wear more light bright colors instead of always black. She looked much cuter too, with her long hair and her pretty half Asian face smiling more. Eventually we drifted away due to the distance but we stayed friends for a long time. One night while we were making love in her cute cozy apartment, her yorky female dog, inspired by our lovemaking, grabbed it's toy bunny and started humping it, duplicating what it was watching, it was the funniest sight I had seen in years.

I also had a couple of not too serious dates with flight attendants who would end up in my room during an overnight somewhere. The Airline had a couple of part time strippers flying for us and they were eccentric and wild at times. On two occasions we had Flight Attendants show us their new acquired implant breasts in the cockpit. It was hard to say "no, not now honey, we're busy" so we just sort of agreed they were pretty and looked very real, sometimes they even let us feel them for better judging.

BRAZIL, RIO DE JANEIRO, AMOR DE CARNAVAL.

We still didn't have a serious relationship with Nena so I considered it an open relationship, I don't know if she agreed with me thou. Every year I would go on vacation to a new exotic destination, Venezuela, Brazil, etc. In Caracas I stayed for about two days and then could hardly wait to get out of the traffic and smog so I rode the bus across the Venezuelan Gran Sabanha, all the way to the border town of Santa Elena and then the Amazon in Brazil. On the bus I met a cool Russian dude called Roma, and later on we hooked up and explored Manaos and the jungle Amazon area. When you're backpacking in risky countries it's good to team up with someone, safety in numbers helps in some countries.

The city of Manaos was an interesting city with many beautiful Colonial buildings, it was hot, muggy and crowded too. I couldn't picture such a big city in the middle of the Amazon forest but here it was and I was in the middle of it. I took a private boat out to the Amazon River and was amazed at the difference in water color and temperature when we crossed the line demarcation from one clear water river to the other more murky one. I even stuck my hand on one side and the other hand on the other and felt the difference in water temperature, both my hands were still intact when I put them back in the boat and away from Piranha Happy Hour. Night life was great in the city, it was also a jungle with lots of young exotic Amazonian Brazilian natives that were very friendly and eager to meet strangers. The whole trip riding on buses, fast private taxis and river canoes had been a great adventure.

I returned the same way and spent a few more days at Isla Margarita off the East coast of Venezuela. However, while waiting for the Ferry at the Port, I ate a chicken sandwich and got really sick. I had food poisoning and was leaking my life fluids away for the next two days. I was really dehydrating fast even thou I kept drinking Pedialite all day. It wasn't until an older lady at the pharmacy gave me some tablets to stop the diarrhea that it all stopped. Still, I hung out at the beach and just relaxed until my energy returned in a couple of more days.

On the last day I was there I met a cute girl from Switzerland, she had deep green expressive pretty eyes and long brown hair below her shoulders, with a very attractive face and petite body. I was sitting at the beach bar and there she was by herself too. We started conversation and spent the rest of the evening talking at an open air beach café, about the philosophy of life in general, traveling experiences, etc. She was a pretty bright girl. I remember she was starting to get cold as we went for a walk so I put my arm around her and kept her warm, it was a mutual nice feeling of romance with a stranger. I didn't push it further because I knew she wanted to get home that night but she agreed to see me the next day. I couldn't tell her that I might have to leave the next day because we had established a good 'feeling' already.

I had to be in Vegas in three days for my next flight and knew I had to leave the next day in order to get there on time. So I seriously thought about reporting myself sick for work, but my responsibility and good ethics didn't allow me to. So I left it up to destiny and didn't set the alarm clock for the next morning, if I woke up on time for the ferry I would go, if not, I would stay and spend another day with Sweet Miss Swiss. That morning there was a very loud and annoying little bird singing right next to my window at 6 am, no kidding. So I took it as a sign and took the ferry back to the mainland Venezuela that morning. I didn't have anyway to notify my new friend and missed out on a romantic experience, yeah, I hate to say it but she also missed out on me. I sort of regretted being so responsible sometimes.

As my luck would have it, I didn't spend my last night in Caracas alone because when I got on the next Mercedes Benz bus back to Caracas, the bus attendant who was a sexy local girl working also part time as a flight attendant was friendly to me. She was serving drinks and snacks on the bus and while the rest of the passengers watched the movie, she would come over and talk to me. First class buses in South America are exactly what they imply, First class with fully reclining comfortable seats, food and drinks and movies on various screens. Exactly like Greyhound in the US, LOL, of course not.

Anyway, when we arrived to the Terminal, I suggested to Fedra the cute Bus attendant with the beautiful ass, attractive face and long dark curly hair to join me on my last night out in the city. She accepted and we took a taxi to drop my stuff off at a Hotel first. I told her she could stay with me in the Hotel since she lived out of town. So she called her Mom and told her she was staying with a girl friend in the city that night. All arranged, no hassles, no cat and mouse game, straight to the point. She showed me the best area of Caracas, the area were the famous Obelisk is, with lots of restaurants, café's and bars.

I had always wanted to see this part of Caracas after reading the second book of Henri Charriere, Papillion II. We had a nice dinner, a few shots of Tequilas and headed back to the Hotel. What a beautiful ass this girl had, her whole body was tight and with the voluptuous curves you find in those parts of the world. We had a terrific bout of hot sex and then in the morning another short session, a shower, a very strong coffee with breakfast and off we went in different directions. "Hasta la vista Baby", was the right term in this case.

Then the following year I went back to Brazil but this time to Rio, I had been invited by Denielle, a flight attendant friend at my Airline, her parents put me up at their friend's Junior's bungalow, or better said Penthouse, facing sideways to Hipanema Beach. It was only me and two American chicks called Melanie and hmmm, I forgot, stayed with Junior at his Mom's (she was a very interesting and generous lady) apartment. My friend Denielle's step Dad, Captain Barth was a retired Captain from Varig Airlines, he was the nicest guy I've known in years and the rest of the family were so hospitable, it was as thou I was part of their Family. They showed me and a few others of their friends around the town, clubs, café's, beaches and of course we all participated and danced at one of the Samba clubs for the World Famous Carnival de Rio de Janeiro.

Dancing in the Carnival with my costume and being part of the whole experience had been so satisfying and energizing, it had also been one of the "things to do" on the top of my list. The later part of the evening of the Carnival when we danced in front of all the International cameras and judges was the best.

It was very physically demanding because the whole thing started in the heat at around three o' clock. We kept marching while keeping up with the Samba step to the rhythm until we made it to the main avenue where we were to be graded by the International judges. The feeling of being on the air in front of all the TV cameras of different countries was exhilarating. All of a sudden I was fully energized all over again from the experience. That's where we all were supposed to show our best smiles while dancing at the same rhythm and timing. That lasted another eternal sixty minutes or so. Then once we cleared the area we could undress and dump the heavy uncomfortable costumes we wore. Later I found out that my little photo camera had fallen out of my boot as I was stomping around, and those were the only pictures I had taken from the whole carnival.

There I met Mini, she was also South American. Hot little tamale, pretty little body with a pretty face and long dyed blondish hair, man, and what a nice round butt she had. We had a passionate affair for about a week and a half and traveled together to Isla Grande. It was like falling in love-lust again, I really dug her. She could make me laugh so hard and we could just talk about anything, even play chess. One night while on the bus back to Rio we started kissing passionately and didn't stop for what I think was 30 minutes or so. There was only one passenger a couple of seats away so we pretty much had the whole bus to ourselves.

She left back to Atlanta were she lived about five days before me, so me and another Israeli guy who was the Family's friend hit the Town in Rio almost every night. We went to a huge, I mean humongous club on Copa Cabana Blvd called HELP. This place had the prettiest hottest girls in the whole city. It seemed that quite a few of them were either free lancing as night social workers, or just plainly out there to have fun or meet a foreign guy to take them out anywhere.

We also went to a very pretty beach town called Buzios just two hours north of the City. Sort of a vacation haven for cute chicks from Ar-

Janine hitting on Brazilian booty at Buzios.

gentina and Chile, man, that place was crawling with them. The Israeli guy Janine was having a ball every night, I on the other hand was trying to recover from a bad cold or bronchitis I had picked up from Mini. We shared a room and one night as I was trying to sleep and recover, Janine and a British chick he picked up, walked in for a quick sex session, they kept the light off but I could hear all the slurping and deep breathing that was going on even with my ear plugs on, so I just pretended to be sleep. I still had a lot of fun and met a few other cute chicks.

I missed my Standby flight twice with Delta Airlines trying to get back to the States because all the flights were full and Capt. Barth picked me back up from the Airport every time. The nicest guy, really.

Then when I finally was able to leave Brazil for Atlanta Georgia, I visited Mini near Atlanta where she lived. I met her family and thought they were very nice people. I continued to visit her once a month but eventually the flame died I think due to her materialistic way of thinking. She seemed to think that a girl was like a little female bird that had to accept only the strongest male bird to build her the fanciest and biggest nest possible. I was disappointed because I hadn't noticed her materialistic interests before. I noticed her loss of interest after I told her that I was probably the lowest paid Airline Captain in the US. She must have thought I was in the $300,000 a year range like some very senior Career guys from other Major Airlines.

I saw the disappointed look in her face when I told her I was still in the five figure number because I wasn't that senior. I was actually close to the six figure but I told her I was in the 60,000 range maybe to test her, I'm not sure anymore. Her attitude changed right after that information was transferred to her mind. It wasn't meant to be more than a passionate vacation affair anyway and I knew it. (I needed a more traditional and down to Earth woman and besides, it was written in the stars that Nena would enter my life again, but I didn't know it at the time.) We had had a very lovely romantic time in Brazil and were never able to duplicate the feelings we had when I came to see her to Atlanta. It had been an intensive, AMOR DE CARNAVAL, passionate and romantic adventure but now it was time to move on.

The last time I saw her was in Miami when we met up there during one of my lay-overs. It turned out pretty chaotic and we ended up fighting and arguing the last night. She wasn't herself and there was no more passion or interest from either one of us, I made love to her just for the sport of it because there was no mutual feeling anymore. I think I had already made up my mind that this was to be the last time we met. So the next afternoon I called her a taxi and sent her back to the Airport so I could get some sleep before my night flight. I remember clearly her big greenish eyes looking at me from the taxi as I put my hand around her small chin, leaned over and gave her a last warm kiss in her sexy lips as I said, "Hasta Luego" meaning, "Until then", but what I really meant was, "until maybe never". Then I went back to my room and took a long nap.

I'm sure every guy and girl on the planet has had experiences like these. Then disappointment sets in, depression, resentment, hate, suicidal tendencies, etc. Why? We should just see it as another learning experience and move on. The trick is not to get too attached. To enjoy the moments of love and bliss and to be aware that it's most likely not going to last forever. Even the happiest couples end up divorcing years later. The human negative qualities sometimes control some people more than others and if we are aware of that, then we won't be so disappointed or hurt. Just don't expect anything and don't try to change a person or expect him or her to change.

In other words, don't expect or demand and you won't be as disappointed. Don't get too emotionally attached and you won't be too unhappy when you get dumped. And finally, don't give all of your love away or you won't have anything for yourself when you do end up by yourself again. Also, always love yourself more than others and don't disregard your health, psyche, or your needs in order to please others more than yourself. I know it sounds selfish but it's a jungle out there and there's always carnivores out there that are willing to devour you if you allow them.

However, don't forget to be honest, be yourself and listen to your inner voice or intuition when you receive warning signs about someone. Oh yeah, and don't forget to have fun and always use protection, you know what I mean.

I've had many good and bad experiences but I see them all as good experiences. Mainly because the not so good ones, taught me a lesson and made me more intuitive with reading or sensing people's true colors.

Some guys just want to use women for sex or money as much as women wanting to use men to take them traveling, buy them fancy gifts or maybe for sex too. It should be a give and give situation to make it fair, an exchange for good love, good sex, good fun and healthy company. It's up to each person to allow how much they're willing to let themselves be run over or used by someone because they think they need their love, or good sex. There are no victims in this arena, there are only volunteers who willingly enter to play with fire knowing they'll end up getting burnt.

Some women just wanna take the roll of cute expensive angora cats, they just wanna lay around and look pretty, enjoy what's offered to them and not give anything in return, if I want an angora cat I'll get a bloody angora cat, they cost less to support and they don't talk back.

I also dated a couple of Flight Attendants with my previous Airline but I couldn't take them seriously.

I can't say I know women or understand them after all the experiences I've had, but I know one thing, "do not try to understand them, just listen to them and pretend to agree, or disagree".

Respect them and don't play with their feelings intentionally, appreciate them and cherish their love when that's all they give you, and love them back if you can.

Picture a pussy cat coming to you for petting, spoiling, feeding, etc. Then, (usually when your bank account is deflating and your wallet is getting lighter) finally after you've figured out how to make it purr, they look you in the eye with such love and wish you wouldn't stop, and the minute you stop they turn around and claw your or bite you. Then they suddenly run away to look for another master who treats them better, sometimes they even return to you much later if they couldn't find someone to feed them more or make them Purr longer, sound familiar?

I am grateful for all the love experiences I've had with women in my life and wouldn't regret anything or want to change things the way they happened, well except when I had to leave early at the wrong moment because of other responsibilities. So I would like to thank all the beautiful women in my life for giving me their Love, attention, spoiling, gifts, affection and passionate moments, and I hope they've all found what they were looking for.

Anyway, all these experiences made me realize that what I had in Nena was something much more fulfilling, she loved me for who I was, simply me, the way I was. Every other girl I'd met had more issues than her and were more materialistic. I started to appreciate her, and to love her more. We fell in love again and started seeing each other more regularly. Plus, she was still beautiful and now I was noticing her inner beauty as well.

Unfortunately, National Airlines, the airline I flew for went out of business. I was out of a job again and welcomed to the meager life of unemployed status. It was all good while it lasted, I had been a Captain on the Boeing 757 for about three years and had really enjoyed the flying we had. From Las Vegas to most Major cities like New York, Miami, Dallas, San Francisco, Seattle, Washington and Los Angeles. All good things come to an end sooner or later.

I was unemployed for about four months and was getting ready to cast off on my boat down to Baja California Mexico, to live off fish and lobster while on unemployment benefits. But my now teenage son Enriko from Germany was living with me and I had to act responsible, so I waited until I got hired by a Japanese Company.

SAILING ACROSS THE PACIFIC TO HAWAII IN THE SUMMER OF 2001.

I got invited to join as crew on a 46 Hunter sailboat for a crossing from San Diego to Honolulu while I was still at National Airlines. That was the opportunity I had been waiting for to get my hands on ocean crossing practices. Although I had the book knowledge, I still wanted to do a crossing on someone else's boat before I would do it on my own boat. Montree (Mon) the owner who was also my neighbor at Marina Cortez in San Diego, Popeye (Harry) and myself were the original crew members, however two days before departure Popeye invited his step son. He was a racer and fisherman so they thought his expertise might help. There were many warning bells that rang before we cast off but I still took the chance to do the trip.

I knew that we didn't have a survival raft (just a dinghy inflatable) but we did have an EPIRB (Emergency Position Indicator Radio Beacon) and the boat was fairly new. Although not a true traditional blue water sailboat in my opinion it did look pretty at the dock. Out to sea it was a different story, it's fin bulb keel and long spade rudder were not that effective at counter acting the crossing seas that started building up and I started getting sick in my stomach for the first two days.

In addition to that, we didn't calculate the right amount of food because we appeared to be on a tight budget. All I wanted was to have good coffee in the mornings but to my surprise we were only supplied with cheap Vons instant coffee, gag, how could they do this to me. Every morning at least one cup of coffee would be ritually offered to Poseidon the Ocean God, all over the cockpit, which used to piss off Montree. It was just the swaying and fish-tailing motion of the boat caused by the crossing seas.

We did catch a few big Mahis thanks to Tim the step son's fishing expertise and that evening we celebrated a great grilled fish dinner with sundowners. However, in the middle of the night my fish managed to escape out of my stomach when I started getting sick with the increasing seas. It was my first ocean crossing and I didn't have my sea legs yet so I was really miserable the first two days. I couldn't even go down below so I stayed in the cockpit day and night rolled up like a dog in my sleeping bag. Eventually my body and mind adjusted to the conditions and I started enjoying the trip.

From the very beginning we had no proper organization or crew synergy. I felt I was being left out of the loop and wasn't taken seriously to do my own night watches. Whenever I would ask Montree if I could help he would answer, "No, it's okay, we got it." I had been originally invited for my weather and navigation expertise but it seemed like now he was letting Tim and Popeye handle everything. Although Tim had never done a crossing he was starting to act like he was in charge and always trying to go fast as thou we were racing, which is what he was used to in smaller sailboats. Bear in mind I had been sailing for nine years, had navigation and weather knowledge but Mon seemed to put all his trust on Popeye and Tim. Not utilizing all your resources is one common mistake many people do during these situations.

Popeye and Mon sort of let him do as he pleased and that worried me. Especially when jibing, he wasn't centering the boom first so the boom would come across with a large slam over to the other side. (The boom is the horizontal mast were the bottom of the sail attaches to). I knew that sooner or later we were going to get in trouble and I tried to convey my message to the owner. Well, eventually we broke the boom vang (which holds to the bottom of the mast and one third down from the boom) when we encountered the squall that caught us with our pants down.

At first Mon didn't seem that interested so I just sort of watched from the observers point of view.

Sure enough trouble was just around the corner. We had been motoring with full sails up because of very light winds all day and when night approached nobody thought about reducing sail (It is recommended to reduce sail by night fall just in case of approaching squalls that can't be seen). It was Popeye's and my watch early one night (we had two hour watches each, two men together for four hours) while we were all looking at the computer screen for the closest Low Pressure

Systems that were South of our position, Popeye stepped down to the toilet while no one else remained in the cockpit.

All of a sudden the boat's speed started increasing and it's heeling angle suddenly increased to almost horizontal levels. It was almost a knockdown and Popeye and I were the first ones out to the cockpit, literally crawling sideways due to the angle the boat was being pushed on down by the increasing gusts generated by a squall that hit us unprepared. Popeye grabbed the wheel and disconnected the Auto Pilot (it probably disconnected itself) while I eased out the mainsheet which in turn released the pressure of the wind on the mainsail and the boom and allowed the boat to right itself up again. (It depowers the main sail while spoiling the wind out of the sail).

Now the seas were churning and the wind was all over the place caused by the squall with it's wind gusts and direction changes. Popeye couldn't see the wind direction in the pitch black night (the lights to the instruments and compass hadn't been turned on yet) and the boat accidentally jibed itself three times.

We must have gone in circles a few times until I suggested to Harry to let me try (I heard him ask Tim to take over but he refused). I had better night vision and I fully understand the qualities and errors of the compass so I took control of the wheel. I pointed the bow or nose of the boat into the wind as best as I could while Popeye and Mon crawled up to fight the Genoa (front sail) that by now had torn itself loose from it's sheet and almost knocked them overboard.

Tim wouldn't go forward or take the wheel, he just barked orders from the safety of the cockpit that were ignored because he really wasn't in charge. That's when the true colors of people show themselves, during critical moments. After about thirty minutes of thrill and adrenalin rush we had the boat under control. We all got a cold beer and tried to relax and talk about what we had just experienced.

I proved myself that I could hold a course as good as anyone else in adverse conditions and now Mon allowed me to steer the boat more often. I suggested we have a meeting and expressed my concerns about Tim's abuse of the boat and Popeye's disregard for his actions.

Also about the lack of proper crew responsibilities and duties. It was obvious that it was Tim's fault for trying to race this boat across the Pacific with full sails up and the motor running all night with squalls around us. But it was also Mon and Popeye's responsibilities for allowing him to do as he pleased with the boat. Tim reacted offended and said he wouldn't touch the boat anymore, (great, that's what I wanted to hear). Now I was included in the loop and was taken more seriously.

We were all tired and sleepy all day from staying up every night for a few hours each and sleeping was difficult with the boat's motion and noises down below. That increased our fatigue levels and could affect our decision making process. We made the best of it and when we started running out of real food after 10 days or so we tried to improvise. I could not believe that we had left with such little food. I had been to Vons with Mon the night before our departure and had tried to buy extra stuff but he had reassured me that he already had enough food on the boat. Fortunately Tim's fishing expertise kept us from near starvation (or cannibalism, yuk) and provided us with fresh fish and sushi for most of the trip. It was both our first ocean crossing so we didn't exactly know how much food to take for the trip. I wanted to take more than necessary and Montree the least amount possible, it's usually better to err on the safe side and take 30% more than necessary but in this case it was the opposite.

About halfway down the trip or around the 1,200 mile point I decided to celebrate and jump in the ocean. The weather had warmed up and the water had this beautiful deep blue color to it. It had been calm for the past two days and as we let the boat sail at around 4 knots, I jumped in the Great Pacific Ocean attached by my safety harness, just in case. On this boat it was easy because we could just walk to the water level from the transom. However, the thought of a great white shark lurking underneath us terrified me and I could almost hear the theme song from the movie Jaws.

I only lasted about one minute at the time before I started crawling and walking on water to get the hell out of it from the panic of the Jaws scenario going thru my head. After that I would take my baths in the ocean every day. I would soap myself while on the transom and then submerge myself and get sort of towed behind by the safety line. On one occasion my shorts left me and only stopped at my ankles when I bent my knees up to avoid loosing them. Jumping in the ocean was also a highlight of the sailing trip.

By know we had been eating fish and rice every evening and when we started eating that for breakfast too I couldn't do it anymore. The typical phrase was, "Not lice (rice) again!" while holding our hands next to our eyes while squinting them. So I decided to improvise and invent a new breakfast on the menu. We did have lots of peanut butter and rice so I mixed it one morning and started trying to down it but it was almost impossible because it was so dry. I felt like a dog eating a chewing gum and the gases from the mixture gave me a bad case of gastritis. I burped so much and couldn't eat anymore while the rest of the crew laughed at me. I started laughing too but I was chocking at the same time so it wasn't that funny anymore. We felt like we were turning Japanese, fish and rice again and again, but it kept us full and when we spotted the Island of Molokai one morning after the eighteenth day, we all hooted out in joy. It was such a beautiful feeling to see land again, an exciting urge to get to land and walk normal again.

Mon had been saving an iced up bottle of very good tequila for the occasion so we popped it open. That was excellent Tequila and it made up for the shitty Vons coffee we got. From morning to night we sipped slowly until we started entering via the Molokai Channel. That was the highlight of the trip, surfing down 15 to 20 foot swells on a double reefed main sail and the motor running. At first, neither Popeye or Tim wanted to steer in the channel, they had a misunderstanding and Tim wasn't cooperating. So Mon and then I started steering it into the Channel. It's a very unpredictable and treacherous channel and we knew it. Then after Popeye was calm he came back up and took over.

By this time we were all happy on Tequila so we enjoyed our last day at sea. It was such a joy to go around the Diamond Head bend and sail across Waikiki towards the Ala Wai Channel. Friends of Popeye were waiting for us and as we docked at the Yacht Club some people started buying us jugs of Rum and Coke, Bottle of Champagne, etc. It was such a nice feeling to be back on firm ground but it took us a couple of days to adjust to our land legs, we were swaying to and fro every where we walked even when we weren't drunk. It had been a great experience and I was now sure I wasn't going to trade my boat in for a motor home, I knew now that I still loved the sea and was going to sail my own boat to Hawaii soon.

Pacific Ocean crossing on tequila, rough day at sea.

Boris and I with pirate flag across the Pacific.

MY SECOND CROSSING TO HAWAII ON TEQUILA, MY WESTSAIL 42 IN AUGUST 2004.

While in Honolulu I joined the waiting list for a permanent slip at the Ala Wai Marina, they had told me it could take up to five years but it only took two years. By then my boat was ready and I planned my crossing. This time I equipped it and planned the trip myself. On this voyage I would be not only the owner, but the designated Skipper as well. My old friend from Frankfurt, Boris the Menace was ready to cast away at my command, (a few years back while we were having some beers in Wiesbaden Germany we made a pact that we would sail my boat to Hawaii in five years from then, we had a contract written and signed on a beer tab so it was official according to us).

I not only wanted 69 year old Harry (Popeye) to come along because he was a good crew member but also because of his mechanical expertise. He had crossed to Hawaii solo twice on his 30 foot Catalina sailboat besides the crossing on Montree's boat so I offered to pay him his ticket back and take up all his other expenses. Harry was a cool guy and was a fun person to sail with (unless he was grumpy). Boris flew over after my boat was ready and was all stoked about this trip.

I had replaced a new Auto Pilot, Radar, GPS, standing rigging, bottom paint, Viking 6 man Life raft, EPIRB with GPS and spent over one thousand dollars (in addition to $20,000 for all the other stuff) on the 85 hp Perkins diesel engine. However, as is to be expected things break down and schedules cannot be kept as wished.

My slip in San Diego had to be vacated within that week so we had to try to fix all the little things as soon as possible. This time I made sure that we wouldn't run out of food and I did buy very good gourmet coffee for the trip (real Gourmet Coffee this time, I must admit that after the trip on Montree's boat, he became a true believer of good coffee and now buys only 100% Kona Coffee). Boris went to Vons one last time the morning before our departure and showed up at the docks with bags full of fruit. Melons, mangoes, and much more of what we already had.

I told him there wasn't anymore room in the icebox and warned him that most of this stuff would end up rotten and dumped in the ocean. And in fact that's exactly what happened, a few days into the trip we were leaving trails of rotten melons behind our wake. I just laughed and reminded Boris of my final words at the dock. We also had boxes and crates with drinks, beer, wine, vodka, rum, tequila, etc. Oh yeah, lots of water too. We wouldn't go thirsty or hungry on my trip, I would make sure of that.

We cast off one afternoon, with our good neighbors at the dock waving us goodbye. Full of food, beer, 200 gallons of fresh water and 200 gallons of diesel. My lovely Tequila West sail 42 purred like a kitten out of the harbor until we shut off the engine and started sailing into the Channel of the San Diego Harbor. Now, some sailors seem to think West Sails are slow so they called them Wet Snails, but that applied maybe mostly to the 32 footers. My 42 had all sails up including the staysail, loaded with liquids and supplies and was doing almost 8 knots right past Point Loma, we were passing other lighter displacement sail boats, so I can prove that the 42s are faster than other boats.

Boris had never crossed an ocean but he did have some local experience in Europe, he also had a sailors license. We had been friends for many years and he was a fun guy to hang out with. Harry and him also got along great so we had a pretty good crew synergy established. We planned the trip for the most part using guidelines that I had read from expert skippers, and good Crew Resource Management that I knew from my Aviation Field so things went by fairly smoothly. I don't want to imply that my previous trip sucked, I'm just saying that it was a great experience because I learned how to improve things during this trip, what not to do, and what to do on my own ocean crossing. We also had a good time with the guys during Mon's crossing.

So on my crossing I applied things that I learned and left out things I didn't like from the other trip.

I made it clear from the start that I would be in charge and Harry also agreed with my plan of action and command decisions. We all had a say but the final word would be left to me since I was the owner and Skipper.

During the trip thou, Boris seemed to take Harry's side sometimes so after reminding him about what we all had agreed to, he seemed to understand and accept the fact that my word and decisions would be considered first. On one occasion Boris and I had a little bit of a confrontation after he started complaining about my boat being un-prepared because the steering wheel was cracking around some parts. I told him that if he wanted to call his Mommy it would be too late and that pissed him off. Also the fact that I made strict rules about their drinking habits due to the cockpit being a mess with their beer cans all over. The first three days we had good weather and we just partied all along. But after the seas started to build and I needed them to remain sober I imposed a no drinking rule after certain time at night.

So they started calling me Captain Blyhe and started hinting that mutiny might arise if they couldn't drink.

They were joking but I also took it as a sign of discontent because they weren't happy with that rule I had made. After Boris and I had a man to man talk, things got back to normal. That kind of helped because we both let out what was bothering us and then we had a cold beer and said cheers to the trip once again. On another occasion Boris the Speedo Man wanted to get some sun by the stern of the boat, with-out clipping his harness on for safety as we had all agreed on as part of the rules. I saw a squall approaching us and thought I would let him wake up to a gust of air, churning seas and loads of rain on him. He crawled back into the cockpit sort of terrified and I just reminded him of the importance of clipping on the safety harness at all times. I think he learned his lesson.

Our names during the trip became, for myself Capt. Blyhe. Boris became Sir Boris the Horrible (also, Galley Bitch) and Harry was Pop-eye.

We had a lot of fun on this trip because we had lots of good mu-sic, musical instruments and games so we all sang along, played guitar or the bongos. Almost every late afternoon, Galley Bitch, Boris's new name, would pop his head out of the galley and take our orders. (Mon-tree did that too, that was pretty cool of these guys to try to improve our morale). We tested him and asked him for complicated drinks,

Tequila sunrise, Margaritas, Martinis, etc. Incredibly, he would create a generic form of the drinks we asked for. For example, for the margarita he would use lemon Gatorade, for the Martinis I don't remember how he made them but Galley Bitch improvised.

The only emergency we had was when Harry and Boris ran out of their beer two days short of arrival. I was hiding one last six pack of my favorite Pacifico Beer under my berth just in case they would empty my beer too, but I did share one last beer with them the day we spotted land.

I had a three liter bottle of the best Tequila El Fogonero you can only get in the heartland of Mexico, and I had that iced up for the occasion. Everything had gone mostly smoothly and only once did we get off course when the boat jibed gently in the middle of the night.

It was Harry's night watch once and he fell sleep with beer and cigarette in hand. I heard from below an unusual bang, any sound from above multiplies itself times ten down below so it sounded kind of loud. I popped my head out like a gopher in the prairie and asked Harry if everything was okay.

He seemed to be awake and he said, "yeah, no problemo". Something didn't look right so I looked around at the rig and noticed the boom on the opposite side of where it should have been. I asked Harry what our heading was and he responded, "What the... we're headed North, how did that happen".

I knew what happened, the wind changed due to a squall and only pushed the boom gently to the other side because we had attached a makeshift boom brake to protect from an accidental jibe.

We got back on course eventually but I couldn't sleep more than 30 minutes at a time. Any sound would wake me up and I'd pop my head out the hatch again over and over.

We did encounter high seas for a few days, well if you want to call 15 to 20 foot seas high.

We didn't catch any fish on this trip but we had plenty of them in comfortable little tin cans from which they couldn't escape. Also, lots of pasta, eggs, bread, pancake mix, fruits and vegetables, soups, cereals and lots of healthy snacks. And we had real gourmet coffee every morning (listen to this Montree), without spilling a cup at all. The older style boats like mine have a full keel and a huge rudder so that makes them very stable in heavy seas. My West Sail just cut thru the seas like a knife thru butter and held a steady course most of the time. The trade winds are generally pretty constant after you reach a certain point into the trip and it wasn't often when we had to reconfigure the sails for wind changes.

I had initially plotted a Rhumb line with a course of around 248 degrees magnetic towards the Island of Oahu. The idea was to stay close to this course line if the wind permitted. With sailboats you can't really go in a straight line when the wind is coming from your desired direction of travel so you have to Tack or zig zag back and forth within 45 (some boats manage close to 30) degrees left and right of your desired course, unless you have the wind on your aft quarter or dead aft. Half way to Hawaii you get the trade winds at a quarter aft angle from you boat, first from the right aft quarter and then from the left as you approach lower latitudes closer to 20 degrees North. We didn't have to go very far from our desired course because we had the winds at our favor most of the time and even when approaching our destination we pretty much went straight into the channel with only two tack changes.

Just as in the previous trip half way across, I dipped myself into the beautiful deep blue Pacific Ocean. Except this time it was a little more difficult because my boat didn't have a low transom or steps to the water. So I had to hang a foldable stair by the starboard side (right side) and step down to be towed and submerged while attached to my life tether. I really loved doing this even thou I had the thought of the brothers in the gray suit possibly lurking somewhere near us. Fortunately, I finished the trip with the same two legs and two arms and everything else attached to me.

We crossed around 2,400 Nautical miles in 18 days and generally averaged about 5.5 knots an hour. Sometimes it was so calm we had to motor for an entire day looking for the wind. I plotted my entry into the channel with the minimum tacks possible and we also surfed our way into the Molokai Channel on 15 to 20 foot swells. This was the most exciting part of the whole trip. It was almost midnight when we arrived but this time we knew where the entrance to the channel was. Harry had hit the 'three sisters' (three rocks on right side of the channel) on his first trip and was very wary about them so he now called them "the three bitches".

This time there was no reception at the Yacht Club, so we headed to the transient dock to clear in but since it was midnight no one was around. A Custom Official told us to tie up to the concrete dock next to the Harbor Pub in front of the Ilikai Hotel. I guess he thought we looked like terrorists because we were all almost full bearded, very tanned and were also flying a pirate flag besides the required flags. That was perfect because as soon as we tied up we staggered to the Pub for a huge hamburger and beers. My friend Montree came out to help us on his dinghy.

During this trip we did break a few little things, metal attachments to the boom called boom buckets, the auto pilots and alternator problems. Three days into the trip we almost had to turn around because we couldn't start the engine due to dead batteries. We hadn't noticed that the alternator fuse had burnt due to a reverse current surge. When we tried to start the engine so we could charge the batteries it wouldn't start.

Fortunately I had bought at the Auto shop store a compact battery charging box and that saved the trip. Then when the seas started building up after the fourth day, the new Auto Pilot started heating up and disconnecting. I had replaced the Auto Pilot with a new one but my mistake had been leaving the old Drive unit on. That was the problem, it was acting up and we couldn't rely on it with building seas. The second Auto Pilot was a pedestal wheel mounted one (Autohelm 3000) and only worked reliably in lighter seas and in proper trim (three days before arrival, the belt popped leaving us without any Auto Pilot at all). So we did a lot of hand steering even at night. That was tiring especially for Popeye and Boris. I was used to observing dim lighted instruments all night from red eye flights but the other guys weren't. We did hand steer at least 40% of the trip and were getting really tired but tried to keep a good crew atmosphere going. Eventually I learned to trim the boat by adjusting sails to keep it trim and at an angle to the wind. Nevertheless, we still had to tend to the wheel often.

I really loved being out there alone at night steering, or just sitting there watching the auto pilot steer itself. Smelling the seas, observing the bright sea life passing by the boat and observing the stars and almost full moon. One night a very loud noise that sounded like we hit a log or flotsam woke me up, I really thought it was something serious but it was only a floating empty bottle of wine that some other boat ahead of us probably pitched overboard. Imagine how it sounds when you really hit a submerged container for example.

Sometimes I even heard sounds coming from the sky, strange sounds that were sort of a mixture of music and voices from far away. It could have been radio waves picked up and bounced off to earth or sea by the ionosphere. Out to sea your senses get really keen so you pick up sounds easier. Oh yeah, we also had flying fish and had company of a beautiful sword fish that had been trailing behind us waiting for food or fish remains to be thrown overboard. It's colors would shift from blue to green depending on how close to us he was, just like a hungry doggy waiting for crumbs off the table.

We really had to conserve water since we only had 200 gallons, so we used salt water to wash dishes and only rinsed ourselves with fresh water after showering with bucketfuls of ocean water. I washed my laundry by tying it to a line that I then threw overboard to trail behind the boat and voila', when I pulled it back in and let it dry, it actually smelled good.

200 gallons of diesel usually carry my boat for close to 1,200 miles on motor only so we arrived with our tanks around one third full, or 70 gallons remaining. We also had lots of food remaining in cans, soups and pasta. Interestingly enough I broke more gear while day sailing in Hawaii than crossing the Pacific. The Ocean around the Islands is basically open Ocean within a couple of miles off shore and because of the Channels between both Islands, gusts and short choppy waves are generated often (venturi effect). So a week after I arrived, I tore up the mainsail, ripped to shreds a staysail and almost tore off the pulpit bow roller while anchored in Waikiki. Maintenance in hot climates like Hawaii, such as bottom cleaning, corrosion prevention and wood varnishing is required more often than in other cooler places. As some old sea dog had once told me, that anything that Flies, Floats or Fondles (f....), is cheaper to rent, I agree with that theory except when you justify the expense of a boat by living in it, or sailing it around the world.

Also, boats are probably cheaper to maintain than a high maintenance demanding attractive woman. At least a boat won't leave you for another wealthier owner, and it won't talk back when you just want to go out and ride it with the wind.

I almost sold my dear TEQUILA but pulled out of the deal after pondering over it for a couple of nights. It was so true what another old salty sea dog had told me, that it's easier to get rid of a girlfriend than a boat. So I decided to keep my West sail 42 and gave my girlfriend away instead, NO, just kidding there, I kept it and have been restoring it as best as I can. Only when I'm ready for my circumnavigation in a couple of years I might trade it in for a 50-54 footer large enough to accommodate my family with three kids. So that's what I did this year, restored the wood, painted the decks professionally and restored the interior. She looks beautiful now, just like the same old girlfriend but with a nice pair of new silicone tits. I also obtained my Master Sea Captain Certificate thru Maritime Institute last summer.

NIHONGO, JAPAN, JOSEI FROM TOKYO.

Well now I was about to fly the long awaited Jumbo, the Big Mama in the skies. It was February 2003 when I started this new gig. I had to put up with the longest training in the world, seven months in Tokyo. The J's treated us as Ab Initio pilots so they insisted on us going thru their detailed flight training into the Boeing 747, I call it Samurai Flight Training. It can be very confusing and frustrating if you don't understand their culture and their different way of thinking. For example, in the western way of training, we get positive reinforcement from our Instructors, such as pointing out the majority of good things we did and leaving the bad thing we did at the end and commenting how we could improve the next time.

In the Asian way, it's the other way around. The Instructor will tell you only the bad thing you did, even if it was something unrelated to flying the Simulator, and he'll dramatize it and point out how dangerous it is if you don't do a Radio check properly on the ground. Where as he'll probably ignore a more important item that could develop into a real problem while flying if he favors you. Also, they generally have the philosophy of negative criticism, it's based on their militaristic training where they use to actually smack their cadets in the head. They don't do that with us because they know from past experiences from training the first foreign pilots that they could get smacked back.

We usually get a partner who has a different background of flying and more or less experience than the other. Then they hold one guy back, making him feel like he really sucks, so that he doesn't advance much more than the least experienced one. (Sort of like mowing the grass down to the same level and then letting it grow all at the same time). Then they disregard basically most of the real mistakes from their favorite guy. It's frustrating for the experienced guys because it starts to reach your psyche, making you feel like you really suck.

It happened sometimes during my Simulator training where I would get scenarios that were much heavier or difficult than my partner's. For example, on one session we were practicing wind shear (strong vertical winds) on final approach followed by a Missed Approach to a safe altitude and when it was my turn, my J Instructor gave me an almost unrecoverable one that almost flew us into the ground, but I recovered. Then after a missed approach with one engine failed, he gave me a Runaway Stabilizer (which is when the aircraft controls along the pitch axis get very heavy and have a tendency to fly itself into the ground due to the tail stabilizer being inoperative). Now, that wasn't part of the training syllabus and a very difficult emergency, but I didn't' crash. I instructed my partner Johnny to hold back the pressure with both hands on the control column while I held the wings level, then once we had it under control I came around and landed without crashing while I could hear the Instructor snickering behind me. Once I landed, I turned around and said to him in a serene voice, "You were trying to kill me weren't you, well it's not that easy, is it?". He just grinned in an embarrassed way.

A few guys walked out of training because they didn't understand what was going on and they took it personal. At first, I almost took it personal and almost quit half way thru but after I vented out I started seeing it as a game. Although, it was becoming kind of personal because it was very obvious that they were trying to harass me more to adjust my character or attitude to a more ass kissing one. But I've always come thru with a good performance and a good attitude without having to bend more than 13.9 degrees. My theory is that, "What doesn't kill me or destroy me, only makes me stronger", and I proved that to the Js.

It took a lot of patience, self control and humbleness to put up with what we had to endure. We were constantly being compared to a 300 hour Japanese Co-pilot, and had to listen to their silly remarks such as one made by one particular frustrated Instructor. "Why you not know that, a Japanese copilot know". Well, I couldn't remain quiet for long and I replied to the Instructor, "yeah, but maybe a J co pilot can't fly", OOHHH, long silence after that one. That's probably why they were picking on me after that.

So it was really a game we had to play, a Kabuki we had to act along to with a good attitude. Fortunately my Simulator partner "Johny be good" talked me into staying. Johny was a lucky guy because the J's liked him, first of all he was blonde, played the Kabuki too well and bended much more than my preferred 13.9 degrees (well past the red arc on the butt kissing instrument dial) . That was something I couldn't do. As I told Johny my theory about the 13.9 degree bow being my maximum he just laughed. According to me, more than that would be ass kissing and it probably wouldn't get respect from them. It was difficult to adjust to the negative reinforcement kind of training from some of the local Instructors and sometimes it was even comical.

It wasn't comical when I was being picked on for insignificant mistakes while Johny was let off the hook with other mistakes. Their typical debriefing was, "Johny okay maybe okay,, Horta san, eto, not so gut, many mistakes", but they wouldn't look me in the eye when they said that. Other times they would compare us and say things to me like," why you not have notepad like Johny, why you not have pen like Johny, why you not this- why you not that," I just laughed it off to myself and told Johny that no matter what I did or said they'd still find something. I told him that the next thing I expected to hear from them would be, "why you not have blonde hair like Johny", so I thought that maybe if I would dye my hair blonde they might like me better. We just rolled in laughter over a few beers there after and restored our morale once again.

Later during the In Flight Training, Johny got the no-respect treatment. His first J Instructor suggested Johny wore his pants too low on his hip, so he approached him and lifted his pants by his belt nearly giving him a wedgy, (because they are used to carrying their pants belt line up above their navels like Charlie Chaplin) then he removed his dark shades off his face and told him he didn't need them in the terminal, then he adjusted his tie like you would with a little kid. Johny was insulted and I just had to laugh because I thought it was funny. Of course I had to rub it in and remind him of my 13.9 degree theory. They wouldn't do that to me, I'll tell you that.

Only on one occasion in the Simulator, a new instructor slapped tapped me in the arm while I was flying, after repeatedly asking me to describe something technical while on a Precision Approach. I was manually flying the approach and trying to configure and slow the airplane at the same time while this dude was distracting me and then hitting my arm, so I turned around to look at him without letting go off the controls, I looked at him with a cold silent look for about two seconds, then I said, "I'll tell you when we land", followed by, "Landing Checklist", to Johnny. My silent cold look told him everything and he remained silent the rest of the session. I guess he expected me to say, "beat me some more master", (my silent cold stare meant, you do that again and I'll push your nose into your brain bro"). When I looked back to my instruments, I was still right on the Glide slope and the Localizer (the vertical and lateral precise track to the runway).

Sometimes when I felt I was getting steamed up by them pushing my buttons too much, I would diffuse it by telling Johny, "I think I'll take door number two Johny", which meant that door number one offered me a job flying the Jumbo, with a descent salary, living in Hawaii, etc. Where as door number two, meant I would be free, sailing to the South Pacific on my sailboat, living off unemployment benefits and catching my own lobster and fish. So when I was stressed out I would choose door number two because it looked more attractive.

Eventually I took the whole thing as a Kabuki only and didn't let myself be bothered. I showed them that I would pass the Final check ride successfully without having to do the pigeon dance, which is when they bow in front of each other over and over again. Later I heard from a source that they had said I had a good attitude and that they agreed we had had the best Check Ride.

In the end the guys with the good attitude always were passed even if they made small mistakes, as long as they corrected their mistakes eventually.

Our last Sim instructor was the nicest one but he was also playing the Kabuki to make me feel like I wasn't ready for the Check ride, so I said to him, "Sir, I am here to pass, do you want me to pass or not, because I came her to finish this training successfully so go ahead and sign me off for the check ride please". He didn't expect this self assurance but he signed me off and I didn't disappoint him.

Once we started flying the line we were introduced to a whole different set of flight procedures and rules by the Gaijin or Western Instructors. It was frustrating because now we had to basically throw eight months of Samurai training out the window and take on new non standard ways that every one had sort of adopted from their previous Airlines. Being a good First Officer means not only flying the airplane but also adjusting like a chameleon. Changing hats from being a new hire Pilot, to a Baby Sitter, a Psychologist or Psychiatrist, and even a marriage Counselor.

We learned to sense what every Captain wanted and expected and sort of played along to more Kabuki. That's why the happiest day in this job was when I upgraded to Captain because now I could set my own pace and become Captain Blyhe, Arrogant or asshole if I wanted. But NO, NO, NO, just kidding here. Now I didn't have to worry about who I would be flying with, is he nice? Is he an asshole? Is he tough? None of that anymore.

I like to set a pleasant and relaxed atmosphere in my Cockpit and very rarely have I had to reprimand a First Officer.

Being a First Officer is neither an easy job nor is it and unpleasant one. You just have to adapt to so many different personalities and try to do an excellent job assisting the Captain. In order to become a good Captain someday, you need to be an excellent First Officer first. There are some F. Officers who think they almost already are Captains and they act lazy as F. Officers not assisting the Captain properly especially in high workload situations. Or they try to get ahead of the Captain to show how good they are which is a big mistake because when it is their turn to fly, then they end up stepping on their own tail.

There are isolated cases of spoiled, lazy and demanding Pilots who expect to pick their favorite leg to fly even when they show up late. They ignore the fact that it is the Captain's decision who gets what leg, based on the Weather conditions on arrival and on the First Officer's level of experience and attitude.

We fly the 300 Mega top which is the same in size as the newer 400 but we have the conventional cockpit, with FMS (Flight management System) and Acars. The planes are kept in excellent clean condition and are a pleasure to fly. However, the transition to the newer B-747-400 is already in progress this year and I should be coming up soon for another four months of transition training in Tokyo (that is if JAL recovers from the economic turmoil). That is basically the same airplane from the outside except the cockpit is all glass, or CRT, Cathode Ray or Liquid Display Tubes as instruments and it has winglets at the end of the wing tips. It also has no need for the Flight Engineer since all the Aircraft Systems are monitored by Computers.

The flight Destinations we had were excellent. We had Brisbane, Sydney, Banghkok, Bali, Manila, Guam, Nagoya, Narita, Honolulu and Kansai Osaka. Normally our lay-overs were only 24 to 28 hours but were usually enough to relax, eat well, have a frew drinks and maybe explore the city.

Banghkok was a longer lay-over sometimes but it was easier to lead us into more trouble. Women there are amazingly exotic and prettier than most Asian women. Probably because of all the mixture they've had over the years in the city (I always say that the most beautiful women are the exotic mixtures, it makes them more interesting).

The typical places to visit were the bar areas or the Massage places, the real massage or the fake ones where your option. There were of course the Fish Bowl Bars where you could stand in front of a large glass and in front of you there sat dozens of pretty girls on benches, like toys on display for you to pick. You then would pay a minimum fee for a normal massage and point at the girl you liked. It was up to you what you really wanted once inside a room with her and it usually took two full hours, of course tips were expected and Happy Endings were the norm. (The girls' English was normally limited to one word "tip, tip").

The bars was another story, huge bars with girls hanging out in their sexy mini skirts trying to lure you towards them. I really didn't see that many attractive women at that particular place and on my first trip there I had a scary experience. Myself, the Captain and Flight Engineer (Rich and Randy) went into Nana Plaza to have a few beers, and after looking around and downing a few cold ones to kool ourselves from the heat, we started talking about heading back to the Hotel. Suddenly across the street from us we noticed four very sexy and attractive young ladies calling us over to their bar.

Those were the cutest ones we'd seen so far so we stood up and headed in their direction like zombies. One of the guys even said, "Now, that's what I'm talking about" and we all agreed. We sat inside and ordered three very cold Heinikens and then the girls started to sit around us.

I hadn't sensed anything yet until one of the 'girls' touched my arm and I felt her skin sort of hoarse and rough. That's when the song from AeroSmith "The dude looks like a lady" came to my head. I looked at him/her and noticed it had an Adam's apple on his throat, then I realized it was a guy converted as a girl. I said to him, "go away, send a real girl", he grinned and let the other cuter petite girl sit next to me. I looked at her and said, "you're not a dude are you"? She grinned and that's when Randy said, " hey guys, we fucked up, ther're all dudes". We stood up and left without paying for the beer (we hadn't even touched it yet).

Now I was paranoid and when we walked into the next bar where they only had real girls, I wasn't too sure anymore. This bar (I think it was called, School Play) was kool because it had a high level dancing floor where the girls danced above our heads, the dancing floor was all see thru glass and the girls weren't wearing any undies so you could see their asses above your head. Then a couple of cute girls came by in skimpy little thongs and tried to persuade us to take them upstairs for a fixed price, "Oh, you so handsome, I love you long time" was the typical phrase.

The one that was hitting on me was very pretty and had a great little body, she was trying hard to convince me and when I said to her that I wasn't too sure if she was a real girl, she grabbed my hand and said, "here, feel yourself that I am a real girl" Next thing I knew she had my hand in between her legs, she pushed one of my fingers inside her vagina and looked me in the eye with the sweetest look and said, "See? I'm a girl". I was convinced now but even thou she was a real woman, I was fighting it not to follow her upstairs anyway. The other two guys said they were leaving and I said to wait for me because I wasn't staying by myself there. And I left back to the Hotel. Phew, that was a little too much for my first Banghkok experience.

Usually, we had more modest socializing than that, usually with our Flight Attendants. For example in Bali, that was a great overnight. We stayed at the Patra Bali right in front of the great reef surf breaks, Airports Lefts, Centers, Kuta Reef, etc. In the morning I usually walked towards the left of the Hotel and talked to one of the boat guys who would then take off on his moped to get me a surfboard to rent. He then would motor me out on his boat and drop me off for a couple of hours by the reef, all for a decent price.

My cute friend Lucy who worked at the Hotel showed me the way to Uluwatu once, that was my favorite place. Kuta town was fun to visit specially at night. A couple of times we ended up there with a few of our F Attendants, the Bounty was a good crew hang out and it wasn't rare for us to end up dancing shirtless (like everyone else) on the podium while our girls cheered us up and took pictures of us (maybe to black mail us).

On one of these layovers in Bali, my other Flight crew member (Canadian Wayne) and I were having lunch at a Café in Kuta as a Major Rugby game was about to begin. Aussies are crazy about Rugby so most of them were glued to the TV. We paid and were about to leave when the couple next to us (the husband) said, "what, you guy aren't watching the Rugby match mate"? Wayne who always has a serious look, leaned over his table with a frown and said, "Fuck no, Rugby is for Pussies". I thought, Oh shit this is gonna be trouble, so I looked over my shoulder to count how many dudes were there ready to pounce on us, but luckily there were only a couple of them at the bar and no one seemed to take notice. The poor guy at the table didn't know how to react and remained speechless, then his wife said to Wayne, " move on, go on, just go away", and we did. Wayne just walked away like nothing happened with a grin on his face. I just shook my head and told him I wouldn't be his bodyguard anymore. We had a good laugh on the flight back to Narita.

Den Pasar Airport in Bali is an interesting and high risk Airport. It has a "black hole" approach from both ends of the Runway, over water and pitch black surroundings. No references except dark water below you at night and high terrain from volcanoes to the North, North West and North East. We would usually approach at night, high over the terrain and then descend at a higher rate to plan to be established for a normal three degree glide ratio by fifteen miles from the Runway. Runway 27 had an ILS Precision Approach which made it easier, but the opposite Runway 09 just had a Non-precision VOR approach which didn't include descend guidance.

It's easy for our eyesight to be misled from the lack of exterior references, so we mostly stick to our Instruments until we're ready to switch to Visuals once we have the Runway completely in sight. Sometimes there was stormy weather all around the Island and with a wet runway the Landing Distance felt pretty short, it was around 9,000 feet long but it felt shorter because there's water on both ends, and also a break water 15 foot high concrete wall on the runway 09 approach side.

It was definitely an Adrenalin Rush Landing every time and I loved flying into there I don't know why. Indonesia is a very interesting country and the people are very friendly, you can also have great shopping and dining.

Needless to say as usual, I got into female troubles again. Before I left for Tokyo, my girlfriend had given me an ultimatum, she said I would have to decide to settle down with her when I got back from Tokyo, for good, to form a Family or else, it would all be over and she wouldn't wait for me any longer. I didn't' think I was ready to settle down yet so I took it as being free again.

I thought maybe it was time to take a break and live in Honolulu, just my teenage son and me first, and then think about her offer.

In the meantime in Tokyo, with all the stress from training I needed a escape, I incidentally met a cute girl who worked at a restaurant near the Haneda Airport. She attended me that day and our eyes locked. It was that eye lock that tells you that something is going to happen, you just know it, you feel it. She had a very pretty face, almost milk white complexion. She didn't look Japanese or full Asian, but she did have some Asian in her, she was half Philippine and half American and Rosa was her name. Very pretty mixture, she had very little freckles and pretty full lips, straight brown hair to her shoulders and a petite cute little figure. And yes, she did have a nice roundness to her derriere too.

Her English was marginal, but we had inner communication, we felt each other. She gladly gave me her number and I gave her mine while I was in line paying at her cashier counter while a few courteous locals waited patiently behind me to close my romantic deal. The next day we went out near the Shinagawa station.

There was something very nice and pure about her. She had been married and had a couple of kids, hadn't been around much and was shy about the whole dating thing. She also had a little girl aura and some innocence mixed with sexuality and she always smelled pretty, sort of like roses. So about the fifth date or so we were ready to take it a bit further. That night after dinner she missed her last train, (I kind of helped her miss it). I suggested we find a Hotel near mine, for reasons I can't explain we couldn't' stay at my Hotel. The Hotels were super expensive in that area and there were no vacancies.

Fortunately a taxi driver took us to a Love Motel near the Gotanda District. They normally charge by the hour but you can also stay all night. Only in Japan, a Love Motel with rooms that have Karaoke, hah, I had to laugh, can you imagine singing to a girl before jumping into bed with her? It also had a coin machine with all kinds of snacks, including sex toys, sexy panties, etc. Needles to say, Rosa and I had a great sexual encounter of the Third Kind. She was a little shy and introvert but that all changed after we kept seeing each other.

She later confessed to me that she didn't know sex could be so satisfying and fun, I guess she had missed out on that because of being married to a local guy. She turned out to be a very willing trainee in the art of sex and eventually quickly became very open minded and always willing to satisfy me. I had no regrets, I had some wonderful times with her and she remained a good friend for quite a while. I loved many things about her, her innocence, her sweetness, her simple ways, and mostly her willingness to always give, share, to always think of the others first. Very few people have I met that show that kind of compassion for others. She had grown up very poor and as an orphan in the Philippines, had suffered much as a child and therefore had developed her loving qualities more than most people I have known. I really admired her for her kindness and loving qualities.

Well, I actually had another great experience with a local girl. Minina was a lovely half breed girl with a South American insertion that made her warmer, sexier and livelier than most. Her physic was better developed because she had round curves all over her cute petite sexy little body. She was a very pretty and intelligent girl, quite a bit younger than me but it didn't seem to matter at first. We met at a Cafeteria having lunch when I established conversation with her. We then went out together with her girlfriend all over Tokyo the first couple of times, then started meeting just her and I for a nice romantic dinner around the Shinagawa area. The communication between us was great thanks to her almost fluent English and her mature personality. She was a lot of fun to hang out with and we explored and traveled together outside of Tokyo on some weekends.

Even thou she was the Material girl, Gucci type, (most J girls are) I fell in love with her because of her easy going personality, her classy appearance and good manners, her sense of humor, her pretty face with her Colgate white teethed (not normally encountered in Japan, it's more often the yellowish piranha teeth) gorgeous smile, her warm and loving qualities and oh yeah, because sex was wonderfully beautiful with her. I could have died and went to heaven and not known the difference every time we made love. She could be very affectionate and then suddenly be very direct and frank, even a little mean sometimes but in a good way.

Whenever I was with her, I felt energized by her and even felt like we were almost the same age. Sometimes it was as thou we had been together before, different life maybe?

No wonder they say that a guy is as old as his girlfriend makes him feel. Minina made me feel in love again and we had very beautiful moments together. I think we could have had a happy life, but then again in the long run, the age difference might have become more of an issue in later years. We maintained a great friendship above all and she stayed in my heart for quite a while and will remain in my mind for times to come.

HAWAII FIVE O.

After training ended I moved to Honolulu with my teenage son, right in the middle of Waikiki on Beach Walk street. It was great for a couple of months because it was summer time and the surf was always breaking somewhere nearby. My son and I were always going out to the best spots, Queens, Kaisers, Bowls, Threes, Pops, Paradise, Rock Pile, In Betweens, etc. There was always good surf in the summer time. But eventually we got tired of the hustle of Waikiki and moved to another apartment outside of Waikiki. By then I had realized that I didn't enjoy this paradise by myself anymore and started missing Nena. I thought I was ready to settle down with her and my other little son. Besides I needed to give my first son sort of a Family life, he needed someone to watch him while I was gone for days up to a week. He kept getting in trouble for ditching school and the school started pressuring me for a Legal Guardian.

So I bought a nice old remodeled two story home near Kaimuki, behind Diamond Head. Nena and Sebi moved over that summer and we started a Family life, at first it took a while getting used to it but eventually we all got along just fine. I was happy to have them with me and I think everybody else was

A mermaid in Waikiki.

happy too. Well, most of us, Rico wasn't quite used to having a full house and sharing his Dad with others, but by then he was pretty much on his own and did his own thing anyway.

That was the best thing I could have done, getting back together with Nena, she gave me two more beautiful children, unexpected, we didn't think she could still have children so we were very happy to have them. First came Kalani, he was like a little alien angel when he was pulled out of his shell. He was in control of the situation and didn't even cry, just grumbled, kicked and punched. Like a little bull pissed off because they pulled him out unexpectedly. He was conceived on my dream boat Tequila, on a loving weekend we had in San Diego just Nena and I. I still remember all the details and I know we made him with lots of love. He was so cute and later on grew curls like me. He was very fair and had brown hair, just like his Mom's Mom and my Dad's Portuguese side of my family.

Then just when we thought that we no longer would be able to have a baby girl, we started talking about maybe adopting one from Indonesia or Thailand in the future. But then Leilani showed up, just like that, we couldn't believe it and were totally happy about her too. The recipe there was also lots of love, a few romantic evenings with great spicy food, red wine and maybe a tequila or two. Also eating protein rich foods such as sea food, avocadoes and chili sauces help procreate. (I gave that recipe to a friend who was having trouble impregnating his wife and it seemed to work eventually.)

Leilani was so cute and chubby and became Kalani's little buddy and partner in crime (so to speak), he wouldn't do anything without her, always by her side whether they were playing or fighting. I called her Queen Kong because she was like a little gorilla baby, knocking everything down and smacking Kalani around or grabbing him from his long curls to get even whenever he took toys away from her.

A few months after Leilani was born, we had a White Hawaiian Ceremony at the beach followed by a nice Reception at our house. It was bound to happen eventually, we just didn't know when and where but it did.

Life is a beach, Corona commercial?

On my days off, I love to take my kids to the beach, the park, sailing or surfing. I usually stay within the South of the Island to surf Diamond Head or the outer reefs in Waikiki. Sometimes in the winter I'll even go to the North Shore surfing when it's not that big.

With the family at Hanauma Bay

It's nice to make new friends that surf and that don't work at my Airline so we don't end up complaining about Airline Management like most Airline Crews do. My friend Jack who I met at Diamond Head when he rescued me and gave me a ride home after I lost my car keys in the ocean, has become a good surfing buddy and is a fun and cool guy to hang out with. Other surfing buddies are my son Riko, Montree and Mark from the Marina who's helped me much with my boat.

Life has been good to me here on the Island, it's given me Ohana, family, great neighbors (Winston and his wife in front of us, Mr. Pang on one side and Sue and Steve behind our house) and a decent financial situation. I must also thank one person who thanks to his good word and referral and my efforts, landed me this great job based out of Honolulu, Ron my ex neighbor from the San Diego Marina who also is a Pilot and a Sea Captain.

These are now very happy days in my life. I was lucky I bought a cute four bedroom Kaimuki house five years ago while the prices were decent, with a pretty yard and lots of fruit trees, safe from the traffic outside and cozy and quiet. Since I couldn't afford an ocean view home I improvised and created my own ocean view, from the kitchen entrance were I extended a lanai from the stairs, about 50 square feet and sort of wrapped around a nice plumeria tree for shade. That's my miniscule ocean view towards Waikiki and it literally cost me blood, sweat and tears when I banged my forehead on the first beam I put up, leaving an eight inch stitch mark on my forehead.

I am very grateful and thank God and the Universe for giving me everything I've had and for the opportunities and privileges I've enjoyed. I try to remember always to appreciate what I have instead of regretting what I don't have or haven't done.

I am also aware that often all good things eventually come to an end, so I try not to "attach" myself too much just in case I suddenly loose my Contract Flying job. As we all know, the Airline Industry is pretty insecure and is directly affected by the countries' economies, so our jobs depend directly on the Economy. It is so true that Airplanes run on fuel and Airlines on money, so to summarize it, "money makes a dog dance and an airplane fly". According to ancient Yogi beliefs, the Hindu believe that the secret to Happiness is "Detachment", I like this philosophy, so I try to enjoy these moments and cherish everything that I have been blessed with, while they last.

It is also true that the best things in life are free, children being part of it. Nature, fruit hanging from your tree in your backyard, a beautiful wave in the ocean, a beautiful smile from a child or a stranger, friends, family, (a fresh brewed coffee?) etc.

My gifts from heaven.

BACK TO THE FLIGHT ACROSS THE PACIFIC. PRESENT TIMES.

So back to the present, over flying the Pacific to Honolulu. We are now past Midway Island and only around 1,000 Nautical miles to Honolulu, nothing can go wrong now, yeah right. At least we know we're going in the correct direction. Honolulu is only around two hours away and the chances of something going wrong are minimized. Statistically, it is during the approaches to landing that some accidents or incidents happen, we are aware of this and put all our effort and concentration into the planning and execution of the approach and landing. As they say, it's not over until the fat lady sings, so we usually have a fresh coffee to wake us up from the grogginess of the night. Usually by this time we feel like Airborne Zombies and after a long night like this, we can be really tired. However, if we've had a magical 20 minute power nap, it increases our alertness and awareness and makes us safer for the approach and landing.

As I said before, the reason for most Pilot induced accidents specially during the approach and landing phase is caused by FATIGUE. Pilot incapacitation caused by a pilot falling sleep is another risk while on the approach to landing (the greater risk of falling sleep is during the cruise phase while on Auto Pilot, I know quite a few Pilots including myself, that have had all crew members fall sleep at the same time for longer periods of time). We are aware of this so we prepare and brief on the whole approach and landing procedures, we also have all eyes on the flying pilot executing the approach. In addition to that, our procedures include call outs and responses from both Pilots in order to guard against Pilot incapacitation.

Prior to briefing and preparing for the approach we checked that the weather is okay for landing, the fuel status is acceptable and that the Cabin Attendants have also been briefed on the arrival time, weather, etc.

Hopefully by now, we've already eaten breakfast or dinner posed as breakfast. See, our Japanese masters don't understand that we don't eat Beef, Chicken or Fish for breakfast, (leather, feathers or gills). We are not Japanese, we are Westerners that require a real breakfast like, toast, eggs, pancakes or something decent, no, they have these same menus for decades and don't dare to change them I don't know why. Having a raw fish jumping around on my plate for breakfast is not my favorite way of waking up to a fishy start, yucky. So I avoid breakfast all together, I just eat the yoghurt, fruit and bread and wait until I get home to have a real breakfast. Bloody airplane food can kill you.

We usually start descent around 100 to 140 Nautical miles out, three times our altitude in feet. (e.g. 35,000, 105 Nautical miles out) plus or minus a few miles for tailwinds, headwinds, hotter conditions, or use of engine anti-ice during descent.

As we descend towards the Island of Oahu we usually pass slightly to the right of the island of Kauai, what a beautiful sight it is. Then we continue towards a few miles off shore from the Waianae coast line, where they clear us to 8,000 feet abeam Makaha Beach, then towards the sandy tip next to Barber point. We then are cleared to descend to three thousand feet until intercepting the localizer and glide slope for runway 08 left, approximately 15 miles from the threshold.

At the same time we are configuring the Aircraft with more flaps and Landing gear down while slowing down to around 160 knots for flaps 20 degrees. By the time we reach overhead Ewabe Beacon or abeam Ewa beach at around two thousand feet we plan to be fully configured for landing. Before one thousand feet all checklists should be completed and we expect to be on a stabilized approach. That is, at our desired Approach speed, lateral path and glide path. Most landing weights are around 500,000 to 520,000 lbs so for the greater weight, that gives us an approach speed of 141 knots for 30 degrees of flaps for landing. Our fuel consumption during the approach approximates 6,500 lbs per hour for each engine, plus or minus a couple of hundred. We have to execute everything with accurate precision and smooth hand flying techniques. Smooth flying is part of being a good stick so it is a good practice to fly manually often to achieve this good feeling for the airplane.

The landing is the last part of the balancing act so at around 30 feet we start the flare technique, which is what birds do when you watch them land, they raise their nose and wing angle a few degrees to slow the descend rate down and slow their speed while touching down smoothly. That's exactly what we must do to achieve a nice landing. If we have strong crosswinds, then we must apply slightly wing down into the wind, along with opposite rudder to counter act the weathervane tendency of the aircraft to point to the wind. This way when we touch down, the Aircraft touches down with it's longitudinal axis, aligned to the runway centerline.

If we cannot achieve a safe approach or landing, or a stabilized one, then we must execute a Go Around or Missed Approach. That is the safest thing to do and we should never force a landing due to rushing the approach or from letting ATC pressure us. Going around is usually a normal procedure and we always have enough fuel to do that, even to divert to an Alternate airport and hold for 30 minutes if the weather deteriorates at our destination.

Once we land, we taxi off the runway into the next available taxiway. While we taxi, which is from the tiller on the side, the non-flying Pilot cleans up the Aircraft, which means to retract flaps, speed brakes (they help decelerate the airplane), lights, radar and transponder off, etc. Then we call for the After landing checklist which the Flight Engineer or First Officer reads and confirms. It generally takes five to twenty minutes to taxi to our gate (specially in Tokyo). In Honolulu it's a quick five minute taxi to our gate, followed by engine shutdown, Parking checklists and final Cockpit tidiness and readiness for the next crew. We then exchange courtesy phrases with the Flight Attendants such as, "Otskare sama-deshta", meaning, "it was a pleasure, let's do it again". Then we must go thru Immigration and Customs before we finally get to our cars.

We can also have a print out done from the AIDS machine which shows us in detail the accuracy of our approach down to the landing, including the G force at touchdown and the landing distance it took until slowing down to 50 knots (close to 7,000 feet total distance). Some J pilots take this very seriously and actually take it to their hotel to study in great detail, to study harder and improve themselves. We the Gaijin Pilots don't take this that seriously except for our own ego satisfaction when we make a nice landing.

Now, this is the part that is the most dangerous to our own selves. Falling sleep while driving home, I've mentioned before how I 've had two car accidents while driving home after flying all night. Like I said, it's not over until the fat broad sings, and it's not until I park my 72 convertible Mustang under it's car port and shut off it's roaring engine that I feel safe again. Then I get totally energized all over again when I hear my little Gremlins playing inside the house.

Capt. Blyhe with Flight attendants partying at the Barge.

CAPTAIN BLYHE.

So eventually after sitting in the right seat as First Officer on the Jumbo for two and a half years, I was promoted to Captain in the summer of 2006. This training again took around 10 months and most of it was line flying. The big difference was, that this time they treated us with more respect, like we finally became one of the boys. All the patience I extended to the limit paid off in the end. The first long eight months of initial training taught me about having patience and becoming more humble, that's what the Asian training is all about, character, humbleness and honor. But it was also ridiculous sometimes because it wasn't really well suited for Western crews.

Getting my hand pushed off the mode control panel, my chart smacked off my hand or being told that I will die if I don't look at a certain cockpit instrument was sometimes more funny than offending. The other hilarious one is when they called the RDMI (Radio Direction Magnetic Indicator) Pilot Killer. Even thou it was sometimes an awkward, nerve wrecking and frustrating flight training it paid off in the end.

It is a satisfying feeling to finally get respect from your peers and Instructors, as well as from the flying public. Every where else in the world, Pilots get more respect for our Profession from the general public or passengers, except in the United States where being a famous and super wealthy drug pusher rap singer would probably impress the general public more.

I have finally made my dream come true, to finally sit in the left seat as Captain of a Jumbo, the almost impossible dream that I had since I was a little child. Sure, some may say we're nothing but Jet Powered Migrant Workers to a Foreign Airline, or Glorified Bus Drivers, but who cares. I do what I do for the satisfaction of accomplishing my childhood dream to fly airplanes. And in my opinion, "Action makes Satisfaction". Besides, I also do it for the quality of family life and the lifestyle, not so much for the money. And the flight adventures we have at interesting and fun destinations around the world.

Exterior inspection of aircraft while in Brisbane.

All the years of perseverance, visualizing to a huge Boeing 747 poster on my wall. Imagining myself walking towards the jet bridge and into the airplane, in my Captain suit, with 4 white bars (epaulets) on it and my Captain hat on. I imagined every detail of it every morning when I woke up.

And that's how I made my dreams and thoughts come true. However, you must also put a date on it because without a date you may never achieve your dreams. A deadline better said.

I had originally told myself that I wanted to become Captain before I turned 40 and I did (much earlier with my previous Airline). I was originally scheduled for my Captain check ride on my Birthday. (that had to be changed for a month later due to our expecting of our baby girl on that particular day). What a coincidence yeah. That by the way, was another dream come true, having a baby girl.

And it doesn't end there, I still have more dreams to achieve, but I can't talk about them until they become reality. Well one of them is to make enough money from the profit of my books to upgrade to a 54 foot sailboat and take the family on a year long sailing adventure of the Pacific Islands. (if, if, if, etc.)

Did I mention that on two different occasions I had been told by two different clairvoyant people a brief description of my life, how many kids I would have and during what circumstances of my life? Well, it all came true. Again, I don't know for sure if it was a psychic preview of my life, or maybe after being told of my so called future I made it happen by thinking about it. Maybe both.

The point is that you can make anything come true, anything realistic that is. I have tried it and it works. But you must keep imagining it, visualizing it, put a date on it and keep dreaming of it every day. It also helps to have visual aids, such as a poster or picture of what you desire. It's all within your reach and it's generated from deep within your inner desires ingrained in your subconscious mind.

Nothing is impossible and everything is possible, it's up to us to achieve a fulfilled life or at least to make the best of it. "So why don't you come and try". And always remember, never forget and never give up.

PS, thank you for buying this book and referring it further to your friends, it's deeply appreciated.

Happy Trails and Sails
Captain (Blyhe) Enrique or Henry (maybe Hank) Horta
Alias, Captain Arrogant

Capt. E. Blyhe Horta inside four engine Cessna

CPSIA information can be obtained
at www.ICGtesting.com
Printed in the USA
BVHW081159210122
626661BV00009B/98/J